D1293386

WHITE PEOPLE DO NOT KNOW HOW TO
BEHAVE AT ENTERTAINMENTS
DESIGNED FOR LADIES
AND GENTLEMEN
OF COLOUR

WHITE PEOPLE
DO NOT
KNOW HOW TO
BEHAVE *at*
ENTERTAINMENTS
DESIGNED FOR
LADIES &
GENTLEMEN
of COLOUR

WILLIAM BROWN'S AFRICAN & AMERICAN THEATER

Marvin McAllister

THE UNIVERSITY OF NORTH CAROLINA PRESS | CHAPEL HILL AND LONDON

© 2003 The University of North Carolina Press
All rights reserved
Manufactured in the United States of America
Designed by April Leidig-Higgins
Set in Monotype Bulmer by Copperline Book Services

The paper in this book meets the guidelines for
permanence and durability of the Committee on
Production Guidelines for Book Longevity of
the Council on Library Resources.

Library of Congress Cataloging-in-Publication Data
McAllister, Marvin Edward, 1969–
White people do not know how to behave at entertain-
ments designed for ladies and gentlemen of colour:
William Brown's African and American theater /
Marvin McAllister.
p. cm.   Includes bibliographical references and index.
ISBN 0-8078-2777-0 (cloth: alk. paper)
ISBN 0-8078-5450-6 (pbk.: alk. paper)
1. African American theater—New York (State)—
New York—History—19th century.
2. Brown, William Alexander.   I. Title.
PN2270.A35 M39 2003
792'.089'9607307471—dc21   2002015820

cloth 07 06 05 04 03   5 4 3 2 1
paper 07 06 05 04 03   5 4 3 2 1

To intellectuals inside and
outside the academy

CONTENTS

ACKNOWLEDGMENTS

IN WRITING AND REVISING this book over several years, I have collected many debts to individuals and institutions. At Northwestern University, I want to acknowledge my dissertation adviser, Professor Sandra L. Richards, for reading chapter drafts and searching for ways to improve an expanding manuscript. I thank other committee members, Professor Tracy Davis and Professor Susan Manning, for their expertise and guidance. During my research, the archivists, librarians, and staff members at the following institutions were most helpful: American Antiquarian Society, Center for Research Libraries, Folger Shakespeare Library, Harvard University's Houghton Library, Library of Congress's Rare Books and Manuscripts and Newspaper and Microfilm Divisions, New-York Historical Society, New York Public Library's Theatre and Drama Collection at Lincoln Center, New York City Municipal Archives, Northwestern University's Special Collections, University of California at Davis's Special Collections, and University of Chicago's Special Collection. For their hospitality during my many research trips to Massachusetts and New York, I extend many thanks to Hadley Morash and Brit Payne. For supplying me with a much-needed, last-minute printer to produce my two-volume dissertation, I am grateful to my mother, Joyce Walker, and her co-workers at North Chicago Community High School.

I amassed even more debts while transforming the dissertation into a publishable book. Tremendous thanks to Professor Ann Elizabeth Armstrong of Miami University, Professor Pamela Sheingorn of the City University of New York, and Professor Margaret Wilkerson for their attentive readings of different versions of the manuscript. I am sincerely grateful for the University of California at Berkeley's Chancellor's Post-Doctoral Fellowship, which provided intellectual space for me to work through my developing theories on whiteface minstrelsy and stage Europeans. Also, I thank Sian Hunter, the staff of the University of North Carolina Press, and the press's anonymous readers for inviting this history into their Tar Heel home. Any errors in this book are solely my own. For late-night inspiration and distraction, much love to Jill Scott, Outkast, Al Green, and João Gilberto; their melodies carried me far away from Richmond, Oakland, and the Boogie Down but always kept me where I needed to be.

Finally, I want to express profound appreciation for my wife, Toni Ola Tildon. While navigating medical school and a difficult pediatric residency program, she managed to peruse portions of the manuscript for coherency. She was there from the beginning of this often bewildering academic journey and she can tell you this "becoming" was rarely fluid, but we finished.

WHITE PEOPLE DO NOT KNOW HOW TO

BEHAVE AT ENTERTAINMENTS

DESIGNED FOR LADIES

AND GENTLEMEN

OF COLOUR

INTRODUCTION

AN ARTICLE IN THE August 1821 issue of the *National Advocate* announced a newly established "African" oasis on Manhattan's West Side: "[A] garden has been opened somewhere back of the hospital called African Grove; not spicy as those of Arabia, (but let that pass) at which the ebony lads and lasses could obtain ice cream, ice punch, and hear music from the big drum and clarionet."[1] The article's author, Mordecai Manuel Noah, also editor of the *National Advocate*, further explained the necessity of such a retreat: "Among the number of ice cream gardens in this city, there was none in which the sable race could find admission and refreshment." William Alexander Brown, a free man of color and former ship's steward, created this pleasure garden for the benefit of black stewards who were barred admission to white pleasure gardens.[2] Nineteenth-century pleasure gardens were private, outdoor summer venues that permitted urbanites to escape the high temperatures and incessant demands of city life and indulge in ice cream treats, alcoholic concoctions, musical entertainments, dramatic recitations, fireworks, and conversation. Brown would entertain a growing population of Afro–New Yorkers, across caste and class, who were desperately seeking more "refined" leisure pursuits. In addition, Brown quickly attracted curious Euro–New Yorkers, thus launching a series of bold social and theatrical experiments that would integrate American theater onstage and offstage.[3]

This interpretive history argues that William Brown's nineteenth-century Manhattan pleasure garden and subsequent theaters were African-engineered but American-focused entertainments that cultivated an inclusive, intercultural, multicultural, and triracial national imaginary. Confronted with the "twoness" of being both American and "Negro" in the United States, Brown demonstrated that African Americans did not have to privilege one cultural identity at the expense of the other. In fact, as a garden host and theatrical manager, Brown would attempt to represent all New Yorkers—African, European, Indian. From 1821 to 1823, Brown successfully but precariously integrated the U.S. stage and audience; provided African American actors complete yet frequently contested access to theatrical representation; rehearsed his black actors and audiences for full participation in public life; explored multiple but often conflicting European, African, and Indian performative identities; and showcased a New World Africanist aesthetic marked by skilled appropriations and unresolved hybridities. Brown's model national institution emerged in four specific stages or phases: an initial backyard pleasure garden on Manhattan's predominantly white West Side; the Minor Theatre on the fashionable and centrally located Park Row; the American Theatre in the remote Greenwich Village; and finally the African Company, featured in a brand-new Village theater. With each phase in this institutional journey, manager Brown encountered artistic, location, and audience challenges that can prove instructive for any truly diverse American theater.

In this study, I also contend that certain disapproving or dismissive Euro-Americans did not know how to "behave" at these mutually African and American entertainments. Although Brown enthusiastically celebrated the young nation's triracial and multiethnic potential, many white pessimists declared this overwhelming pool of multiplicity unworkable and undesirable.[4] During America's early national period — the formative years between independence and the early 1830s — many Euro-Americans were unwilling to imagine an openly heterogeneous national character that embraced African Americans as legitimate cultural claimants. Specifically, competing white theatrical managers, incensed white newspaper editors, insecure white circus workers, and overzealous white patrons vehemently rejected Brown's intrepid participation in national self-definition. Even as this black impresario designed his entertainments for the pleasure of all Manhattanites, escalating racial divisions in nineteenth-century New York transformed his Minor, American, and African Theatres into exceptionally volatile and even dangerous social spaces. After a physical assault in August 1822, an irate William Brown allegedly responded to the rioters with a provocative sign, claiming that "Whites Do Not Know How to Behave at Entertainments Designed for Ladies and Gentlemen of Colour."[5] The second objective of this project is to analyze those misbehaving whites who attempted to divest Brown's black company of its artistic agency and to erase these legitimate producers of national culture from Manhattan's theatrical landscape.

This study combines North American history, Caribbean history, U.S.

theater history, performance theory, and theories of cultural identity to situate William Brown and his mercurial institutions within the country's early years of national and cultural formation. Despite the extensive archival work of many researchers and historians, personal information on this nearly forgotten American theatrical innovator remains extremely rare. Some scholars speculate that William Alexander Brown was born a free man of color in the Caribbean, perhaps on the island of St. Vincent, which was once inhabited by the Garifuna or Black Carib Indians.[6] We do know that Brown earned a respectable living as a steward working aboard passenger packets bound for Kingston, London, Manhattan, and other transatlantic seaports. In the early 1800s he retired from this maritime trade, settled on the island of Manhattan, and rented an apartment in a predominantly white West Side neighborhood. Reluctant to sever his maritime associations, a retired Brown elected to spend his twilight years managing a pleasure garden for black stewards, their wives, other leisure-minded Afro–New Yorkers, and eventually curious Euro–New Yorkers.

However, I am concerned less with Brown's personal history than with the cultural identities or personas he cultivated through his unfolding entertainment institutions. Stuart Hall contends that cultural identity is a "matter of 'becoming' as well as of 'being,'" and that New World identities are "far from being eternally fixed in some essentialized past" and "subject to the continuous 'play' of history, culture, and power."[7] Hall's process-focused definition of cultural identity is especially appropriate for the United States' unbounded early national moment, and Brown's multifaceted, ever evolving institutional journey was partly a product of an incredibly fluid early national theater. With his initial pleasure garden, Brown embarked on a significant institutional "becoming" that mirrored the young nation's struggle with plurality and its difficult sojourn through a defining period.

Throughout this institutional "becoming," Brown's entertainments were shaped by powerful forces from the dominant culture, including the aforementioned white newspaper editor M. M. Noah. When it came to the critical business of naming Brown's initial summer retreat from Manhattan's hustle and bustle, Noah stepped to the foreground. With his pleasure garden article published in August 1821, Noah christened this new retreat the "African Grove" because it was managed by an impresario of African descent and originally catered to black stewards. The act of naming can grant or deny power, notes performance scholar Brenda Dixon Gottschild, and "what is not named, or misnamed, becomes an impotent backdrop for someone else's story."[8] We lack a record of how the retired black steward originally identified or envisioned his first garden, so it would appear that Noah was telling his particular version of Brown's story. However, this interpretive history will demonstrate that Brown's "becoming" was also a product of his own managerial self-construction, which was marked by an eclectic or hybrid aesthetic and an intense commitment to social integration. Despite Noah's campaign to circumscribe or "ghettoize" the African Grove and Brown's subsequent "African Amusements," the black entrepreneur initially rejected such racially restrictive monikers. When he first advertised an identity in New York newspapers and on printed playbills, Brown brazenly selected provocative yet inclusive titles like Minor Theatre or American Theatre. As for theatrical locations, Brown tended to favor real estate close to the entertainment district of Park Row or the affluent West Side. Nearly all the documentation on his managerial twists and turns points toward one conclusion: this ambitious ex-steward turned theater producer coveted a place in the center, not on the margins, of Manhattan's leisure landscape.

America's amazingly fluid theatrical and extratheatrical performance landscapes had a profound impact on national definition.[9] With multiple ethnicities populating this New World nation, especially in an emerging metropolis like New York City, Americans needed performative outlets to process an unprecedented and increasingly problematic level of diversity. The country's emerging theaters and other extratheatrical venues provided coping mechanisms or processing laboratories through which American social identities could be constructed and transmitted.[10] Whether dressing as natives and dumping tea into Boston Harbor or "blacking up" and parading as Callithumpian Bands, a cross section of early nationalists repeatedly borrowed racial and ethnic personas. In his essay "Change the Joke and Slip the Yoke," Ralph Ellison explains that "[f]or the ex-colonials, the declaration of an American identity meant the assumption of a mask."[11] Before the well-documented national fascination with blackface minstrelsy, newly emerging Americans vigorously appropriated redface, or the mask of Indianness, to declare their national identity.[12]

From the colonial moment forward, transracial, transclass, and even transgender performances became national theatrical and extratheatrical pastimes. In his study of circum-Atlantic New World performance, *Cities of the Dead*, Joseph Roach explains that when "confronted with revolutionary circumstances for which a few precedents existed," New World subjects "invented themselves by performing their pasts in the presence of others" and

INTRODUCTION

by performing "what and who they thought they were not."[13] Roach contends that American moderns, from North America to South America, had to master and perform Indian, African, and European "others" in order to create new selves and new nations. So from the beginning, cross-racial appropriation or mimetically embodying the "other" proved to be a thoroughly necessary American theatrical and social practice. Cultural theorist Michael Awkward contends that much of contemporary American life is still a "meeting ground" where cultural crisscrossings around race, gender, class, sexuality, and religion transpire.[14]

In this highly experimental and variable cultural context, William Brown and other American artists learned to separate color from culture and produced distinctive national forms, one of the most notable and instructive being blackface minstrelsy.[15] Writing about the nation's earliest excursions into blackface performance, theater historian William J. Mahar explains how stereotyping "others" is a normal process of "classifying individuals from different nations" because it helps one understand how the "other" fits into more familiar patterns of behavior. Mahar also warns, however, that artistic efforts to understand the "other" through performance can devolve into acts of representational exclusion or expropriation.[16] As blackface minstrelsy embraced and popularized its commodified version of blackness, this white-authored performance tradition simultaneously denied social legitimacy and artistic agency to African Americans. Ironically, the mere existence of Brown's African American company made minstrelsy in America a theatrical possibility, but the ascendancy of blackface signaled the unfortunate end of Brown's producing career.

Cross-cultural or transracial performance in the early national United States was marked by such dualities. Postcolonial theorist Homi Bhabha further defines stereotyping as a kind of fetish that "gives access to an 'identity' which is predicated as much on mastery and pleasure as it is on anxiety and defence, for it is a form of multiple and contradictory beliefs in its recognition of difference and disavowal of it."[17] As evidenced by blackface minstrelsy and Indian-inflected masking, early national performance embodied these contradictory impulses toward mastery and anxiety, pleasure and defense. According to Bhabha, the colonial subject and colonizer, dominant and subordinate groups, reconcile their multiple or contradictory beliefs about the "other" and the "self" through accumulated stereotypes. Therefore, he cautions that any examination of stereotyping "should shift from the ready recognition of images as positive or negative, to an understanding of the process of subjectification."[18] Bhabha claims that if we study the colonial interaction of dominant and dominated without judgments, stereotypes become "a complex, ambivalent, contradictory mode of representation, as anxious as it is assertive."[19] This project endeavors to approach the nation's cross-racial performance—blackface, redface, or whiteface—with an appreciation for its complexity, ambivalence, and contradiction.

Another significant theoretical assumption of this study is that Americans of African descent were uniquely qualified or perhaps ideally suited to participate in the nation's theatrical and extratheatrical laboratories. Like their fellow New World arrivals, nineteenth-century African Americans were remarkably proficient at multiracial appropriations and representational contradictions. Early America's commitment to mutability and masking partly explains Brown's institutional phases, which metamorphosed from African Grove to Minor Theatre to American Theatre and finally to African Company. However, the profound impact of slavery and the retention of distinct Old World African values may have rendered New World Africans even more skilled than the average Euro-American. W. E. B. Du Bois's early twentieth-century theory of "double consciousness," being both American and "Negro"—or African—ascribes a potentially liberating "second sight" to African Americans.[20] More recently, black Atlantic theorist Paul Gilroy traces this doubleness, in particular its performative component, back to enslavement and colonialism. Gilroy writes, "Survival in slave regimes or in other extreme conditions intrinsic to colonial order promoted the acquisition of what we might now understand to be performance skills, and refined the appreciation of mimesis by both dominant and dominated."[21] For enslaved and free African Americans, it was paramount to accept and perform the role of dominated while also understanding and mastering the characteristics of the dominant classes. Brenda Dixon Gottschild also recognizes an intrinsic duality at the core of New World African performance, both theatrical and extratheatrical. This duality "can be understood as a precept of contrariety, or an encounter of opposites. The conflict inherent in and implied by difference, discord, and irregularity is encompassed, rather than erased or necessarily resolved."[22] Gottschild maintains that African American cultural claimants never completely resolve the various dualities created by their slave or colonial experiences. Instead, black performers maintain an Africanist "precept of contrariety" and continue to embrace opposites and multiple possibilities.

Within the slippery world of postrevolutionary U.S. theater, New World

Africans crafted complex, contradictory, and multilayered performances that celebrated, parodied, and even historicized Indian, African, and European others. Before blackface minstrelsy imposed substantial limitations on the African American image, no established rules delineated which roles black actors could perform. Within the supportive confines of Brown's African garden and theaters, the range of representation for the black performer was unbounded. At the African Grove, black social performers indulged in a preexistent tradition of whiteface minstrelsy—blacks performing white privilege—which was seemingly designed for mere entertainment but was potentially a rehearsal for future racial equality. On his stage, Brown would encourage a versatile company of black actors, singers, dancers, musicians, choreographers, and dramatists to explore a range of theatrical material; in particular, Brown introduced stage Europeans—blacks performing white dramatic roles—to the national laboratory. In the same way that European immigrants looked to Indianness for national and personal definition, Brown's black audiences and actors performed whiteness to construct African American identities. Beyond conventional stage Indians and stage Africans, Brown's featured performers like James Hewlett and S. Welsh presumed they could effectively embody a dynamic sampling of stage Europeans, from English royalty to Scottish rebels.

To summarize, early American theatrical and extratheatrical spaces functioned as laboratories where three races—Indians, Europeans, and Africans—performed one another in order to comprehend and conquer the "other," discover new "selves," and "become" an unparalleled New World nation. African American performers, equipped with endless dualities and a healthy appreciation for contrariety, proved the ideal clinicians for these performative labs. Once these early national African American cultural claimants are restored to their rightful place in the theatrical narrative, a truer profile of nineteenth-century U.S. performance emerges. The first four chapters of this interpretive history advance the argument that Brown's aesthetically "African" garden and theaters were the most "American" institutions in Manhattan's nascent theatrical landscape. Throughout these chapters, the focus is more thematic than chronological. Each chapter concentrates on a particular aspect of Brown's "becoming," one of the four phases, but continues to monitor ongoing institutional developments, such as Brown's ever evolving hybrid repertoire and his increasingly integrated yet volatile audience.

Chapter 1 introduces Brown's first venture, a semiprivate pleasure garden where ladies and gentlemen of color gathered to appropriate and parody

Euro-American privilege. Rooted in a "second sight" predicated on African-ness and Americanness, Brown's culture-craving black patrons nightly performed a kind of cross-racial "becoming" that I term whiteface minstrelsy. This underestimated extratheatrical tradition, firmly rooted in master-slave or dominant-subordinate relations, entertained, but also trained, the emergent Afro–New Yorker community for an expanded role in American society.

In Chapter 2, I analyze Brown's Minor Theatre, the phase in which he ventured into theatrical production, appropriated Shakespeare, and dared to challenge Manhattan's Park Theatre. The Park was Manhattan's previously undisputed "major" theater and was managed by Stephen Price, a lawyer who became America's first noteworthy theatrical producer. Price would prove an important and debilitating rival for Brown's upstart African American theater. The chapter introduces and examines the company's unique contribution to American theater, the stage European. As the theatrical complement to extratheatrical whiteface minstrelsy, this strictly dramatic vehicle allowed black actors to investigate and complicate white dramatic roles, including the Duke of Gloucester and Lady Ann in Shakespeare's *Richard III*.

Chapter 3 chronicles the American Theatre phase during which William Brown proclaimed his national pride, constructed a brand-new theater catering to all New Yorkers, and staged various Native American identities from North America to South America. This section features a discussion of Afro-America's first known drama, William Brown's *Drama of King Shotaway*, which recreated a Carib Indian rebellion on the West Indian island of St. Vincent. For Brown and other early U.S. dramatists, the consummate New World spirit was not naturally embodied by the European or African arrivals but was fully represented by the initial inhabitants: Native American nations.

Next, Chapter 4 concentrates on the African Company phase, the most conflicted leg in Brown's institutional "becoming." In the company's final year of existence, Brown experimented with a brief yet provocative exploration of black characters or caricatures crafted by European writers. By the early 1820s, white theaters had become increasingly enamored with stage African material, and Brown's African Company joined that popular trend by featuring "real" blacks performing stage African roles free of brown or blackface. Brown's two documented stage African performances achieved a precarious balance of comic and dramatic blackness that, compared with most Euro-American appropriations of Africanness, communicated a more intricate and nuanced portrayal of slavery in the New World.

Chapter 5 and the Conclusion concentrate on white misbehavior and Brown's legacy. For many Euro–New Yorkers, Brown's dualistic theatrical vision and integrationist experiments never registered as significant threats to their Manhattan. Tolerant whites merely indulged these African entertainments as pleasurable artistic and social curiosities. But for more observant or perhaps paranoid whites, the company's fresh perspectives on the culturally and politically dominant "other"—as exhibited in whiteface minstrelsy and stage Europeans—undermined previously unquestioned assumptions of white supremacy. The "colored" company negated Euro-America's self-image as the primary claimant on national definition, thus causing certain displeased and powerful white citizens to attack its productions and hasten Brown's managerial demise. Chapter 5 reconstructs and examines a range of white unruliness that materialized as political, cultural, physical, and metaphorical assaults on the theory and reality of an African and American theater. These attacks were directly or indirectly engineered by the company's two primary detractors: M. M. Noah, editor and political operative, and Stephen Price, manager of the "major" Park Theatre. Finally, the concluding chapter recovers verifiable nineteenth-century black responses to the misbehaving white patrons. The Conclusion also summarizes Brown's potential legacy by examining the theatrical activity of Brown protégés Ira Aldridge and James Hewlett. This black theatrical first was not simply a short-lived, "colored" aberration destined to be displaced by blackface minstrelsy; rather, Brown's "becoming" can serve as an invaluable blueprint for an inclusive national theater. In the face of constant white resistance to African American cultural claimants, Brown's boundless black performers designed and staged multiple New World identities for all Americans.

Late-Night Pleasure Garden
for People of Color

NOAH'S AFRICAN GROVE

FOR A MID-1980S GUEST appearance on NBC's *Saturday Night Live*, Eddie Murphy and comedy writer Andy Breckman created a satiric short film, *White Like Me*, in which Murphy disguises himself as a Caucasian complete with whiteface makeup, a greeting card vocabulary, a straight blond wig, tight buttocks, and an intensely nasal voice. After mastering "white" form, Murphy discovers a "hidden" Manhattan where white fellows can do amazing things such as leave stores with free newspapers and secure bank loans without a whiff of collateral. Murphy's stiff posturing and exaggerated Caucasoid dialect blatantly ridicule and caricature whiteness, but his whiteface mask generates more than easy laughs. The short film exposes and critiques the excessive entitlements, real or exaggerated, enjoyed by Euro-America, and it engages the larger problem of racial assumptions that link whiteness with plenty and blackness with lack.[1] At the core of Murphy's virtuoso performance are seemingly natural associations between whiteness, prosperity, opportunity, and educational achievement that pervade U.S. media and classrooms.[2] Murphy's performed whiteness is part of a long-standing but underdocumented performance tradition of whiteface minstrelsy.

This chapter interprets the African Grove pleasure garden as a semiprivate entertainment that deployed whiteface minstrelsy to elevate socially, and perhaps politically, the position of Afro–New Yorkers in Manhattan's cultural landscape. In this "becoming" phase, Brown encouraged an extratheatrical performance of whiteness that allowed New World Africans to construct a distinctly black urban style and to rehearse their most coveted social aspirations. This underestimated tradition of whiteface minstrelsy first emerged in seventeenth-century New World slave cultures, eventually reached the streets of nineteenth-century New York, and finally surfaced in Brown's African Grove. As a site of social performance, Brown's first venture perfectly reflected Manhattan's mutable social context marked by multiple acts of cross-racial, cross-class, and cross-caste appropriations. In white theaters and pleasure gardens, Euro–New Yorkers explored the self-creative potential of stage Indian and stage African "others." Not surprisingly, Brown provided an attractive space for free and enslaved blacks to "other" Euro–New Yorkers and their dominant culture.

M. M. Noah initially dismissed Brown's garden as a collection of social-climbing "colored" gentry who "generally are very imitative" and live to "ape their masters and mistresses in everything."[3] Many years later, Afrocentric scholars Carlton and Barbara Molette also dismissed Brown's efforts, claiming his theatrical exploits "do not fully expose the beginnings of Afro-American theatre" because his company did not offer "pure African art forms."[4] But were there any "pure African art forms" available to manager Brown and his leisure-starved black patrons, and what exactly did it mean to be "African" in the early national United States? According to anthropologist Melville Herskovits, "African" in the New World signified a composite identity rooted in common cultural denominators shared by slaves from diverse West African ethnicities. Historian Sterling Stuckey further develops this composite model of "African" and claims that West and Central Africans began reconstructing an interethnic cultural identity during the traumatic Middle Passage. Aboard seventeenth-century slave vessels traversing the Atlantic Ocean, disparate groups merged religious values, linguistic elements, and artistic predilections into a syncretic "African" culture for their new home. More recently, historian Earl Lewis has extended Stuckey's thoughts on African identity: "In the midst of the Middle Passage, words were shared, customs exchanged, and dreams of freedom planted. There and in the Americas, these ethnic people became, first, Africans and then African American — that is, they came to see and think of themselves, in relational terms, as members of a larger collective."[5] Lewis redefines or restates the composite model as an "overlapping diaspora" that resists the notion of an essential "African" and advances a diversified conception of New World blackness.

Slightly divergent from Herskovits's, Stuckey's, and Lewis's composite model or "overlapping diaspora," anthropologists Sidney Mintz and Richard Price warn that any discussion of "African" culture in the New World should not be grounded in surviving sociocultural forms but in shared values. A central "African" value that Mintz and Price emphasize—as does Brenda Dixon Gottschild—is a fundamental dynamism, a shared sense that cultural change, not stagnation, is an integral part of life.[6] Mintz and Price argue that interethnic "Africans" not only recreated their Old World cultures but freely incorporated values and practices from European ethnicities in the Americas. Mintz, Price, Stuckey, Lewis, and Herskovits would all agree that New World slaves actively assimilated into an undeniably predominant Euro-American culture. Therefore, there were no "pure African art forms" for Brown's colored actors and audiences to cultivate, and, more important, "African" in this New World could easily embody European cultural material. As an "African" value, this fundamental dynamism was best exhibited through whiteface minstrelsy.

Early national Africans in the Americas may have been exceptionally proficient at interethnic and interracial appropriation, but it would be misleading to view their various syncretisms as seamless, uncomplicated fusions of multiple African and European cultures. Historians, anthropologists, and cultural theorists have all articulated the persistent and intriguing tensions embedded in the African and American binary, as well as the potentially hybrid dynamics prevalent in colonial contexts, postcolonial moments, or other systems of domination. African American scholar W. E. B. Du Bois first articulated the New World African tension—or duality, depending on one's perspective—of being both culturally "American" and "Negro" in the United States. For Du Bois, "American" and "Negro" represented competing directions that the "talented tenth," those African Americans active in both white and black worlds, would have to resolve. More recently, theorist Homi Bhabha examined this encounter of seemingly competing cultures and found a hybrid fusion of the binary, a "third space," which can serve as a transgressive mode of cultural production. Cultural critic Stuart Hall theorizes that diasporic black identities—especially Caribbean identities—are produced by three distinct cultures or "presences," Présence Africaine, Présence Européenne, and Présence Americaine. Hall considers the American presence, his third space, the "beginning of diaspora, of diversity, of hybridity and difference" and a metaphoric "primal scene" where diasporic identities constantly produce and reproduce themselves.[7]

If combined, these different historical and theoretical perspectives define "African" in an early nineteenth-century United States as a complex convergence of multiple Old World African and European cultural practices and values, a fundamental dynamism that embraces difference, and a diasporic hybrid identity constantly in the act of reproduction. As for "African" institutions in the early nineteenth century, Sterling Stuckey claims some black organizations selected or were assigned the name "African" with no cultural association implied, whereas other institutions embraced the name to celebrate a continued connection to the Old World. Elizabeth Rauh Bethel argues that certain "African" societies, churches, or schools in the urban North intentionally used the term as a defining act that "publicly claimed and proclaimed both their freedom and their African ancestry."[8] In 1780s Manhattan, prompted by discriminatory practices at communion and baptisms, three African American ministers—Peter Williams Sr., James Varick, and Levin Smith—proclaimed their freedom and defected from the majority-white John Street Church. By 1795 their African Methodist Episcopal Zion Church was conducting separate religious services in a converted stable at Leonard and Church Streets on the city's West Side. In June 1808 independent-minded Afro–New Yorkers, led by John Teasman, founded New York's African Society for Mutual Relief to counter the perception of free black dependency on white philanthropy. This society's primary responsibility was to keep its members and their families out of the almshouse— New York's home for the poor and destitute—but the institution extended its resources to nonmembers.[9]

Culturally speaking, Stuart Hall theorizes a Présence Africaine for diasporic blacks and their institutions. Although Old World customs are ever present in African American religious and secular practices, this cultural presence is a deferred Africa, or Africa "as a spiritual, cultural, and political metaphor."[10] The African Grove, whether named by Noah or Brown, was undeniably a secular institution that personified Old World African values, and, in fact, the Grove merged a metaphoric Présence Africaine with elements of a dominant Présence Européenne to produce a most American tradition of whiteface minstrelsy.

Whiteface Minstrelsy

Whiteface minstrelsy can be understood as extratheatrical, social performances in which people of African descent assume "white-identified" gestures, dialects, physiognomy, dress, or social entitlements. Whiteface is a mimetic but implicitly political form that not only masters but critiques constructed versions of whiteness. Attuned to class as much as race, these acts tend to co-opt prestigious or elite representations of whiteness. From the time of their arrival in North America, African slaves "acted white" or mastered, celebrated, and even satirized "superior" European fashions, leisure pursuits, and other cultural forms. As Paul Gilroy suggests, "Apart from the work involved in enacting their servitude and inferiority while guarding their autonomy, people found significant everyday triumphs by mimicking and in a sense mastering, their rulers and conquerors, masters, and mistresses."[11] These "everyday triumphs" through social performance were not limited to slaves mastering masters and mistresses; free African Americans, North and South, mastered and mimicked other variations on privileged whiteness.

The term whiteface minstrelsy is an obvious play on blackface minstrelsy, but beyond the derivation of its name from blackface, my working definition owes much to recent revisions in minstrelsy scholarship. A number of performance theorists and historians have reconsidered the performative roots and social unconscious of blackface minstrelsy, and in the process these scholars have exposed minstrelsy's working-class roots, located an attraction-aversion duality in this tradition, identified the separation of a commodified "blackness" from black culture, and even argued that minstrelsy was a forerunner to contemporary hip-hop.[12] Musicologist Dale Cockrell offers this illuminating observation: "To black up was a way of assuming 'the Other,' in the cant of this day, a central aspect of the inversion ritual. Some of the most compelling evidence that this is in fact what happened comes from eighteenth- and nineteenth-century Caribbean John Canoe rituals, where slaves generally put on ritual whiteface theatricals personifying their Other."[13] Cockrell links blackface and whiteface in the same natural process of "othering" and understands that all New World moderns, not just Euro-Americans, constructed versions of neighboring races.

A distinct difference between whiteface and blackface lies in the dissemination and reception of these cultural products. Blackface minstrelsy, backed by the cultural sanction of white supremacy, enjoyed unlimited access to literary, visual, and theatrical outlets that circulated this uniquely U.S. form nationally and internationally. By contrast, whiteface minstrelsy—and its companion, stage Europeans—have yet to be fully recognized as legitimate forms and are only recently appearing on the radar screen of performance studies. Anthropologist John Szwed explains that white "high status minstrelizers," in everyday life and onstage, can appropriate blackness more easily than blacks can co-opt whiteness. In fact, when blacks and other "low status" Americans adopt "the high status group's cultural devices, [they] always risk . . . discrediting."[14] Therefore, blackface, which performed socially downward in terms of class and caste, was more readily embraced than whiteface, which performed upward. Nevertheless, before white blackface minstrel artists popularized their Zip Coons and Jim Crows, Brown's garden patrons and his "colored" acting company were marketing their commodified versions of whiteness. Nineteenth-century audiences may have been curious about black Shakespeareans, but they were not completely aware of what they were witnessing. Some white critics, like M. M. Noah, dismissed this "low status" usurpation as simple mimicry, thus discrediting Afro-America's tradition of performed whiteness, but whiteface was vastly more complicated.

Cockrell theorizes whiteface minstrelsy as a companion to blackface, but Joseph Roach, in his work on transatlantic performance, identifies this social practice more explicitly and distinctly. Through an insightful reading of the 1895 *Plessy v. Ferguson* racial accommodations case, Roach defines whiteface minstrelsy as "stereotypical behaviors—such as white folks' sometime comically obsessive habits of claiming for themselves ever more fanciful forms of property, ingenious entitlements under the law, and exclusivity in the use of public spaces and facilities."[15] The all-white Louisiana train car serves as an outstanding example of what Roach considers "fanciful" white privilege or property. According to Roach, mulatto Homer Plessy also engaged in whiteface minstrelsy when he attempted to "pass" into that all-white conveyance and partake in the "ingenious entitlements." These extratheatrical whiteface minstrel acts, in which whites construct entitlements and blacks appropriate them, demonstrate how African Americans could aggressively assume the privilege and cultural prestige enjoyed by Euro-America.

The relationship between Homer Plessy's social expropriation of white entitlements, or whiteface minstrelsy, and passing is a complex one. Racial passing is a social practice by which legally defined black citizens, who visually appear white, take advantage of their biological windfall and attempt to assimilate into the majority culture. For many African Americans, in slave and postemancipation contexts, passing provided an avenue for advancement and conditional acceptance by the dominant group. Scholars have queried whether passing as a social practice represents a definitive political strategy, and they have generally agreed that it does not. Cultural theorist Amy Robinson, who has also examined the *Plessy v. Ferguson* case, writes that "the social practice of passing is thoroughly invested in the logic of the system it attempts to subvert."[16] A passing individual rarely challenges the "high status" culture but instead consciously dissembles to become an accepted member within that prevailing cultural group.

A passing individual must execute an exact replica of "whiteness" without the slightest deviation; remaining inconspicuous or undetectable marks a successful pass. Racial passers ultimately conform to the preexistent political-racial order or symbolic hegemony because they are conditioned by what Antonio Gramsci terms "false consciousness." On the level of ideas, this consciousness prevents subordinates from ever thinking themselves free.[17] At best, racial passing can expose the unreliability of racial categories predicated on visual markers; what you see and assume is not what you get.

Cultural theorist Michael Awkward claims that while passing reveals "the ease with which racial barriers can be transgressed," other "texts of transraciality," such as Murphy's *White Like Me* film short, generally insist on "the impenetrability, the mysteriousness, of the racial other's cultural rituals and social practices."[18] To the contrary, I contend that both passing and whiteface minstrelsy can demystify and familiarize white social and cultural practices. Awkward misreads Murphy's performance of white privilege, which does comically reveal the secrets of Euro-America but ends with a satirically ominous warning that the borders can and will be transgressed by subsequent African Americans with "tons of makeup." In fact, the whiteface minstrelsy of Homer Plessy and Eddie Murphy, more so than the implicitly invisible passing, suggests that the dominant culture's rituals and entitlements can be penetrated or invaded.

Without question, both whiteface social performers and racial passers acknowledge the cultural primacy of Europe in the United States, and both view the dominant culture as a target for invasion. New World slaves came to identify Europeanness with a better way of life because whites rested atop the colonial and national power structures. With the passage of time, rapidly acculturating American blacks, both slave and free, came to associate European features, values, cultural practices, and speech patterns with prestige and success.[19] By comparison, blackness was strongly linked to primitivism and underachievement—racial assumptions that still operate today. Given the degradation of slavery and postemancipation, institutionalized racial discrimination, an assimilating African American unconscious is understandable.

However, many nineteenth-century African Americans chose not to pass but still "penetrated" privilege by refusing to concede Euro-Americans an exclusive hold on refinement. Observations by two English visitors, Frances Trollope and Charles Mathews, indicate that early national African Americans did not consider white skin a prerequisite for gentility. Trollope, who traveled through the United States in the late 1820s, noticed among New York "Negroes" a "very superior air of gallantry assumed by the men, when in attendance on their *belles*, to that of the whites in similar circumstances." In her journal, *Domestic Manners of the Americans*, Trollope lauded "Negro" men for removing their hats in the presence of their women and chastised Caucasian men for wearing their chapeaux and even smoking in the presence of the fairer sex. In his memoirs, English comedian Charles Mathews characterized the "lower order" of whites as "blackguards" and claimed that blacks were above them in "being genteel." Both English observers highlighted important class distinctions in their observations and concluded that African Americans were more attuned to elite fashion and decorum compared with working-class white Americans.[20] Culturally, these genteel blacks questioned the presumed associations of whiteness with progress and blackness with backwardness, thus contesting absolute claims of white supremacy.

When compared, both passing and whiteface minstrelsy raid white privilege, question the reliability of visual markers, and partly acknowledge white cultural dominance. However, these practices diverge on the levels of conscious intention and execution. Joseph Roach implies and Amy Robinson explains that Homer Plessy never intended to remain a passing individual; but, as part of a legal ploy, he planned to infiltrate, invade, or "pass" onto that segregated train car and announce his blackness. Therefore, Homer Plessy should be read as a whiteface minstrel performer, not a racial passer. His calculated action was a mimetic intervention designed to question white supremacy by interjecting his legally defined black identity into an exclusively white context. Unlike passing's demand for conformity to the existing order, extratheatrical whiteface acts are free to demystify, challenge, comment on, and even recreate dominant conventions. In fact, as much as blackface practitioners commodified blackness by separating culture from race, whiteface minstrel performers commodified whiteness by successfully disconnecting refinement from race and potentially from economic class as well. Such critical and reconstructive, as opposed to simplistic or reactionary, appropriations of the dominant culture challenge the extent of "false consciousness" and diverge from the social practice of passing.

Literary studies scholar Houston Baker Jr. has developed a theory of mastering and "blackening" white forms that further explicates the relationship between the dominant culture and whiteface minstrelsy. Baker coined the term "mastery of form" as a way to explain how African Americans as different as Booker T. Washington and Charles Chesnutt manipulated minstrel masks to "sound" an "authentic" African American folk voice. Borrowing freely from Muhammad Ali, Baker writes that "mastery of form conceals, disguises, floats like a trickster butterfly in order to sting like a bee."[21] He claims that black artists have mastered and concealed themselves behind European forms, nearly passing or assimilating, but ultimately emerge to exhibit notable differences. Baker singles out the "*standard* artistic postures" of two Harlem Renaissance writers, Claude McKay and Countee Cullen: "[O]ne can contextualize such efforts by saying that McKay's 'sonnet,' like Cullen's 'ballads,' are just as much mastered masks as the minstrel manipulations of Booker T. Washington and Charles Chesnutt are."[22] Through McKay's and Cullen's literary work, the mask of a standard sonnet or ballad became trickster tools sounding a uniquely, and perhaps essentially, African American voice.

Additionally, Baker and his former student Michael Awkward have introduced a differentiating step after "mastery of form" that they term "denigration of form." They define this revisioning process as a necessary or "forced" adoption of the standard that results in an effective "blackening" of white form.[23] In using the term "denigration," I doubt that Baker wishes to imply African American appropriations of white forms signal the death or literal denigration of artistic genres. Rather, when Cullen, Chesnutt, and McKay "blacken," denigrate, or remodel standard structures, they produce a fresh and distinctly African American artistic product and perspective.

Extending these theories of differentiation, revision, and penetration, literary scholar Henry Gates's much cited theory of signifyin(g) as textual revision provides an excellent theoretical vehicle for understanding what whiteface minstrelsy produces. Gates's concept of "motivated signifyin(g)" not only parodies and revises the original form but "functions to redress an imbalance of power, to clear a space, rhetorically."[24] Both Gates's and Baker's theories of textual revision highlight processes that have the potential to displace white forms and introduce new black forms. If we simply replace the literary text with the body as text, we can use both theories to illuminate whiteface minstrelsy. As performance traditions, whiteface minstrelsy and, by extension, stage Europeans are not content with revealing the complexity of Euro-America; they propose new black performative models.

As a social performance tradition, whiteface minstrelsy exhibits important differences and similarities with extratheatrical inverse rituals, saturnalias, or misrule revelries. Traditionally, these carnival moments are predicated on a communal contract that publicly sanctions, at a set time of year, the suspension of societal norms. During these topsy-turvy annual events, for example, a cross-dressing male peasant may knock on the door of a wealthy family and demand money, or an African slave may parade as royalty and command monetary homage from his temporary subjects.[25] Whiteface minstrelsy diverges from these inverse rituals on the important issue of permission. Before promenading down the streets of New York City or Charleston, South Carolina, the African American social performers did not seek or receive official sanction to "blacken" or reconstruct certain white forms. There was no social contract permitting a black pleasure garden to co-opt the cultural prestige and social privilege seemingly reserved for Euro-Americans. So understandably, when these "colored" impositions on the dominant culture went too far, they were verbally and even physically attacked by offended and threatened Euro-Americans.

Connected to this issue of communal sanction is the question of how inverse rituals function in relation to regular life. Scholars continue to debate whether these regular social rituals constitute safety valves that ultimately affirm the existing structure or represent mounting acts of resistance that gradually destabilize civic order and offer alternative paradigms. Ex-slave turned abolitionist Frederick Douglass proclaimed unequivocally that plantation Christmas parties were designed to quell insurrectionary sentiments: "These holidays serve as conductors, or safety valves, to carry off the rebellious spirit of enslaved humanity."[26] The holidays to which Douglass referred were plantation gatherings sanctioned, financed, and monitored by the planter class, so his definitive statement rings true. Anthropologist Victor Turner would consider this position the "conservative view of ritual disorder," which underestimates the insurgent potential of these rituals. Historian Natalie Zemon Davis maintains that the carnival moment can embrace both resistance and accommodation. She writes, "It is an exaggeration to view the carnival and Misrule as merely a 'safety valve,' as merely a primitive, prepolitical form of recreation," and further argues that "the structure of the carnival form can evolve so that it can act both to reinforce order and to suggest alternatives to the existing order."[27]

Whiteface minstrel acts, crafted by free and enslaved African Americans, evolved into a performance form that co-opted and reinforced certain elements of the dominant culture, but the most highly developed versions of this tradition clearly fostered an alternative social model. These extratheatrical acts differed from Douglass's sanctioned Christmas parties and similar saturnalias because they were active components of a growing, unsanctioned, black-dominated counterculture. They progressed toward an alternative social model where everyday blackness could represent liberation, refinement, and even cultural dominance. Much of whiteface social performance did not relieve or resolve social tensions between divided populations, but rather intensified cultural and spatial confrontations between Afro- and Euro-America.

Finally, to understand the full import of whiteface minstrelsy, it is necessary to reveal the inherent power dynamics operating in the public, private, and in-between spaces where African Americans cultivated this counterculture and performed their unsanctioned social disruptions. Political scientist James Scott provides the best theoretical model for discussing power in semiprivate spaces like a pleasure garden and public spaces like Manhattan's major thoroughfares. Scott divides the everyday social performance spaces of dominant and subordinate groups into the public transcript or onstage arena and hidden transcripts or backstage arenas.[28] Onstage, majority and minority cultures jointly construct a public transcript that portrays the majority culture as all-powerful, all-knowing, and even magnanimous. Backstage or offstage, removed from majority surveillance, the minority group creates hidden or private transcripts that contradict the public transcript and proffer alternative versions of civic order. In crafting backstage versions of the public transcript, the subordinate group often borrows gestures, social practices, and speech patterns from the dominant group. As we shall see, Manhattan's whiteface minstrel performers created private or semiprivate transcripts but did not confine their alternative visions of the public transcript to these somewhat hidden spaces. They boldly interjected their hidden transcripts into the most public spaces and purposefully blurred distinctions between private and public, white and black, majority and minority.

Black Dandys and Dandizettes

Brown's African Grove provided a perfect location for the public exhibition of Afro–New York's hidden transcripts of white privilege and position, but his pleasure garden was not the first Manhattan venue to showcase white-face minstrelsy. Prior to this colored Arabia, nineteenth-century Afro–New Yorkers paraded their appropriations of whiteness along the city's most visible streets, especially Broadway. More than a century before the "Great White Way" emerged as a center of commercial theater and tourism, Broadway was literally a broad street that snaked from Battery Park in lower Manhattan through Greenwich Village on the outskirts of town. Well before the *Lion King* dominated a Disney-inflected jungle, this broad street itself served as an entertainment outlet for a diversity of restless, leisure-seeking Manhattanites. New York's Common Council, the governing municipal body, decreed that gardens, theaters, and circuses could not open for amusement on the Sabbath.[29] Therefore, following Sunday services, Broadway became the site of a most spectacular extratheatrical performance as families, couples, and single youths amused themselves with pleasurable strolls along the thoroughfare. Without first requesting white approval, stylish Afro–New Yorkers joined and eventually dominated this weekly ritual. In the aforementioned article of August 1821, Noah dubbed the promenading black extratheatrical performers "black dandys and dandizettes." Costumed in the latest fashions, they devoted every Sunday—their one day off—to transforming Broadway into their very own civic showcase. They constructed a public transcript that severed the seemingly natural connections between whiteness, dominance, and refinement and, more important, advanced a new urban black style. Far from endorsing white superiority or exhibiting false consciousness, their whiteface acts rejected the negative connotations associated with blackness and advocated an alternative, more self-possessed African American identity.

Initially, white young men and women were the dominant promenade performers, engaging in informal fashion shows and coy courting rituals. One prominent player in this sporting, courting dance was the foppish male rake known as the "dandy."[30] In a series of newspaper articles, M. M. Noah exposed "Dandyism," beginning with an article satirizing a fictional "Dandy Committee of Young Men." Based on actual dandies, Noah imagined an all-male association of well-dressed characters who sported "shammy gloves" and assumed outlandish, pseudomilitaristic names. Noah's dandies were not merely interested in the latest fashions; they were superficially attuned to the political scene as well, convening to pass resolutions on the political viability of General Andrew Jackson and Governor Yates of New York. In a second article entitled "Dandyism," Noah reported the true story of a real-life "spark of the first water" who possessed the same last name as General Andrew Jackson. Using the fact that Jackson was campaigning for the presidency, this dandy pretended to be a relative and ordered tailors to make "his tippy coat, his blue silk sham, his cossack pantaloons, his corsets and shammy gloves."[31] For his readers, Noah captured the typically vacuous and opportunistic dandy with questionable political and familial associations. Dandies were rarely men of great means, but that did not deter these resourceful rakes from plotting economically advantageous schemes and starring in the sartorial Sunday promenades.

As for female counterparts to the dandies, Christine Stansell, working-class historian, reports how white domestics indulged in the Saturday evening and Sunday afternoon habit of "walking out." Not to be confused with prostitution, "walking out" was an elaborate courting-flirting ritual that allowed young women to escape the surveillance of families, neighborhoods, or employers as they explored romantic possibilities. Middle- and upper-class female employers of white domestics perceived their well-dressed servants as signs of class erosion and precursors to domestic insubordination. They also feared that the social practice of "walking out" would lead to the ruination of their workforce. Consequently, concerned employers created the Society for the Encouragement of Faithful Domestic Servants to admonish their young ladies to "dress in a manner becoming your station."[32] But admonishment could not dissuade Manhattan's stylish white domestics from devoting their leisure hours to promenades and coquetries with "sporty" dandies.

Eventually, white dandies and domestics were forced to share this public stage with Noah's "black dandys and dandizettes," and by the late 1810s Afro–New Yorkers were becoming the major attractions or distractions during the Sunday spectacles. Much like cunning social-climbing white dandies and class-transgressing white domestics, black domestics, cooks, stewards, and day laborers exhibited the elite attitudes and privileged posturing denied them during the workweek. Noah's first African Grove article explained that, because blacks were denied admission to white pleasure gardens, these Sunday outings became tremendously important occasions: "Their modicum of pleasure was taken on Sunday evening, when the black dandys and dandizettes, after attending meeting, occupied the side walks in Broadway, and slowly lounged towards their different homes."[33] For many black servants and slaves, Sunday remained significant, beyond religious rites, because it was their only day completely devoted to leisure.[34]

In general, New Yorkers accepted "walking out" and promenading as natural products of a restless youth culture and simply enjoyed the spectacles. However, some Euro–New Yorkers perceived fully possessed black promenaders as a direct challenge to a white-constructed public transcript and sensed progress or regress toward an alternative symbolic world. One concerned citizen wrote a letter to the *New York Evening Post* describing the increased black presence on Broadway: "Two gentlemen, on Sunday afternoon last had the curiosity to count the number of Negroes, males and females, that passed a house in Broadway, near Washington Hall. In about two hours they amounted to fourteen hundred and eighty. Several hundred passed in the course of the evening. It was observed that these people were all well drest, and very much better than the whites. The men almost without exception, wore broadcloth coats, very many of them boots, fashionable Cossack pantaloons, and white hats; watches and canes. The latter article was observed to be flourished with inimitable grace, to the annoyance of all the passengers."[35] What stands out in this portion of the letter is the substantial, perhaps exaggerated, number of Afro–New Yorker males passing by the two spectators. Also the "two gentlemen" reveal that the blacks were uniformly better attired than their white counterparts, which suggests that black dandies were supplanting white dandies as the star performers on this common stage. The anonymous letter mirrored many commentaries published in the *Evening Post*, the *Spectator*,[36] and M. M. Noah's *National Advocate*, all of which related, in obsessive detail, the actions and carriage of male and female black promenaders. We should be thankful that these concerned citizens took the time to register their reactions, because without their written complaints we would have no records of these weekly social rituals.

These well-documented fashionable strollers and their New World African sense of style embodied Henry Gates's theory of "motivated signifyin[g]" because they addressed a definite imbalance of power in the broader society by clearing rhetorical space, along a major thoroughfare, and establishing or repositioning blackness at the center rather than the margins. Beyond mastering or imitating the white dandy, black promenaders reconfigured whiteness and the latest European styles to promote their much maligned blackness as dominant and self-possessed.[37] Contrary to claims of "false consciousness," these Afro–New Yorkers did not approach white fashion as inviolable or sacrosanct but proceeded to revise Old World attire by widening the bottoms of pantaloons, replacing white hats with colored headdresses, or brandishing incredibly ornate canes. On the level of cultural signifiers, self-assured black bodies attacked essential notions that granted whiteness an exclusive hold on authority. New York's signifyin(g) promenaders and similar black social performers in other U.S. cities—notably Charleston, South Carolina—authored an expressive product that temporarily separated privilege from whiteness and inserted black bodies into the center of civic life. If the nineteenth-century letters were any indication, this resistant, repositioning campaign was a success, and Africans were now the Sunday superstars.

Each Sunday, "black dandys and dandizettes" metaphorically breached racial and class boundaries to reposition blackness in the social hierarchy, but the resistance went further. They physically challenged the dominant group's authority over Manhattan streets and literally intimidated Euro–New York. The concerned—presumably white—citizen quoted earlier noted that, although "Negro" males flourished their ornate walking canes "with inimitable grace," they also used their walking sticks to annoy other "passengers." The writer further recounted how "[t]he blacks usually walk four or five a breast, arm and arm, with segars in their mouths, bid defiance to all opposition, and almost universally compel our most respectable citizens, returning from church with their families, to take the outside of the walk, and sometimes to leave the side walk altogether."[38] Trapped in servile positions during the week, on their special day, emboldened blacks refused to genuflect before whites or "our most respectable citizens." As a matter of informal convention, blacks were supposed to "give the wall" to whites and allow their social superiors the privilege of walking closer to the buildings and clear of the street's muck and mire. Black promenaders moved in lines of four or five and dominated the entire sidewalk to establish, literally, their unequivocal command of this weekly ritual and the entire public transcript.

In fact, these "black dandys and dandizettes" demolished the boundary between private and public transcripts, which was never a solid wall to begin with.[39] According to James Scott, subordinates generally performed their masters offstage, in hidden spaces where they could freely revise and critique the official or public transcript. Broadway's black promenaders may have formulated their critiques and revisions of white privilege backstage, using dominant cultural material, but their Sunday performances ushered this commentary to center stage. The signified and blackened white fashions, the self-assured black bodies, and the intimidating lines of domineering Afro–New Yorkers figuratively and literally seized control of the public transcript and spoke their version of truth to power. Such instances in which the hidden or private transcripts pierce through the public transcript represent significant collision or explosion moments; Scott terms these intrusions a "symbolic declaration of war."[40] On Sundays, Broadway witnessed a collision of private and public, black and white, confrontations of unresolved opposites. Such symbolic declarations of war triggered a temporary collapse of racial polarities, cultivated a hybrid New World African identity, and produced a dominant version of blackness in Manhattan's public spaces.

Noah's African Grove?

Broadway's "black dandys and dandizettes" staged the possibility of substantive change in the social relations between Afro– and Euro–New York, a potential further developed in the African Grove. M. M. Noah, a Republican newspaper editor, local sheriff, and American playwright, introduced this colored playground to New York and subsequently developed a complex relationship with Brown's other institutions.[41] Noah's initially curious and benign coverage of these "African Amusements" would develop a more satiric and adversarial tone as Brown's entertainment interests expanded. Nevertheless, the neophyte manager continually invited Noah to his events and published his first theatrical advertisement in the *National Advocate*. Furthermore, during the lengthy American Theatre phase, Brown supported and popularized native-born writers by producing Noah's dramatic work. Whether ubiquitous friend or necessary foe, Noah's published reviews and editorials represent the most significant primary source materials on Brown's first phase and its attendant performance conventions, specifically whiteface minstrelsy. For his nineteenth-century readers, Noah introduced the African Grove in the distinctly racial terms most consistent with prevailing stereotypes and assumptions. For historians, the cunning editor has submerged Brown's amusements beneath enough political and cultural bias to make any reclamation project nearly impossible. But for better or worse, Noah's raucous and ridiculing accounts constitute the basis for any performative reconstructions.

We have no official record of how William Brown identified or advertised his garden, but the African American manager and his initial supporters may have informally adopted the name African Grove. Given Brown's largely black clientele and the fact that his establishment was the lone Manhattan garden amenable to people of color, this racially particular moniker seems appropriate. However, the best indication of how Brown envisioned his institutional identity rests with his choice of location: Manhattan's West Side. In the early 1820s the West Side was a generally affluent neighborhood northwest of City Hall Park, Manhattan's major municipal landmark. The community was removed from the business district of lower Manhattan and featured elegant homes, an educational institution like Columbia College, and a European-quality hotel like Astor Place. Providing balance to these elite attractions, the neighborhood also harbored its share of late-night gambling establishments, exclusive upscale brothels, and mildly boisterous taverns.[42] At some point between 1816 and 1821, Brown settled into retirement by renting a house at 38 Thomas Street on the West Side. This was a noteworthy, even bold real-estate decision, given that tax records and city directories reveal few Afro–New Yorkers in this area.[43] Brown not only created a lively pleasure garden for people of color in his Thomas Street backyard but also further integrated the West Side. Noah's August article placed the garden "back of the hospital" or behind the City Hospital. Municipal maps from the period show that this hospital literally separated the wealthy West Side from the economically depressed and allegedly "black" Five Points district.[44]

Five Points acquired its name because the center of this residential area rested where Cross, Orange, and Anthony Streets converged to create five corners or points. The original Points residents were wealthy Euro–New Yorkers, but the low-lying, marsh property proved poor real estate. As housing values rapidly declined, the wealthy sold and relocated. Attracted by inexpensive housing and discouraged from moving into other sections of the city, poor Irish immigrants and freed slaves converged on Five Points. By the 1820 census, Irish Americans followed by African Americans were the two largest groups in this last resort for the ostracized and impoverished, and despite the circumstances, they developed profitable, often contentious, but always intimate relations in the Points. As one of the few neighborhoods with substantial social and residential integration, Five Points became notorious for its interracial sex trade. White-owned and black-owned brothels located primarily along Anthony Street provided interracial, exclusively white, or strictly black clienteles with prostitutes of varying shades and sizes.[45]

Beyond the variegated sex trade, black entrepreneurs created a cottage industry by transforming their cellar apartments—residences below street level—into a thriving subculture of dancing cellars, cellar kitchens, and underground grog shops in Five Points and other areas. Unlike white pleasure gardens, the black cellar hosts refused to practice discriminatory admission policies, and their subterranean leisure outlets afforded slaves, free blacks, and whites the space to congregate, converse, consume, and dance well into the evening. Amenable working-class whites, especially Irish Americans, were mainstays in the late-night, black-operated dancing cellars, and these whites attended to drink alcohol and to master particularly complex African American dance steps.[46] In the late 1820s John Russwurm and Samuel Cornish's *Freedom's Journal*, America's first black newspaper, published an article condemning Five Points dancing cellars. Their article on "Dancing Houses" characterized the working-class dance hall scene as filled with prostitutes, pickpockets, and disreputable young men bent on ruining "thoughtless servant girls."[47] Such comments reinforced the increasingly infamous image of Five Points and echoed the sentiments of a group like the Society for the Encouragement of Faithful Domestic Servants, which was equally concerned with the despoiling of "servant girls." As more young men, black or white, ruined reputations and as foreign visitors toured the Points, this community earned an international reputation as America's disreputable and unpredictable red-light district. Even though Irish Americans outnumbered African Americans, the Points also developed the reputation as a "black" slum. A significant African American presence coupled with black-owned brothels and cellar entertainments gave Five Points the appearance of a playground for darker New Yorkers.

By establishing personal and professional residence on the primarily white and more affluent West Side instead of the dispossessed, felonious, and "black" Five Points, Brown deviated from racial and residential expectations. From the perspective of many Euro–New Yorkers, including Noah, Manhattan's first black pleasure garden should have surfaced in the city's first distinctly black area, Five Points, but Brown's contrarian real-estate decision exhibited the same resistant tendencies as Sunday's black Broadway promenaders. Like "black dandys and dandizettes," Brown brazenly staged his New World Africanist spectacle in the middle of affluent whiteness, or at least in its backyard. In lieu of an official name, his choice of location established a distinctly integrationist tone for the garden entertainments and later "African Amusements." Ironically, his tone amplified the integrationist spirit of the cellar-dwelling black entrepreneurs who refused to practice discrimination, and like his Five Points predecessors, Brown's institutions catered to presumably "second-class" Afro–New Yorkers while cultivating an interracial Manhattan.

As a retired steward, William Brown acquired his profound appreciation for integration not from Five Points or the West Side but rather from his maritime experiences. Historians from Peter Linebaugh to Paul Gilroy have recovered an eighteenth- and nineteenth-century transatlantic maritime culture that incubated and transported radical ideologies such as abolition, democracy, and racial equality between Old and New World seaports. Aboard passenger packets, cargo ships, or whaling ships, black and white maritime workers developed inclusive worldviews often in direct conflict with oppressive policies practiced ashore. On a small scale, after the War of 1812, the Park Theatre invited a crew of American sailors to a performance honoring their heroism. Although the Park restricted blacks to the gallery, that population comprised half of this naval crew; therefore, the sailors disregarded Park seating policy, and all assumed seats in the pit. On a larger scale, maritime workers also spread the seeds of revolution among working-class whites in Europe and the Americas and among slaves and free blacks throughout the African diaspora.[48]

William Brown cultivated a comparatively egalitarian atmosphere throughout his managerial career, but at first glance, his initial pleasure garden may have appeared deficient in certain democratic principles. By definition, nineteenth-century pleasure gardens were elitist entertainments designed to provide the most possessed New Yorkers with an escape from the undesirable aspects of urban life. For Euro–New Yorkers, these urban undesirables included the noise, the filth, the summer heat, Afro–New Yorkers, and lower-class Irishmen. As a companion to the Broadway promenade, the semiprivate, semipublic Thomas Street garden provided leisure-seeking Afro–New Yorkers with their own privileged escape. Brown originally opened his garden for the benefit of his fellow black stewards, who constituted early Afro-America's elite class. Amateur historian and black physician James McCune Smith describes the prestige attached to this particular group in African American communities and characterizes black stewards as "a class which, at that time and for years afterwards, even to the present day, occupied a respectable and responsible position. The steward was then, next to the captain, the most important personage in the ship."[49] Brown risked his life savings so that an esteemed class of Afro–New Yorkers could have a pleasant space to congregate, and according to McCune Smith, these genteel blacks gave Brown their "full share of patronage."

Brown's primary allegiance rested with this economically privileged black subculture, and his star attraction, James Hewlett, also occasionally worked as a ship's steward.[50] However, his garden quickly attracted leisure-deprived Afro– and Euro–New Yorkers from other economic classes and castes, thus creating an ideal "meeting ground" for cultural crisscrossings. In his article introducing the African Grove, Noah claimed to have overheard Afro–New Yorkers using phrases like "our gentlemen" and "our young ladies," which suggests that these particular patrons were domestic servants or even slaves. Social historian Edwin Olson claims that wealthy Manhattan masters routinely gave their slaves money and permission to attend entertainments like Brown's garden.[51] So, land-loving domestic workers and slaves mingled with esteemed stewards and their wives at this colored "oasis," not to mention curious whites like M. M. Noah, who were equally welcome at the African Grove. Through this motley mixture of classes, castes, and races, Brown successfully elevated the Five Points working-class dancing cellar to a higher, more middle-class standard.

A common denominator among Brown's black garden patrons and the Broadway promenaders was an aspiration toward middle- or upper-class status. Noah articulated the connection between this garden and the promenaders: "As their number increased, and their consequence strengthened; partly from high wages, high living, and the elective franchise; it was considered necessary to have a place of amusement for them exclusively."[52] The "high wages" were figments of Noah's active imagination, but the appetite for "high living" among Manhattan's ever increasing colored population was very much in evidence each Sunday. Not content with their one day, "black dandys and dandizettes" desired, or perhaps demanded, a more consistent, reputable, and prestigious leisure outlet. Five Points subterranean taverns and dance halls were available most of the week, but those entertainments lacked the cultural cache that a pleasure garden could offer. Brown avoided all the negative associations with Five Points by creating a more respectable leisure environment in a presumably safer West Side community. Furthermore, while black cellar hosts were forced to transform poorly ventilated basements into dance halls, the adventuresome impresario had a spacious backyard and an evening breeze at his disposal.

Traditionally, garden goers enjoyed orchestral or vocal musical acts, dramatic recitations, and rudimentary fireworks. Noah claimed that Brown's garden entertainments were no different and noted that they featured a small garden band performing music similar to that heard at the white-owned Chatham or Vauxhall Gardens. Among the garden populace, Noah noticed direct parallels between Sunday promenaders and this garden gentry. He described one colored gentleman wearing "a blue coat fashionably cut; red ribbon and a bunch of pinchback seals; wide pantaloons; shining boots, gloves, and a tippy rattan and a colored lady sporting her pink kid slippers; her fine Leghorn, cambric dress, with open work; corsets well fitted; reticule, hanging on her arm."[53] Similar to Sunday rituals, this social performance centered around an informal fashion show in which garden patrons competed with one another for the best attire. Noah found that "these black fashionables saunter up and down the garden, in all the pride of liberty and unconsciousness of want. In their address; salutations; familiar phrases; and compliments; their imitative faculties are best exhibited." Ever the astute editor, Noah recognized the self-consciousness or artificiality of these "free" attitudes and recognized the thoroughly performative nature of this "imitative" whiteface show, fertile ground for a "becoming" identity process. He registered how the proud black patrons were infused with a sense of liberty and equality that they did not manifest daily in the public transcript. Whether Noah acknowledged it or not, Brown had successfully extended the fleeting yet liberating self-esteem of the weekly promenades to these daily gatherings.

Joseph Roach partly defines whiteface minstrelsy as creating fanciful, even excessive entitlements, and such a description captures the ultra-exclusive posturing practiced in Brown's garden. His black garden goers embraced the unseemly attitudes that accompany exclusivity, specifically snobbery, nativism, regional prejudice, and class-caste animus. In particular, they behaved as if they were more refined than select Euro–New Yorkers. Noah allegedly overheard an affected conversation between four garden patrons and recreated their exchange: "Harry, who did you vote for at de election? De federalists to be sure; I never wotes for de mob. Our gentlemen brought home tickets, and after dinner, ve all vent and woted."[54] In spite of Noah's unfortunate German-inflected "Negro" dialect, the "recreated" conversation reveals a few important social and political truths. First, the conversation reveals that Afro–New Yorkers were voting in 1821, an electoral practice that would eventually come under attack. Also, the Federalists for whom "Harry" voted represent the Federalist Party, which was the party of New York's wealthiest citizens. The Federalists also acquired a reputation as

"Negrophiles" because several slave owners and ex-slavers in this party lobbied to end slavery throughout the state.[55] Finally, in line with Federalist elitism, the colored foursome articulates a frightening strain of nativism when they decry "the mob," which is a reference to the Irish immigrants flooding into Manhattan. Federalists were stridently anti-immigrant and refused to embrace propertyless Irish Americans.

Of course, a politically savvy editor like M. M. Noah could have imposed this "mob" animus on these four patrons. In reality, Irish New Yorkers and Afro–New Yorkers resided in the same dispossessed communities, like Five Points, which meant urban blacks had more materially in common with poor Irishmen than with monied Federalists. However, because wealthy Euro–New Yorkers owned, once owned, or employed many Afro–New Yorkers, it is conceivable some blacks gravitated toward this nativism in their social posturing and politics. Also, African Americans did develop their own anti-Irish sentiments, which were expressed through physical confrontations with Irish Americans and an extensive repertoire of Irish jokes that ridiculed this "lowly" white population.[56] So, the idea that Noah's garden patrons chose to align themselves politically and socially with the richest New Yorkers is plausible. The garden foursome's identification with Federalism against the unrefined Irish accomplished the important work of separating gentility from whiteness. This "mob," the object of black and Federalist derision, represented whites who could hardly claim refinement, whereas the colored gentry in Brown's backyard surely could and did.

Difficult to contain once unleashed, this elitist and dismissive whiteface posturing derided another "low status" group—black migrants. Noah's foursome blackened "white" snobbery by replacing the Federalist whipping boys, Irish immigrants, with an intraracial target: southern or "country" blacks. Noah recalled this exchange: "Miss how you like to go to de Springs? I shouldn't like it; too many negers from de suthard, and such crowd of folks, that decent people can get no refreshments."[57] The foursome now turned their noses up at the "negers from de suthard" overrunning the "Springs," or Saratoga Springs, New York, a summer resort thirty miles north of Albany. "Negers from de suthard" refers to the southern blacks, free persons and escaped slaves, streaming into New York State. The remark can also be read as city blacks distinguishing themselves from "country" blacks, which suggests this garden gentry, like Broadway's African trendsetters, cultivated a distinctly urban black identity. With privileged white gardens as models, elitist "black dandys and dandizettes" needed targets to disdain, and native

Afro–New Yorkers made rural "negers" the unfortunate outsiders. That is the risk Brown ran by cultivating a retreat where an aspiring "colored" gentry could freely indulge in excessive entitlements.

To reiterate, there seems to be an undeniable tension between this foursome's exclusive disdain for less refined blacks and Brown's egalitarian agenda. His garden catered to free blacks, slaves, domestic servants, and stewards, so any hint of social stratification could have undermined that desired inclusiveness. But the artificial nature of the garden social performances can partly resolve this apparent conflict. Implicit in Brown's backyard whiteface gathering is an abrogation of clearly defined class, caste, regional, or other borders; such distinctions are already porous because they can be appropriated and performed—much like that white dandy posing as Andrew Jackson's relative proved. Far from promoting strict definitions of class or an unyielding tripartite hierarchy—upper, middle, lower classes—Brown's garden embraced and embodied the notion that class was about relations and activities.[58] In this "becoming" playground, Brown's garden attendees were never forced to assume their everyday economic or social identities, so conceivably a group of newly arrived "negers from de suthard" could have been the very same foursome Noah overheard belittling rural blacks. Or perhaps a well-heeled slave, owned by a Federalist, was a member of this small cabal, and despite her lower-caste status, she could gleefully deride a free black from the "country." Although they might be owned, impoverished, or hopelessly "country" during the week, while luxuriating in their African Grove slaves could transcend caste, servants could transgress class, and migrants could outdistance region.

One possible reading of Noah's African Grove article would suggest that these allegedly transracial, transclass free-for-alls lacked resistant potential and did not advance a politicized blackness engaged with the symbols or markers of dominant whiteness. Noah would have us believe that "black dandys and dandizettes," much like white dandies, were vacuous pretenders with no social, political, or cultural substance. He maintained that the superficial garden performers were never truly attuned to the politics they discussed; rather, their discourses simply parroted the conversations of "white folks." To open his pleasure garden article, Noah characterized most Afro–New Yorkers as "very imitative, quick in their conceptions and rapid in execution; but it is the lighter pursuits requiring no intensity of thought or depth of reflection. It may be questioned whether they could succeed in the abstruse sciences, though they have, nevertheless, some fancy and humor, and the domestics of respectable families are complete facsimiles of the different branches of it, not only in dress but in habits and manners."[59] Noah would have us believe that members of this "colored gentry" dressed the part but were mentally incapable of serious political thought or social action. He concluded, "Thus they run the rounds of fashion; ape their masters and mistresses in everything; talk of projected matches; rehearse the news of the kitchen, and the follies of the day, and bating the 'tincture of their skins,' are as well qualified to move in the *haut ton*, as many of the white dandies and butterflies, who flutter in the sun shine." Again Noah highlighted the artifice and rehearsal involved conceding blacks were well schooled in "Dandyism," but he maintained they lacked a serious investment in current events and public life.

Another reading of the same pleasure garden report reveals cultural resistance in this colored oasis. Noah's constant references to a lack of black intellectual capacity or political aspiration were intended to infantilize Afro–New Yorkers, but ultimately his comments exposed a politically aware colored community. His article demonstrated that this largely servant crowd assembled to display the latest fashions, deride social inferiors, and weigh in on a range of current events from the Missouri Compromise to suffrage rights. In closing his article, Noah wrote: "They fear no Missouri plot; care for no political rights; happy in being permitted to dress fashionable, walk the streets, visit African Grove, and talk scandal." True, the patrons were attuned to scandal, but a national issue like the Missouri Compromise, which designated slave and free states, was an incredibly relevant topic for this particular assemblage of free blacks and slaves. As for whether they cared about political rights, throughout the article there are various references to blacks exercising the "elective franchise," and a black garden dandy named "Harry" made it a point to vote against the populist Irish immigrants. The garden gentry revealed a topical interest and awareness of local and national developments directly affecting the lives and interests of Afro-America.

Editor Noah employed an interesting phrase to describe these conversations, "rehearse the news of the kitchen," suggesting he understood exactly what was transpiring. Breezy conversational engagements with a combination of scandal talk and political happenings, "the news," were extracted from private or hidden spaces, "the kitchen," and "rehearsed" in this new semiprivate, semipublic leisure outlet. In short, the Thomas Street garden constituted a training ground or rehearsal hall for greater political and social participation in public life.[60] With slavery slated to end statewide on July 4,

1827, these whiteface social performers had a specific date targeted, and they used this space to "become" postemancipation African American citizens.

George Lipsitz, in his work on American popular culture, explicates the meaningful relationship between culture, politics, and rehearsal: "Culture can seem like a substitute for politics, a way of posing only imaginary solutions to real problems, but under other circumstances culture can become a rehearsal for politics, trying out values and beliefs permissible in art but forbidden in social life."[61] In a racially polarizing Manhattan, Afro–New Yorkers needed supportive gathering spaces like Brown's garden in which to rehearse dominant social sensibilities and to "self-create" a liberated Afro-America. Without question, free and enslaved African Americans had to rely on their fertile imaginations to generate these new attitudes, but if members of Manhattan's "colored gentry" could pretend to be politically aware and socially self-defined for four or five nights a week, they might develop a taste for further liberation. They would eventually strive to become civically attuned and active citizens in their real, everyday worlds.

In addition, Ralph Ellison, writing on masking in an amazingly fluid America, contends "that which cannot gain authority from tradition may borrow it with a mask. Masking is a play about possibility and ours is a society in which possibilities are many. When American life is most American it is apt to be most theatrical."[62] By borrowing or co-opting privilege through the mask of whiteness, Broadway's "black dandys and dandizettes" aggressively established physical and figurative dominance over a public transcript customarily defined by Euro–New Yorkers. Colonized African Americans adorned in flared pantaloons, fitted corsets, or free-swinging parasols flattened the distinction between public and private, challenged presumptions surrounding whiteness, and showcased a liberated version of blackness. Consistent with this notion of the United States as a laboratory replete with possibility, this distinctly black urban style carved rhetorical space for an African American sartorial splendor that still remains a major force in fashionable circles to this day.[63]

In Brown's garden, similar whiteface practitioners balanced a semiprivate, semipublic pursuit of elitist leisure with nightly "becoming" rehearsals for full participation in political and social life. After retiring from a uniquely egalitarian maritime culture, Brown created a complex, integrated, but African-dominated entertainment rooted in two monumental and self-defining managerial decisions. His first defining step was to open an inclusive pleasure garden in a white neighborhood where blacks were scarce and therefore most conspicuous. Instead of drawing curious whites and blacks into a black-dominated cellar subculture in an allegedly black neighborhood like Five Points, Brown crossed the tracks and brought his fusion of different races, classes, castes, and regions directly to the majority community. For all concerned this was a training or "becoming" ground where whites nervously eavesdropped on blacks, where slaves trafficked with free blacks, and where simple domestics entertained with "revered" black stewards. Not surprisingly, Euro–New Yorkers like Noah were quick to notice, and as soon as the *National Advocate* announced the African Grove behind the City Hospital in August 1821, Brown's integrationist action was a success. The second significant decision was to encourage an atmosphere where Afro–New Yorkers could radiate their emergent sense of hybrid style, even disdain those less fabulous, and rehearse for "new symbolic worlds." Afro–New Yorkers were firmly in control of this partly hidden, partly exposed transcript; and over the course of an evening, they "masked" frivolous entitlements and prejudices such as high-sounding language, white dandy pretensions, anti-Irish nativism, and even antiblack regional prejudice. However, the black garden goers also explored distinctly political positions or possibilities like unchecked liberty and freedom from want. Although some would have us believe that this colored gentry simply gloried in being fabulous, their fantasies were never limited to outward appearance, but were attuned to the potential for substantive social and political change in the near, postemancipation future.

Charges of mindless mimicry aside, M. M. Noah firmly identified Brown's African Grove and subsequent theaters as rehearsals for increased political engagement, and he would eventually use his editorial position to sabotage this training. A month after heralding the garden with its nocturnal breeze, light refreshments, and whiteface performance, Noah would warn Manhattan of the political danger inherent in these entertainments and similar black usurpations of white privilege.[64] As a member of the competing Republican Party, Noah believed black voters, allegedly controlled by their Federalist "white folks," represented a serious threat to his party's interests.

Less than a month after its opening, the backyard amusement drew complaints from disgruntled neighbors. Noah reported: "We noticed, some time ago, the opening of a tea garden and evening serenades for the amusement of our black gentry; it appears that some of the neighbors, not relishing the jocund nightly sarabands of these sable fashionables, actually complained to the Police, and the avenues of African Grove were closed by authority."[65] Despite this closing at the behest of Brown's white neighbors, other avenues remained open to this creative entrepreneur, and Broadway's original "black dandys and dandizettes" continued making rhetorical room for their fabulous, fully possessed African American identities.

Hung Be the Heavens with Black

TOWARD A MINOR THEATER

AN EDITION OF THE *Spectator* for January 1822 reprinted portions of a play-bill announcing William Brown's first self-articulated institutional identity, the Minor Theatre.[1] Brown's declaration of this particular, but not racially specific, identity was the result of hierarchical struggles with Stephen Price's Park Theatre. This aesthetic hierarchy of major and minor theaters originated with English theatrical censorship. Queen Elizabeth I (1533–1603) fully appreciated the seductive power of the stage and therefore restricted "official" theatrical production to her most loyal subjects. Nearly two centuries later, the link between ruling bodies and theatrical institutions intensified, as the 1737 Licensing Act designated two patent or major theaters, Drury Lane and Covent Garden. London's patent theaters were authorized by the crown to perform "legitimate" dramas and comedies, and the remaining nonpatent or minor theaters were restricted to "illegitimate" pantomimes and ballad operas devoid of spoken text.[2]

In her work on the British major-minor patent system, theater historian Jane Moody contends that the patent theaters and their "legitimate" dramas claimed "to be public guardians of the nation's dramatic heritage and cultural life."[3] Major theaters represented political and cultural authority, the seat of power; however, Moody argues England's patent system operated under the "illusion that a theater without spoken dialogue was a theater without power." She maintains that minor theaters and the unsanctioned artistic communities that developed around them functioned as formidable "counter-public spheres" or alternative theatrical cultures to the politically or royally sanctioned theaters.[4] Even under the constraints of the 1737 Licensing Act, London's major and minor theaters developed a competitive relationship. English melodrama may have first appeared in London's patent houses, but this innovative form flourished in the minor theaters. As an "illegitimate" theatrical genre, melodrama blended dumb shows, music accompaniment, and elaborate spectacle to create a highly entertaining and emotionally affective experience. The form would become so popular with working-class English and U.S. audiences that many theaters, major and minor, favored melodramas over traditional dramas, and when the licensing act was lifted in 1843, London's minor theater audiences still preferred their "illegitimate" entertainments.[5]

Although municipal officials and religious leaders in North American cities from Boston to Charleston mistrusted theaters and regulated this dangerous diversion, U.S. political authorities never instituted a major-minor licensing system. Within the nation's fluid entertainment industry, it would have been extremely difficult to restrict, officially, Brown and other ambitious theatrical managers to minor or "illegitimate" theatrical material. Therefore, it was left to local theatrical communities to reconstitute, unofficially, England's aesthetic hierarchy. In New York, an informal version of the patent system emerged, primarily through the strategic efforts of Stephen Price and his Park Theatre. From the late eighteenth century, this theater was located on Park Row directly across the street from City Hall Park—hence its name—and for decades the Park Theatre was the only permanent theater in the city, prompting many New Yorkers to refer to this revered cultural institution as simply "the Theatre."[6] Price, a lawyer by training, comanaged the Park with an actor named Edmund Simpson, and as the dominant force in this partnership, Price envisioned an undeniably major theatrical institution with an international reputation. Within his own theater, Price restricted the second-rate or "minor" Park stock company actors to leads in musicals and comedies, whereas he reserved the Shakespearean leads for "major" European stars. Beginning in the early 1810s, Price began importing and featuring well-known British stars such as George Frederick Cooke, James Wallack, Edmund Kean, and Charles Mathews in major productions of Shakespearean and contemporary plays. Price even perfected a "star" system by which he supplied leading performers to other "major" theaters in Philadelphia, Boston, and Baltimore. Theater managers paid Price directly for the services of "his stars," thus earning him the transatlantic moniker of "Star Giver General to the United States."

This chapter clarifies the artistic and political distinctions between major and minor in a Park-dominated theatrical universe and, in the process, defines Brown's institution as a "minor" theatrical venture with "major" aspirations. Consistent with the notion of U.S. theater as a site of social and aesthetic experimentation, neophyte manager Brown promoted a potentially combustible aesthetic combination of "legitimate" dramatic material and "illegitimate" musical material. In terms of social experiments, Brown's Minor Theatre pursued the first known national exploration of unrestricted theatrical integration by expanding his white patronage and by mingling working class with middle class, free with enslaved. Ironically, his merger of white and black audiences with wildly divergent expectations would ultimately ensure Brown's status as the "minor" theater. Artistically, during this stage of "becoming" Brown introduced stage Europeans to the nation's cultural laboratory by unapologetically casting black amateur actors in white dramatic roles crafted by white writers for white performers. The final section of this chapter interprets the signifying practices of Brown's first leading lady, S. Welsh. Her complicated reconstruction of Shakespeare's Lady Ann identified with and against the dramatic original to produce fresh perspectives on *Richard III*. At first glance, Welsh's stage European seemed merely to celebrate the best of majority culture, but, on closer inspection, her distinctly "womanist" or prototypically feminist revision of Lady Ann spoke directly to the social conditions and aspirations of nineteenth-century African American women.

Major or Minor?

Manhattan's major-minor struggle began in May 1820 after a mysterious fire destroyed the Park Theatre. Price promptly raised funds to construct a new and improved theatrical shrine at the same Park Row location, and for this new structure he envisioned a marble exterior rivaling the elegance and beauty of any public building in Manhattan.[7] As Price rebuilt, a few aspiring theatrical managers, including Brown, perceived the theater's lengthy absence from the entertainment landscape as an opportunity to expand the market.[8] Brown troubled tranquil theatrical waters with the less-than-spectacular opening of a makeshift theater in his cramped upstairs apartment at

38 Thomas Street. Noah reported, in an article on "African Amusements," that "after mature deliberation" Brown made his theatrical debut with Shakespeare's *Richard III*.[9] Starting with this minor establishment featuring a major Shakespearean tragedy, the resourceful manager would struggle to build the best acting company possible, establish a prime location, and manage an integrated patron base.

For his managerial debut, Brown assembled a company of amateur black actors who spent their days headlining as servants. Noah identified Brown's first leading man as "a little dapper wooly-headed waiter at the City Hotel" who "personated the royal Plantagenet," meaning he played the scheming Duke of Gloucester turned King Richard in *Richard III*.[10] The "wooly-headed waiter" was Charles Taft, alias Charles Beers, an ex-slave who was freed after relentlessly disobedient conduct. Taft was so invested in his evening engagements with the Duke of Gloucester that he violated the law to present this role in the most immaculate attire. In late October 1821 authorities arrested Taft for stealing more than one hundred dollars and some cravats from a private house. At trial, Noah—also sheriff of New York—recognized Taft and concluded that the waiter stole the items to improve his Richard: "This fellow belonged to the black corps dramatique; it seems he wanted cloathes to dress in the character of Richard the 3rd, and therefore stole them." Taft never enjoyed a second opportunity to impress as Richard because, on November 5, he was convicted of grand larceny and sent to prison.[11]

As for Brown's initial leading lady, she also spent her days serving Manhattan, but at night, she played multiple roles. The review from September 21 mentioned that "Lady Ann was sustained with great spirit by a young sable lady, chambermaid in a family near Park Place." A playbill dated September 24 for a second *Richard III* production revealed the maid's name was Welsh, and another playbill dated October 1 referred to her as S. Welsh.[12] We have no evidence of what the S. stood for, but we do know that Welsh was compelled to perform both male and female roles.

Similar to the African Grove whiteface acts that traversed region, caste, and class, Brown's first acting company transgressed gender boundaries on a routine basis. Noah explained that "from a paucity of actors, some doubles occurred and thus: King Henry and the Duchess Dowager were represented by one and the same person, while Lady Ann and Catesby were sustained by another."[13] Females playing male roles were surprisingly common on the nineteenth-century Manhattan stage. Theater historian Claudia Johnson found that in New York theaters, from 1821 to 1858, at least twenty-six different women assumed nearly forty different male roles, including the Duke of Gloucester, Romeo, Marc Anthony, Macbeth, and Shylock. These female actors generally assumed lead male roles for their much anticipated benefit nights,[14] but Welsh and Brown's future female leads did so out of necessity. Most important, Brown's small and overextended company provided servants such as Taft and Welsh with a space to develop their artistic sensibilities.

Following Taft's incarceration, Brown inserted another passionate young performer named James Hewlett as the leading man in the next performance of *Richard III*.[15] Unlike other company members, Hewlett aspired to become a full-time, professional actor. According to a biography published in the *New York Star* and *National Advocate* in 1825, Hewlett billed himself as a serious Shakespearean actor, singer, and dancer who imitated the best European talents in hotels and theaters throughout the nation. The biography reported that Hewlett's "imitations of Kean, Mathews, Phillips and others were recognized as correct, and evincing a nice discrimination and peculiar tact on his part, which ought to recommend him to every lover of pure acting."[16] Hewlett was not simply "aping" white thespians, but, like most aspiring nineteenth-century actors, he mastered and repeated the scenes and acting styles associated with the era's most celebrated performers.

Unfortunately, Hewlett encountered two major difficulties on his sojourn to stardom. First, like Taft and Welsh, he found it difficult to commit himself totally to artistic pursuits. Between stage engagements, Hewlett worked as a steward aboard transatlantic packet liners, in addition to other occupations.[17] Second, Hewlett suffered from educational deficiencies. Historian Martin Delany recalled witnessing a "colored" comedian named James Ulett — more accurately Hewlett — who performed with Brown's company. Delany recalled that this "Ulett" tended to stumble over certain words in his recitations, due to a lack of education, yet still managed to succeed on the U.S. and British stage.[18] Actually, Hewlett was never a major success on either side of the Atlantic Ocean, and apparently Delany confused him with Ira Aldridge, who briefly appeared with Brown's company in the inaugural 1821 season.[19] And Delany was not the only observer to notice how Hewlett's educational shortcomings hampered his performances. The largely flattering newspaper biography of 1825 mentioned that "Hewlett is yet young enough to receive some of the advantages of education."[20] In spite of his deficiencies, Hewlett instantly assumed a leadership role as the premier actor, singer, dancer, and choreographer for Brown's fledgling company.

As a unit, Brown's acting ensemble was spirited, extremely versatile, untrained, and passionate to the point of criminality. Apart from being part-time performers and relatively new to the stage, this amateur troupe was primed to cultivate that counterpublic sphere which Jane Moody theorizes. As an alternative to the Park Theatre's "major" foreign imports and "minor" regular company, Hewlett and company tackled "legitimate" material like *Richard III* and contested the Park's status as Manhattan's only major theatrical outlet. However, the phenomenon of eager performers appropriating the best of European drama was not enough to secure a respected place in Manhattan's emergent theatrical landscape. Brown understood that a prime location, or at least a theatrical space apart from his residence, and a strong audience base were equally important factors in determining whether his institution would become a major or minor player.

Barely a week after opening a theater in his cramped upstairs apartment, an ever enterprising Brown relocated his entertainments to a larger space on Mercer Street in the remote Greenwich Village. In the early nineteenth century, Greenwich Village was literally a village, inhabited primarily by lower-class Euro–New Yorkers and newly freed slaves in search of affordable housing. Brown needed more space to mount a serious theatrical venture, so the Village's reasonable real estate was a definite attraction. Also, the only other leisure options in the area were a periodically operational circus building and Vauxhall Gardens, a strictly summer pleasure garden associated with Price's Park Theatre. Brown's theater was a welcome addition to the emerging area and even encouraged solidarity among the growing population of black migrants to this rural community.[21]

The Village was far removed from the locus of New York's cultural life, which was centered around City Hall Park, and, more important, this remote neighborhood was rapidly gaining the reputation as a popular retreat for unruly youths.[22] Some Village residents resented the Bohemian atmosphere overtaking their remote community, and earlier in 1819 they had complained to the Common Council of "certain persons of color practising as Musicians with Drums and other instruments."[23] Ironically, similar complaints from neighbors closed Brown's West Side pleasure garden. Without question, the African American impresario moved into an area ripe for counterculture leisure activity, an unpredictable milieu that could potentially have a detrimental effect on Brown's institutional identity, especially with regard to his audience experiments. By moving to this rural address, Brown abandoned a comparatively more secure audience base of curious Euro–New Yorkers and leisure-starved Afro–New Yorkers.

In particular, Brown jeopardized his mutually beneficial relationships with his brother stewards, their wives, fashionable slaves, domestic servants, and, of course, Broadway's "black dandys and dandizettes." Would they travel to this literal village on the margins of Manhattan to continue their support of Brown's entertainments? On his first Village playbill, Brown attempted to sustain his prior associations: "Mr. Brown, respectfully informs his Friends of Colour in this city, that on Monday Evening, September 24, 1821 at half past seven o'clock, an Opera will take place, corner of Mercer and Bleecker streets."[24] The playbill language concedes that black Greenwich Village residents, primarily newly freed slaves, were not substantial enough to sustain a theater, and therefore Brown had to rely on his "Friends of Colour" from throughout the city. After alerting all Afro–New Yorkers to his new location, the announcement further reassured: "Mr. Brown has neither spared time or expense in rendering this entertainment agreeable to the Ladies and Gentlemen of Colour." This last portion sought to reassure his former patrons that, like the pleasure garden, this new theater intended to serve and respect African American leisure seekers.

Brown expanded to a legitimate theatrical space and "neither spared time or expense" in outfitting that theater, but the African manager may have priced his Afro–New Yorker friends, those willing to make the long trek, out of the new establishment. A larger theater meant more onstage and offstage space to fill; consequently production expenses related to advertising, scenery, costumes, and lighting escalated. Also, rent was now an expenditure because Brown was no longer using his residence as a theater but was leasing a separate building. Out of economic necessity, Brown had to increase his ticket prices. At the pleasure garden, Brown never charged an admission price, but the Thomas Street playbill for September 24 listed a ticket price of thirty-seven and a half cents, and his Village playbill for October 1 advertised an even higher admission charge of fifty cents. Brown's new prices were noticeably higher than a twenty-five-cent seat in the Park Theatre's gallery, the only section in which blacks were allowed.[25] In the early 1820s, Afro–New Yorker salaries, with ship stewards at the top and domestic servants at the bottom, ranged from roughly ten dollars to one dollar a week.[26] For an unskilled black laborer or chambermaid, fifty cents was nearly half of a week's salary, a considerable price to pay for leisure activities. Brown may have charged these inflated prices expecting that many Afro–New Yorkers would travel and pay more to support a theater where people of color were respected.

The racial profile of Brown's audience changed drastically with this relocation to the Village. A month after the move to the new theater, Brown embarked on a complex and volatile social experiment to integrate two audiences with vastly different perceptions of "African Amusements." A pleasure garden originally instituted as a retreat for "elite" black stewards and their wives transformed, seemingly overnight, into a counterculture playground for carousing white voyeurs. Due to increased prices and a remote locale, manager Brown could not survive unless he cultivated and accommodated this new patron base. In late October 1821 the *National Advocate* published the following comments on Brown's affirmative actions: "The gentlemen of colour announce another play at their Pantheon, corner of Bleecker and Mercer streets, on Monday evening. They have graciously made a partition at the back of their house, for the accommodation of the whites."[27] Although this managerial decision may smack of discrimination, Brown's approach to integration, beginning with the African Grove, was decidedly more fluid than Price's Park Theatre, which sequestered blacks to the balcony. Dr. McCune Smith noticed immediate results from this social experiment and described Brown's audiences as "composed largely of laughter-loving young clerks, who came to see the sport, but invariably paid their quarter for admission."[28] The term "sport" implies these young clerks perceived this "colored" company as "minor" or amateurish entertainments, not serious theatrical productions. Partition aside, Smith reported the Village theater was increasingly dominated by these presumably white clerks with "minor" expectations.[29]

Brown's experiment with audience integration, specifically catering to whites with "sporting" intentions, was a potentially calamitous miscalculation. New York theater historian George Odell opined a century later that "this partition, erected by a race so long segregated in the negro gallery of playhouses, strikes me as pathetic and ominous."[30] Odell was correct—the partition and a dramatically increased white presence would prove "ominous." In August 1822 a group of riotous whites nearly destroyed Brown's second and more impressive Village theater. The partition can be interpreted as an unfortunate business concession made by a somewhat desperate novice manager on the margins of Manhattan who needed to attract white patrons. Based on Park Theatre policies, Brown understood that many Euro–New Yorkers were accustomed to or preferred some form of segregation in their entertainment experiences, and so he attempted to make them comfortable in order to maintain their support. A partition allowed uncomfortable whites the option of sitting apart from blacks.

Rooted in his historical moment, Odell assumed that early nineteenth-century blacks were completely opposed to segregation; however, if considered in the context of October 1821, the partition was not as "pathetic" as Odell imagined. The crucial question to consider is who was the partition benefiting? From an alternate perspective, the same partition can be read as Brown's reversing the racial hierarchy on Euro–New York, inverting its white supremacy. Despite the relocation, Brown continued to advertise his institution as an African-controlled theater, or counterpublic sphere, targeting culture-starved Afro–New Yorkers. This partitioned section for "laughter-loving" white clerks was located in the rear of the Mercer Street theater, so Brown and his faithful ladies and gentlemen of color essentially usurped white exclusivity by segregating and relegating whites to the back of his establishment. Such an elitist gesture is not entirely surprising, given that two English visitors, Mathews and Trollope, characterized African Americans as more mannered than most Euro-Americans. Under Brown's partition arrangement, the "Friends of Colour," who came to admire the histrionics of "their" James Hewlett, could be separated from the "laughter-loving" clerks who attended merely for the "sport."

Whether the partition is read as pathetic or counterpublic, successful or unsuccessful, manager Brown dared mingle "sporty" clerks with the "colored" gentry, a truly Africanist "encounter of opposites."[31] The conflicting perceptions and receptions of his white and black patrons profoundly affected, even molded, Brown's institution during this "becoming" phase. Beginning with this first Village theater, an undeniable symbiotic relationship emerged between his white patrons, his developing repertoire, and his African American acting company. In his 1849 memoir, Ira Aldridge recalled how "people who went to ridicule, remained to admire, albeit there must have been ample scope for the suggestion of the ridiculous."[32] Aldridge's forked remembrance implies that the untrained amateur actors may have warranted some ridicule, yet the company still managed to convert a portion of that derision to admiration. Other reports reveal that when white patrons were intent on ridiculing the performers and dictating the program, Hewlett and company endured arduous evenings. Eventually, the question became, were the amateurish productions attributable to wretched acting or uncooperative, overly involved patrons? As we examine in later chapters, Brown's unique entertainments and his utopian vision of a multiracial audience would be overwhelmed by a demanding cadre of "laughter-loving clerks" who refused to accept these "African Amusements" as "legitimate" productions.

With the initial Village relocation, Brown may have secured more real estate and embarked on a profitable but contentious social experiment with integration, but he still had to solve his visibility problem. His first nonresidential theater was nearly marooned in the suburbs, far from the promenaders, museums, pleasure gardens, hotels, and theaters encircling City Hall Park. Discontented with his position on the margins, in January 1822 the ex-steward moved his company of African American thespians to the center: Hampton's Hotel on Park Row, right next door to the Park Theatre.[33] According to a performance playbill, Brown made significant institutional changes to compete with the "major" Park Theatre, such as extending the number of performances. In the Village, the troupe performed strictly on Mondays, but now it appeared on Monday, Wednesday, and Friday evenings. Also, the all-African company expanded its Shakespearean repertoire beyond *Richard III* to include scenes and speeches from *Julius Caesar* and *Macbeth*. Finally, Brown advertised a fifty-cent admission price for all seats at Hampton's Hotel, which equaled a pit ticket—the middle-tier admission price—at the new Park Theatre. The new Park Row address, repertoire expansion, and other institutional changes greatly increased Brown's visibility in Manhattan's entertainment landscape and boosted attendance.

Amateur company and audience experiments aside, Brown opened on Park Row to compete with Price's Park Theatre for the mantle of Manhattan's "major" theater. But ironically, this move to the theatrical center submerged Brown's theater into a distinctly minor-inflected counterpublic sphere. An alternative theatrical culture was alive and well in Manhattan, an expansive community of eager amateurs and aspiring performers that reached well beyond conventional theater spaces into museums and hotel ballrooms. New Yorkers flocked to these other performance spaces to witness amateur dramatic recitations and more exotic oddities, such as exhilarating gas exhibitions—performers taking nitrous oxide or laughing gas. By selecting Hampton's Hotel for his residency, Brown settled into this counterpublic sphere of curiosities, and, of course, few events were more peculiar, novel, or exotic in 1822 Manhattan than all-African productions of Shakespeare. Given the city's appetite for the unusual, Brown's stage Shakespeareans and other stage Europeans could expect considerable economic success, at the expense of being identified as quaint and hopelessly "minor." Either in the Village or on Park Row, Brown's ever expanding public, especially the white patrons, viewed his theater as an eccentric diversion from the more refined and "major" Park Theatre.

Major or minor, Price's new neighbor proved a substantial rival, forcing the Park Theatre and its allies to take immediate action. As for the hotel performances, M. M. Noah reported that the "audiences were generally of a riotous character, and amused themselves by throwing crackers on the stage, and cracking jokes with the actors."[34] Such disruptive behavior was fairly standard practice for certain segments of early nineteenth-century audiences, but Noah's observations hinted that Brown's actors interacted with or responded favorably to this audience involvement. He further reported that due to the large crowds and increasing rowdiness at these hotel performances, municipal authorities dispatched watchmen to arrest the black company under the charges of "danger from fire" and "civil discord." With unrestrained dramatic flare, Noah recounted how, on January 7, 1822, "Police Magistrates" stormed the stage, stopped the production, and apprehended the entire company. In the only surviving account of these now infamous Shakespeare arrests, Noah openly accused Brown of invading Park Row to increase his profits and rival the "great Park Theatre."[35] Noah was correct on both counts; Brown moved to Park Row to rival Manhattan's "major" theater and, more important, to siphon some of the Park's excess patrons. Compared with his theater in the remote Village, a hotel next to the Park offered greater visibility and increased profits, but, sadly, the residency proved temporary. The magistrates released the company from jail only after it "promised never to act Shakespeare again."

Brown registered the political and cultural message embedded in these outrageous Shakespeare arrests: an African-managed theater would never be accepted as a legitimate theater. As ordered by the "authorities," he temporarily refrained from producing Shakespeare as part of his regular repertoire and, for the first time, publicly named his entertainments. Several days after the Hampton's Hotel closing, the *Spectator* printed the playbill announcing: "Mr. Brown manager of the Minor Theatre respectfully informs the public, that in consequence of the *breaking up* of his theatrical establishment, there will be no performance this week."[36] One could read Brown's Minor Theatre playbill as capitulation, a black manager accepting his second-class status in a suddenly competitive entertainment industry.

Alternatively, there were always subversive possibilities in being the "minor" theater. The italics included in the printed playbill suggests that Brown believed the "breaking up" to be dubious or unwarranted, and although Brown publicly agreed to play minor to the Park's major, his Minor Theatre never restricted itself to "illegitimate," nondramatic material. On the same bill introducing the Minor Theatre, Brown announced a world premiere drama, *Shotaway; or the Insurrection of the Caribs of St. Domingo*. This production marked the first known drama written by an African American; unfortunately, we know very little about this black first because Brown never published the play. From Caribbean history, we do know that a Carib Indian chief named Shotaway lived on the island of St. Vincent—not St. Domingo—and led native soldiers in a 1795 uprising against the British. The insurrectionary subject matter indicates that Brown probably crafted an intensely dramatic piece with spoken text, thus breaching the assumed minor theater restriction to "illegitimate," music-oriented productions. According to an *Evening Post* article, Brown originally intended to debut the drama on Park Row at Hampton's Hotel, but the January 7 arrests postponed the premiere. The aforementioned *Spectator* article on the Minor Theatre praised this dramatic first: "Thus it seems that these descendants of Africa are determined to carry into full practice the doctrine of *liberty and equality*, physically by acting plays and mentally by writing them."[37] Officially minor or major, an upstart African American company staging a new drama about a Carib insurrection could not have been more defiant and progressive.

In total, this second phase in Brown's "becoming," his Minor Theatre period, exhibited major and minor tendencies. As for major, this African American troupe staged several Shakespearean productions and an original drama; established a permanent, nonresidential theatrical space in the Village; even moved onto the profitable Park Row; expanded its evenings of performances; and charged ticket prices competitive with the Park Theatre. As for minor, the company comprised strictly amateur actors; performed temporarily in a nontheatrical hotel; capitalized on the subcultural allure of novelty; and encouraged an integrated but conflicted audience. Brown's Minor Theatre had the potential to function as a powerful counterpublic sphere where the seeming opposites of "legitimate" and "illegitimate" mingled onstage, while black "Friends" and "laughter-loving" white clerks peacefully coexisted offstage—that is, if the Afro–New Yorker manager could maintain control over this alternative theatrical subculture. Brown's eclectic repertoire fostered an elaborate counterpublic sphere somewhere between Shakespeare and exhilarating gas exhibitions, but the Park Theatre remained the major theatrical institution in the minds of most New Yorkers. At the conclusion of this major-minor showdown, Brown may have been forced or expected to play "minor" to the Price's "major"; however, the Minor Theatre was never a completely imposed, reactionary, or even transitory identity to be abandoned during his more patriotic American Theatre or more racialized African Company phases. This "minor" period would leave a significant impression on Brown's brief managerial career and introduce his most significant contribution to early American theater, the stage European.

Stage Europeans

The stage European, theatrical cousin to whiteface minstrelsy, can be succinctly defined as black actors performing whiteness through white characters. This underresearched performance convention first emerged when manager Brown debuted an all-African production of Shakespeare's *Richard III*.[38] Recently, theater and performance scholars David Krasner and Nadine George-Graves have historicized specific incidents of black performers staging whiteness, primarily in black vaudeville and musicals.[39] Within early national theater, the stage European was comparable with the stage Indian or stage African character in terms of its "masking" function. Yet there was a major difference between those white-authored, cross-cultural appropriations of available others and stage Europeans: Brown's actors performed white characters never intended for them. Despite S. Welsh and James Hewlett's theatrical aspirations and mimetic skill, Shakespeare never envisioned *Richard III* with blacks playing King Richard and Lady Ann. By contrast, white actors assumed a range of African or Indian roles constructed for them by white writers.

Although partly produced by whites and restricted to the traditional stage, the company's assumption of white roles was potentially as liberating and subversive as whiteface minstrel acts. Whiteface implicitly challenged racial and class distinctions by revealing their performativity, and stage Europeans confronted the same constructed social categories by exposing their artificiality. The company's range of stage Europeans facilitated two distinct processes of disidentification and cross-cultural identification with various European cultures, experiences, and histories. Brown's counterpublic sphere provided space for combinations of seeming opposites, such as an African

American steward playing a Scottish insurrectionary leader or an Afro–New Yorker chambermaid performing an English queen. These creative acts allowed black actors and audiences to move beyond performing whiteness as privilege to isolate and investigate specific issues and values integral to Afro-America.

A most instructive theoretical approach to performed whiteness — or stage Europeans — can be found in José Muñoz's work on disidentification and queer performers of color. By disidentification Muñoz means "the survival strategies the minority subject practices in order to negotiate a phobic majoritarian public sphere that continuously elides or punishes the existence of subjects who do not conform to the phantasm of normative citizenship."[40] The surviving and negotiating queer performers of color upon whom Muñoz bases his theory tend to identify with and against a dominant or majority culture that demands "normal" behavior. They work within and outside the public sphere, employing some of the dominant's normative assumptions, codes, and paradigms. Muñoz's theory of disidentification has much in common with Gates's notion of motivated signifying and Baker's concept of blackening "standard" white forms. A noteworthy distinction embedded in Muñoz's theory is the admission that disidentifying performers do partially identify with the phobias or prejudices of the majority culture.

Muñoz further argues that by intervening in the majority culture, disidentifying queer performers of color produce a counterpublicity or "minoritarian space."[41] His concept of counterpublicity or minority space seems to restate James Scott's theory of public and private transcripts; however, unlike Scott, Muñoz completely dismantles the thin wall dividing the private, offstage transcripts of the minority and the public, onstage transcript largely defined by the majority. Disidentification and the resulting counterpublicity demonstrate how minority performers can openly work within the public transcript, using the dominant's assumptions and phobias. Finally, Muñoz's theory recalls Moody's concept of a counterpublic sphere centered around London's minor theaters. Muñoz recognizes a similar alternative culture developing around disidentifying performers of color. More than two centuries removed from Moody's counterpublic marked by class and artistic hierarchy, Muñoz's counterpublicity concentrates the division between majority and minority communities around racial, gender, and sexual differences.

To illustrate a disidentifying performance of whiteness that generates counterpublicity, Muñoz examines the solo performance work of Vaginal

Davis, a black, gay, transvestite performance artist who has constructed a neo-Nazi, racist, homophobic white stage persona named Clarence. This white character, or caricature, represents both the object of and threat to Davis's sexual desire. Interestingly, in constructing this aversion-attraction duality, Davis does not choose an obviously privileged member of the white majority but rather a white supremacist who feels dispossessed—rightly or wrongly—by minority populations. Whether Clarence is privileged or deprived, Muñoz argues, "Davis's disidentificatory take on whiteface both reveals the degraded character of the white supremacist and wrests 'symbolic controls' from white people."[42] By forcing this militant white identity to "share" the body of a black drag queen, Davis's whiteface act—or stage European—exposes the absurdity and illegitimacy of white supremacy. An angry white image, potentially threatening to people of color and homosexuals, is stripped of its presumed power and ridiculed. Furthermore, in the largely white and masculine subculture of hard-core, speed metal music, this "terrorist drag" performer commands or expropriates "punk" representation to accomplish this kind of disidentifying work. Muñoz terms Davis's performances "terrorist drag" because she performs the entire nation's internal terrors surrounding issues of race, gender, and sexuality. Her seizure of "symbolic controls" not only undermines the supremacy of Clarence and the white masculinity of this alternative "punk" culture but also challenges the majority culture, which is understood as white, male, and heterosexual.

Within Brown's nineteenth-century counterpublicity, his Minor Theatre, the stage Europeans were comparatively less satiric and terrorizing than Vaginal Davis's whiteface act. Nevertheless, his black actors accomplished a similar expropriation of symbolic controls, especially with the dramatic work of William Shakespeare. In an article on Shakespeare, blackness, and Brown's black actors, theater historian Joyce Green MacDonald argues that by "performing Shakespeare, the black actors were also enacting and appropriating the cultural sanction bestowed by his works."[43] MacDonald implies that Brown, his company, and most Americans attached great cultural significance to Shakespeare, which was partly accurate but not the full picture.

For most early national Americans, the Bard's cultural sanction did not translate into artistic hierarchies or class distinctions; rather, Shakespeare represented a shared national treasury free to be identified with and against. Americans did not view Shakespeare as an inaccessible or sacrosanct highbrow deity, but as "Brother William," one of the family.[44] U.S. theater's egalitarian, familial, and occasionally experimental relationships with Shakespeare explain why an African American company would elect to produce and personalize a popular tragedy like *Richard III*. Shakespeare was respected as common property, a populace poet to be read, interpreted, and performed by any and every American. Brown's stage Europeans tested that theory. On a base level, black Shakespearean productions illustrated Afro-America's natural identifications with an English heritage and American popular culture. More strategically, Brown's deliberate decision to perform the Bard ushered his company and its blackened versions of a beloved dramatist into the center of the majority culture's public space.

Additionally, on the transatlantic theater scene—at least in England and the United States—a revolution in Shakespearean performance was emerging, led by the highly innovative English tragedian Edmund Kean. During the late eighteenth century, most English critics regarded George Frederick Cooke's somber and solemn Richard III as the proper portrayal. Therefore, when Kean emerged with a highly emotional Duke of Gloucester in the early 1810s, critics labeled his "naturalistic" or "romantic" approach a "flashy" departure. As an alternative to Cooke's solemnity, Kean introduced playful stage business like rubbing his hands together in self-congratulation when the Duke sensed things were going well. One nineteenth-century critic, Leigh Hunt, endorsed Kean's innovations and explained that by departing from the "usual solemn pedantry of the stage," Kean strove to "unite common life with tragedy." Another critic, William Hazlitt, called his inventive stage business the directions Shakespeare neglected to write.[45] An anonymous 1830 promptbook claimed Kean's freshly conceived approach to *Richard III* was successful because his shamelessly ambitious Duke generated admiration rather than animosity from an audience. Another 1860 promptbook, ascribed to J. C. Cowper, detailed how Kean crafted a Duke with dual personalities, ingratiating at first, but full of fury when necessary. Cowper, a stage manager, advised actors to follow this example of a "positively light and playfully sarcastic" Duke of Gloucester who disarmed his audience in the opening scenes, but in the final scenes, shifted dramatically into a maniacal, fully enraged King Richard.[46]

Kean's flamboyant, dualistic, and revolutionary innovations rapidly became the model for many aspiring American-born actors, including Brown's African American performers. In particular, Charles Taft, the ex-slave turned waiter turned actor turned petty larcenist, crafted a distinctly counterpublic Duke of Gloucester who identified with and against "Brother

William"'s original. Noah's September 1821 review of the premiere *Richard III* production recalled how the dapper waiter immediately played to his crowd, especially the fawning "black ladies" waving handkerchiefs on his entrance. To romance his public, Taft allegedly spoke these revised lines: "Now is de vinter of our discontent / made glorious summer by de son of New York." Noah then noted, "Considerable applause ensued, although it was evident that the actor had not followed strictly the text of the author."[47] The original lines read: "Now is the winter of our discontent / Made glorious summer by this sun of York."[48]

One could dismiss Taft's alteration as a product of Noah's vivid imagination; however, let us assume that Taft did make these revisions. By calling himself a "son of New York," Taft highlighted the fact that he was a native New Yorker performing a much heralded role dominated by British imports. Taft's native status would have endeared him to New Yorkers, black or white, male and female, and elicited "considerable applause." Also, one can read his textual alteration as an extreme act of hubris in that this "son of New York," not the "sun of York," transformed a discontented winter into summer through his glorious presence in Brown's makeshift theater. These revisions marked a successful departure from Shakespeare, a disidentification with the author's text that the audience at Brown's makeshift theater heartily endorsed.

Noah's review also suggests that Taft positively mastered Kean's split dispositions. After romancing his fans and stroking his ego, Taft released a fully enraged Richard in the final scenes: "The tent scene was the *chef douvre*: the darkness of the night, the black face of the king, the flourish of the drums and clarionets, the start from the dream, the '*Gib me noder horse*,' and, finally, the agony of the appalled Richard, the rolling eye, white gnashing teeth, clenched fists, and phrenzied looks, were all that the author could have wished."[49] Taft elevated his intensity for the tragedy's most demanding moments, and Noah believed Taft's suitably appalled and distressed King Richard was exactly what Shakespeare had intended. Following Kean's lead, Taft seized control of this well-known and much-loved character, but he also remodeled a few lines to highlight his particular identity as American and New Yorker.

Beyond disidentification, the stage European can be understood as a cross-cultural identification with European culture that can result in an enriched African American identity. This concept of cross-cultural identification in U.S. performance has been discussed extensively in revisionist scholarship on blackface minstrelsy. White working-class blackface minstrel actors and audiences employed blackness to formulate and broadcast socio-political grievances against the upper classes.[50] These Euro-Americans freely expressed their working-class sentiments or resentments from behind a black mask associated with but not limited to blackface minstrelsy. Other minstrel revisionists have traced this liberating black mask to folk parades, carnivals, and similar social rituals that predate the minstrel stage. Eric Lott claims that blackface processional masks paid tribute to the subversive power and potential of blackness. Musicologist Dale Cockrell adds that ex-theatrical disguises allowed lower-class or working-class whites "to speak the unspeakable" in the face of powerful forces.[51] From behind the mask of whiteness, the stage European provided Brown's troupe with similar opportunities for individual and communal expression.

Brown's actors donned white masks other than those of English nobility to identify across cultures and "speak the unspeakable" to America. In many of his vocal performances, James Hewlett exploited Scottish folk music traditions, especially Robert Burns's historical ballad "Scots, wha hae wi' Wallace bled," to express the African American condition. This Scottish anti-colonial anthem, alternatively titled "Bruce's Address to His Army" and "Robert Bruce's March to Bannockburn," pays homage to Scottish national heroes William Wallace and Robert Bruce.[52] On two different benefit nights, in October 1821 and January 1822, Hewlett performed the piece with his best and most requested material.[53] In many respects, the nationalist anthem was becoming his signature song, and through Burns's anticolonial anthem, Hewlett provided African Americans with a sociopolitical context to reflect on their current condition.

Scotland's history of colonial oppression under the English crown mirrored Afro-America's encounter with slavery and therefore provided ample space for cross-cultural identifications. In Burns's revolutionary ballad, Bruce inspires the Scottish forces with rhetoric that juxtaposes freedom and bondage:

> Wha for Scotland's king and law
> Freedom's sword will strongly draw,
> Free-man stand, or Free-man fa'
> Let him follow me!

By oppression's woes and pains!
By your sons in servile chains!
We will drain our dearest veins!
But they shall be free![54]

Provocative references to oppression and chains balanced with talk of free-dom and freemen surely resonated with Brown's black patrons and triggered immediate connections to their own circumstances. Afro–New Yorker slaves and servants in attendance could easily transpose the English oppressor–Scottish oppressed model to the United States and contemplate their own white master–black slave or servant relations. While appearing to sing about English colonial tyranny a world away, Hewlett's Scottish appropriation launched a direct attack on slavery and similar oppression at home. This transracial performance did not view Scottish culture as impenetrable, mys-terious, or even foreign; rather, via Burns's Bruce, Hewlett issued a symbolic call for substantive freedom that surely resonated with an African American audience.[55]

Hewlett's melodic yet revolutionary rhetoric, no matter how often per-formed, failed to incite uprisings, and his implicit cross-cultural identifica-tion could never substitute for concrete political action by African American citizens. Nevertheless, these stage Europeans served a significant cultural function, illustrating George Lipsitz's observation that "culture exists as a form of politics, as a means of reshaping individual and collective practice for specified interests, and as long as individuals perceive their interests as unfilled, culture retains an oppositional potential."[56] Burns's anthem ap-pealed to or resonated with this black company and black patrons because their interests remained unfilled. Slavery in the state of New York would not be officially abolished until July 1827, and, in the meantime, Hewlett would continue to include this protest song in his repertoire. Burns's ballad identi-fied Afro-America's sense of continued oppression and expressed a people's oppositional potential in a manner Shakespeare's *Richard III* never could. The nationalist anthem highlighted shared political aspirations and rallied African American, and perhaps Euro-American, support for complete black liberation and full U.S. citizenship. In the absence of municipal uprisings and complete emancipation, Scottish stage Europeans served as freeing vehi-cles to "speak the unspeakable" about the United States' peculiar institution.

S. Welsh's Lady Ann

Ballads lamenting the chains of colonial or racial oppression may have identified with Scottish rebels and against English royalty or U.S. slave owners, but the most textually subversive black Shakespearean was S. Welsh, the chambermaid from Park Place. In a scene from Carlyle Brown's play, *The African Company Presents Richard the Third*, a character named Mr. Brown advises James Hewlett to "[f]orget what them fancy-full people think, them high-blowin' elitists, and say ya Shakespeare like ya want."[57] Historically, Hewlett was the company's most conscientious performer in terms of fidelity to the text. The aforementioned 1825 biography stated that his "imitations of Kean, Mathews, Phillips and others were recognized as correct, and evincing a nice discrimination and peculiar tact on his part."[58] Hewlett's correctness aside, Lawrence Levine explains that for most Americans "Shakespeare was seen as common property to be treated as the user saw fit."[59] American-inflected Shakespearean productions were notorious for tailoring England's prized playwright to local tastes and social conditions.

In keeping with the view of Shakespeare as common property, Welsh's conception of Lady Ann altered the Bard to her specifications. The amateur actress identified with and against Shakespeare's tragedy to transform Lady Ann into a resilient heroine who vigorously resists the Duke of Gloucester and, when faced with shame, discovers her redemptive possibilities. Welsh identified with the queen's feelings of blindness and betrayal but revisioned *Richard III*'s Lady Ann to expose a contemporary version of the wronged queen who could speak directly to and for working-class women. Welsh disidentified with the Bard by infusing "Brother William"'s text with an upbeat tempo and popular music that produced a more familiar or demystified stage European. Also, her performative renovations and textual additions undermined Shakespeare's customary conception of the tragic woman, ultimately suggesting an alternative ending for the beleaguered queen. Welsh's protofeminist perspective is not surprising in light of cultural critic bell hooks's claim that "[n]ineteenth century black women were more aware of sexist oppression than any other female group in American society has ever been."[60] My reading of Welsh's nineteenth-century performance relies on hooks's black feminist study, *Ain't I a Woman*, which examines this historical era's contrasting images of black females — especially the masculinized "Amazon"—and the feminist potential of this doubly oppressed group.

Noah, in reviewing Welsh's performance in *Richard III*, noted that compared with Taft's Richard "she had not as correct a conception of the part, as she always danced on the stage, instead of the pensive march of the afflicted Queen."[61] In her first scene, the funeral procession, the queen is traditionally arrayed in mourning attire and visibly distraught at the loss of her husband, King Edward V. From her first appearance, Welsh's "dancing" Lady Ann marked an extreme departure from the solemn and bereaved tone seemingly required by the text. Noah next marveled at the courting scene, act 2, scene 1, which also diverged from convention:

> The courting scene was inimitably fine, particularly when Richard confesses his passion.
>
> > "Ah take de pity in dy eye
> > And see um here.— Kneels.
> > Ann—Would dey were brass candlesticks
> > To strike de dead."
>
> This Lady Ann accompanied with a violent action, such as seizing the king by his wool, shaking him furiously, and finally dashing him on the earth, which was certainly very characteristic.

If these lines sound unfamiliar, that may be because "brass candlesticks" reads as "basilisks" in the original text. Her lines — as Noah recalled them — may have lacked elocution, but Welsh did not lack energy. Customarily, after the Duke of Gloucester admits to his gruesome deeds and begs for her forgiveness, Lady Ann responds by spitting on him, calling him a devil, and requesting that he leave. At the scene's apex, Richard extends his sword to Lady Ann imploring her to impale him. When the sword appears, the actors seesaw the blade back and forth as Richard delivers a lengthy speech intended to assuage Ann's burning hatred. His assuaging usually prevails and typically the struggle ends with Ann dropping the sword, as one critic described, like "a figure in a puppet show."[62] Welsh, and her manager-producer Brown, again refused to conform to "correct" portrayals of the mournful queen. "This Lady Ann" shook Richard violently "by his wool"— his hair — and threw him to the ground; and despite this apparent reversal in the power relations, Noah termed the scene "inimitably fine" and appeared to be titillated by the violence.

Edmund Kean's "flashy departures" and dualistic approach must have had a direct impact on Welsh's stage European. His more "naturalistic," playful interpretation supplanted Cooke's somber model, and Welsh's disidentification did the same for Lady Ann. She declined to pursue a traditionally mournful and meek Lady Ann but, rather like Kean, abandoned the "solemn pedantry" of tragedy. With an upbeat conception of this character, complete with a little dancing, Welsh immediately subverted audience expectations, especially Noah's. Her bereaved lady with considerable pep in her step downplayed the seriousness of the queen's recent loss and transformed the mourning widow into a more composed, likable, and perhaps identifiable figure. Welsh's electrifying and energetic Lady Ann reduced Taft's Richard to the "puppet" by shaking him back and forth. By refusing to submit and physically dominating the silver-tongued misogynist, Welsh complicates the gender dynamics of the scene; this is not totally surprising for an actress who was also called upon to play male roles. By the end of this scene, the Duke does dominate Lady Ann, but Welsh's conception of the role raised certain questions: who truly won round one? And did she let him win? Surely, Shakespeare never imagined the scene ending with such queries, but Welsh refused to be limited by Shakespeare's intentions—if we assume those can be known from the text—or traditional theatrical interpretations, and instead, she pursued her own logic. As a result, Welsh created a "counterpublicity" in the public sphere of nineteenth-century theatrical production and offered her alternative interpretation of this well-known queen.

To close his vivid account of act 2, scene 1, Noah described Welsh's choices or actions as "very characteristic." What did this theatrical and cultural critic mean by "very characteristic" in this review? Was he simply suggesting that Lady Ann's aggressive reaction was consistent with Welsh's upbeat conception of the role? Or gesturing beyond the stage, was he implying her performance was "very characteristic" of a black female in nineteenth-century New York? In order to answer these questions and further illuminate Welsh's divergent Lady Ann, we might cautiously apply a black feminist or womanist reading to her performance. The emphasis is on caution because it is always precarious to read and interpret the actions of historical agents through the limited and presentist prism of contemporary theory.

Early in her career, bell hooks successfully theorized nineteenth-century female slave experiences from a black feminist perspective. Unlike sociologists and historians who focus on slavery's emasculation of the African American male, hooks examines how slavery "masculinized" black females. She argues, "The institution of slavery forced black women to surrender any prior dependence on the male figure and obliged them to struggle for their individual survival. The social equality that characterized black sex role patterns in the work sphere under slavery did not create a situation that allowed black women to be passive. Despite sexist myths about the inherent weakness of women, black women have had to exert a certain independence of spirit because of their presence in the work force."[63] Hooks proposes that white men feared their women might gather ideas about social equality by simply witnessing black women working in the fields. Therefore, to explain how unprotected black females performed "male" work, "white males claimed black slave women were not 'real' women but were masculinized sub-human creatures." In the white male imagination, synonymous with Euro-America's cultural logic, black women were Amazons, powerful matriarchs possessing "masculine-like characteristics not common to the female species."[64]

I contend that this "Amazon" was the "very characteristic" black female Noah recognized in Welsh's resistant Lady Ann. Although hooks concentrates on female slave experiences in the plantation South, this notion of "masculinized" females also surfaced in northern, urban contexts in relation to working-class black and white women. Historian Christine Stansell found that young white females in New York's working world "contributed to a cultural imagery betokening a prideful working-class female independence distinct from the imagery of female virtue produced by bourgeois culture."[65] Similar to hook's "Amazon" imagery, these women projected a social and economic independence at odds with upper- and middle-class codes of feminine virtue, vulnerability, and dependency. When Welsh's Lady Ann manhandled her Richard rather than wilt under his charms, this actor rejected the dictates of "bourgeois culture" and embraced an "unladylike," urban, and working-class alternative. Surely this was not the model Noah or the Society for the Encouragement of Faithful Domestic Servants would advocate for Manhattan's emerging young women; nevertheless, a self-assertive Lady Ann could resonate with black and white domestics. Through Welsh's rough treatment, mistreated and forlorn female audience members could identify with and vicariously expel accumulated frustrations. This deceived yet assertive nineteenth-century black female is what Noah may have meant by "very characteristic."

The *National Advocate* editor was intrigued by the unconventional courting scene, but he took great offense at Welsh's artistic alterations in Lady Ann's other significant scene. In act 3, scene 2, Richard bluntly informs Lady Ann that he detests her and intends to wed another. Noah reported that Welsh reacted by singing a popular nineteenth-century melody, "Eveleen's Bower," which he conceded was "tolerably well sung" but a "rather inappropriate" musical addition. Noah may have deemed it "inappropriate" or, in minor theater terms, "illegitimate" for Welsh to marry a popular song with a Shakespearean drama, but this kind of intertextual combination was common practice on the early U.S. stage. As mentioned earlier, national audiences and performers treated Shakespeare as one of the family. Actors and theater managers inserted popular songs such as "Yankee Doodle" between the acts of tragedies, including *Hamlet*, and even adapted the Bard's originals into socially relevant travesties and burlesques on national themes and issues.[66] By no means did those equally "inappropriate" American productions intend to denigrate the Bard; rather, they sought to further integrate "Brother William" into the nation's fluid representational laboratory. The intertextual tenor of Brown's *Richard III* featuring Welsh's Lady Ann was "most American" and most accessible for Brown's actors and his expanding Minor Theatre audience. Speaking of accessibility, given Brown's amateur company and his variegated audience, a popular ballad would have been Welsh's most effective method for communicating Shakespeare's ideas. Like Hewlett, educational deficiencies may have prevented Welsh from fully commanding Shakespeare's language, but she could certainly express the Bard's meaning through song. In addition, Brown's patrons, with their own educational and attention deficits, may have had difficulty comprehending Elizabethan verse unless it was set to music.

Welsh's fusion of the Bard and popular music stretched beyond singing "Yankee Doodle" between acts, because she performed her "Eveleen's Bower" during the natural course of the scene. Welsh introduced "illegitimate" musical material directly into "legitimate" Shakespeare, which prompted an authority like Noah to claim that her "inappropriate" addition degraded his dramatic deity. If we take a closer look at the scene and the song, however, we find her addition was an illuminating dramaturgical choice. To close act 3, scene 2, Ann laments:

> Forgive me, heaven, that I forgave this man!
> Oh, may my story, told in after-ages
> Give warning to our easy sex's ears!
> May it unveil, the hearts of man, and strike
> Them deaf to their dissimulated love!

She recognizes her grave error in falling for Richard and now hopes that her story can become a cautionary tale for future generations of women. Welsh identified with this sentiment and realized that the comparable lyrics of "Eveleen's Bower" could amplify Lady Ann's circumstances, essentially setting the play's cautionary tale to music. One pertinent verse from the ballad reads:

> Oh! Weep for the hour
> When to Eve - leen's bower
> The Lord of the Val - ley with false vows came;
> The moon hid her light
> From the Heavens that night,
> And wept be - hind her clouds o'er the mai - den's name.
> The clouds past soon
> From the chaste cold moon,
> And Heav'n smiled a - gain with her ves - tal flame;
> But none will see the day
> When the clouds shall pass a - way,
> Which that dark hour left up - on E - ve - leen's fame.[67]

The "Lord of the Valley with false vows" resembles the deceitful Duke of Gloucester who made false vows of love to Lady Ann but then betrayed the vulnerable widow after clawing his way to the throne. In the same way that King Richard stripped Lady Ann of her honor, this "Lord of the Valley" stole Eveleen's fame, which she perhaps can never reclaim. By interjecting an "inappropriate" melody, Welsh successfully united "common life with tragedy" and illuminated a striking correlation between a royal personage and a common chambermaid. Lady Ann's feelings of despair and isolation were hardly mysteries to S. Welsh; she surely felt and lived that pain. Through this transracial, transclass stage European, Welsh identified with this royal personage and demonstrated how any impressionable and vulnerable female, including a "very characteristic" black woman, could be duped by a womanizing gentleman.

Welsh's unconventional Lady Ann may have been assertive, but her interpretation never completely effaced the vulnerability of Shakespeare's original. Her stage European could be submissive, a trait many considered uncharacteristic for nineteenth-century black females. As a counterpoint to the "Amazon" image of the female slave, bell hooks examines the submissive side of nineteenth-century black womanhood as envisioned by slave women. Initially, female slaves did not stigmatize field labor, but as the "cult of true womanhood" emerged in the nineteenth century and "they assimilated white

American values," enslaved black women adopted the position that it was "degrading for women to work in the fields."[68] Within the slave subculture, black women increasingly desired to be treated like white ladies and assumed "womanly" qualities such as modesty, sexual purity, innocence, and a submissiveness. Sadly, the constant threat of rape rendered some of these qualities unrealistic or unattainable for black women. Welsh's Shakespearean stage European was essentially a womanist rendering of Lady Ann that challenged the dominant Richard but also undermined the perception that women of color were purely "masculine" creatures unresponsive to love or pain.[69]

Beyond Welsh's softening of the black female image, her addition of "Eveleen's Bower" challenged Shakespeare's implied connection between female vulnerability and inescapable tragedy. She disidentified with the Bard's well-worn conception of the tragic female lead destined for death by proposing a more optimistic and resilient end for Lady Ann. Shakespeare's tragic women, such as Lady Macbeth, Desdemona, Ophelia, and Lavonia, are all marked by a kind of metaphoric or literal shame that ultimately ends in suicide or, in the case of Lavonia and Desdemona, murder at the hands of a sorrowful father or a jealous husband. In act 3, scene 2, Richard suggests that the distraught and shamed queen, or queen-to-be, consider suicide. Lady Ann dies, and in the popular Inchbald edition of the play, we are led to believe she commits suicide to avoid her superficial coronation as queen. In contrast, the final verse of "Eveleen's Bower" resonates with an entirely different potential:

> The next sun's ray
> Soon melted away
> Every trace on the path where the false Lord came;
> But there's a light above,
> Which alone can remove
> That stain upon the snow of fair Eveleen's fame.[70]

Welsh undermined the high tragedy of Lady Ann's impending suicide by proffering the possibility of redemption. Although the ghost of Lady Ann appears in act 5 with pointed words for King Richard, Welsh's act 3 musical interjection of Eveleen, a misled maiden who outlived her shame and restored her fame, is no less powerful. Her song suggested that a new day and faith in a higher power could restore a young woman's fame and, by extension, circumvent an ominous ending. By including this sentimental melody, Welsh demonstrated that black women were not callous creatures desensitized to real emotion and that women, even Shakespeare's women, were not fated to become hopeless victims.

Always the astute reviewer, Noah quickly realized that Welsh was acting in a "very characteristic" manner, like a willful, audacious womanist. She breezed by theatrical convention to communicate the self-reflexive power, transcendent potential, and vulnerability of black females. If Kean's Richard could be both playful and maniacal, Welsh's disidentifying stage European could be both aggressive with her suitor and susceptible to his guile. In essence, Welsh disagreed with Shakespeare's ultimate vision, and the bold chambermaid's solution was to expropriate the Bard's symbolic controls and reconstruct an enlivened version of the mournful queen and an alternative future for a fallen lady. After mastering "Brother William"'s meaning, she bridged the divide between common life and tragedy by introducing Lady Ann to a relatable musical heroine, Eveleen. Through an encounter of multiple opposites, vulnerable and assertive, royal and common, Welsh produced a working-class queen who had the potential to reject suicide and survive.

Years after Brown's stage European experiments, other black theatrical ventures would continue combining the seeming opposites of European and African, "illegitimate" melodies and "legitimate" Shakespeare, common life and tragedy. Two famous productions are the Ethiopian Players' jazzed-up version of *Comedy of Errors* in 1920s Chicago and the Federal Theatre Project's vodoun-inflected version of *Macbeth* in 1930s Harlem.[71] Like Brown with his *Richard III*, the producers of twentieth-century black Shakespeare understood that one cannot simply assume Shakespeare speaks directly to contemporary circumstances; it must be made relevant. Beyond appropriating the Bard's cultural sanction, Taft and Welsh expressed their specific conditions and aspirations by personalizing these texts to include local issues like gender relations and "glorious" native actors. In general, Brown's stage Europeans, like whiteface minstrel acts, demonstrated how fearless black artists could exercise dramatic choice, remodel difference, and command social space. Furthermore, the company's multiple versions of whiteness revealed Europeans as heterogeneous and, by extension, black cultural production as equally diversified. Through co-opted English queens and Scottish nationalists, African American performers demonstrated in the most public spaces that a black "self" could identify and disidentify, subvert or celebrate, and ultimately speak their truth to power.

As he entered this second artistic phase focused on theatrical production, William Brown proved resourceful enough to gather a company of committed amateur actors and was fortunate enough to establish James Hewlett, an undereducated part-time tailor, as his star attraction. With stage Europeans as the primary performance form, Brown fostered an alternative counterpublic sphere or site of counterpublicity committed to a cross-cultural identification and disidentification with the best of European drama. Whatever Brown's artistic and managerial intentions, if he meant to challenge Stephen Price on Park Row, if he meant to transform amateurs into professionals, or if he meant to accommodate ridiculing whites and admiring blacks, his quest for a more conspicuous institutional identity taught Brown two hard lessons. First, Price's Park Theatre would remain the "big dog" on the block and Brown's venture would always play the "minor" to the Park's "major." Brown wisely accepted that harsh reality, publicly advertised his venture as the Minor Theatre, and even refrained from Shakespeare for several months, but he continued to produce "legitimate" material, including Afro-America's first drama. Second, he learned the social experiment with audience integration would have a profound impact on the tone of his entertainments. In increasing numbers, Euro–New Yorker patrons were attending for pure "sport," the novelty, and eventually the mayhem. Overwhelmed by "laughter-loving clerks," this immature African American company would struggle to maintain control over its institutional and artistic identities. In the next chapter, this study updates Brown's precarious integrationist project and the effects of divergent white and black perceptions on an increasingly eventful institutional "becoming."

American Taste and Genius

BUILDING AN AMERICAN THEATER

HISTORIAN BENEDICT ANDERSON proposes a working definition of nation in the New World: "[I]t is an imagined political community—and imagined as both inherently limited and sovereign."[1] Anderson further explains that this imagined community is limited geographically because a country traditionally develops borders or boundaries with other nations. In the case of an initially colonial and later national United States, the first border nations were Native American tribes. The Dutch colony of New Amsterdam began the process of national creation and expropriation in 1625, when Dutch settlers purchased the island that would become New York City from its inhabitants, the Manhattan nation of the Wappinger confederacy, for roughly twenty-four dollars. In a short time, Dutch, English, French, Irish, German, Scottish, and Spanish immigrants populated a colony characterized by lucrative commerce, linguistic diversity, and a potentially volatile amalgam of European ethnicities. Anderson contends that despite such diversity and regardless of "actual inequality and exploitation" within the confines of an emergent nation, the imagined community is always "conceived as a deep, horizontal comradeship."[2]

New York historian Joyce Goodfriend confirms that Manhattan's primary ethnic groups struggled to construct a "pluralistic social order combining Dutch, English, and French ethnoreligious communities."[3] If merging heterogeneous European ethnicities into a "horizontal comradeship" was not demanding enough, in 1626, Dutch colonists began importing Africans, of various ethnicities, as "bond-servants." Combined with the continued presence of native nations and a steady traffic of white immigrants, the Dutch created an Indio-Euro-Afro–New York awash in multiple languages and cultures. After a British takeover in 1664, Manhattan remained a triracial colony, and even with the birth of an independent United States of America, the city's disparate cultures continued to work toward a new national imaginary.

Early national clergyman and intellectual Timothy Dwight toured Manhattan in the early 1810s and was astounded by the proliferating ethnic groups, especially the burgeoning Irish immigrant population. In his *Travels in New England and New York* (1822), Dwight warned of the inherent dangers in Manhattan's potentially volatile amalgam of European ethnicities. He cautioned that finding a common "American" character in a multicultural metropolis, or the nation, would be impossible given the divergent political styles, religious values, social standards, and artistic tastes of multiple white ethnicities.[4] The "melting pot" was yet to emerge as a national metaphor for ethnic assimilation, but Dwight advocated a coalescing process in which European immigrants detached from Old World connections in service to a more unified, homogenous "American" community.[5]

Rarely, if ever, does a nation "officially" envision itself coterminous with all of mankind; in plainer words, nation builders "naturally" erect ethnic and racial borders. Culturally and philosophically, borders defining the "other" or "outsider" are imagined alongside the concept of nation or political community.[6] At this pivotal juncture in its national identity formation, "America" as imagined community could have embraced an unequivocally triracial, multiethnic, and multilingual comradeship. Unfortunately, Euro-American revolutionaries were incapable of imagining African Americans and Native Americans as full participants within the boundaries of their sovereign nation. Literary scholar Werner Sollors distills this contention over "American" identity down to the "problem of ethnic heterogeneity: how inclusive and how exclusive could America be?"[7] Dwight answered that question by envisioning an ethnically diverse but racially specific America. The diversity and mutability of early American culture disturbed Euro-Americans like Dwight, so to make America's already troublesome pluralism more manageable, he proposed excluding African Americans and Native Americans from the national imaginary. True, his "America" was a nation of immigrants, but he imagined a uniracial community in which European ethnicities confronted the difficult tasks of forging a political system, social fabric, economic structure, and cultural logic. Historian David Roediger characterizes this limited, horizontal "America" as a "herrenvolk republic" in which Euro-Americans excluded blacks and Indians from the ranks of culture producers and political participants, thus allowing whites to forge alliances across class and ethnic divisions. Euro-Americans who shared Dwight's multiracial phobia would cultivate a "herrenvolk republic" or "horizontal comradeship" centered around a valuable whiteness as contrasted to a dispossessed Afri-canness or an increasingly invisible Indianness—hence the birth of white supremacy in the United States.[8]

The "official" position for Native and African Americans was on the mar-gins, with no legitimate claims on this "American" project, whereas Euro-American performers, playwrights, and politicians were allowed unfettered access to the New World cultures of marginalized others and the nation's many representational outlets. Of course, the national concept of an Amer-ica completely disconnected from Indianness or Africanness is nearly im-possible to imagine, and some would argue that English colonists forged their national identity based on Indianness more than on European or Afri-can cultures.[9] As Euro-American theatrical artists appropriated and recon-structed Indianness to forge New World selves, an ambitious federal govern-ment established a manageable, white-dominated "herrenvolk republic" by conquering, exterminating, or relocating Indians. This "America" deceived and decimated native nations, ultimately pushing the first Americans to the margins of an ever expanding, ever manifesting United States. In addition, their "America" systematically excluded Americans of African descent from the social fabric, cultural logic, and political process, often casting these in-voluntary immigrants as "problems" in need of extreme solutions such as enslavement.

In this chapter, I defend William Brown's claim on a version of "America" that was decidedly more inclusive than Euro-America's imagined commu-nity. At this self-proclaimed "American Theatre," Brown constructed and marketed a cultural institution at odds with the emerging "white" republic. His American phase tested the dominant culture's "herrenvolk republic" by continuing the social experiments with an integrated audience, by intro-ducing a racially diversified company, and by embracing a range of Native American representations. Because Brown's national theater maintained that true "American genius" was inextricably linked to indigenous cultures throughout the Americas, this chapter briefly outlines the conventions of Indio-constructed and Euro-constructed stage Indians in nineteenth-century Manhattan. These competing but mutually constitutive approaches to "playing Indian" both reveal a significant conquest-creation duality at work in the national performative laboratory. Consistent with their Africanist aesthetic, dramatist William Brown and choreographer James Hewlett exploited but never resolved this defining American duality. The final section of this chapter examines Hewlett's and Brown's complicated fusions of Africanness, Indianness, and Europeanness that produced the New World's first black drama and first black ballet. By combining Indio-constructed and Euro-constructed Indianness, these African American cultural claimants staged not only persistent U.S. dualities but cultural hybridities from other parts of the Americas.

The American Theatre

The "problem" of African American citizenship intensified in the late eighteenth century as various northern state legislatures passed immediate or gradual abolition bills. This legislation created a growing class of transitional blacks situated somewhere between chattel and citizen in an essentially white republic.[10] In the early 1810s the United States government and private entrepreneurs began exploring strategies to solve their free black dilemma. One proposed solution was returning black noncitizens to the Old World. By 1816 a federally funded and ironically named American Colonization Society (ACS) prepared to launch a ship "returning" black volunteers "back" to West Africa. Historian Elizabeth Bethel claims that "African Americans uniformly met the American Colonization Society agenda with outraged protests," and black economic and religious leaders like James Forten, Peter Williams Jr., and Richard Allen "led a solid opposition to the American Colonization Society proposal for the resettlement of all free African Americans in an independent colony on the African west coast."[11] Through the 1820s the ACS transported fewer than one thousand blacks to Liberia in West Africa, a colony that Russwurm and Cornish's *Freedom's Journal* described as located in "an unhealthy region."[12] Despite this criticism of federal efforts, emigration ignited a significant intraracial debate that exposed divergent black opinions on the possibility of full participation in American society. In December 1815, a year before the federally sanctioned ACS program materialized, a black sea captain named Paul Cuffee independently transported a small group of free blacks to Sierra Leone in West Africa.[13] The families aboard Cuffee's 1815 voyage, as well as many other despondent free blacks, were dissatisfied with the United States and did not foresee economic, political, and social progress for African Americans.

The African colonization question became a litmus test prompting African Americans, including theatrical manager William Brown, to reveal publicly where their allegiances resided, in Africa or America. After the American Colonization Society's back-to-African plan surfaced, many black institutions began discarding the term "African" and instead affirmed their American citizenship. For example, in 1830 African Americans congregated in Philadelphia to create the American Society of Free Persons of Colour. Black institutions intentionally avoided the term "African" because of the growing public perception that organizations which adopted "African" in their titles favored Africa over America.[14] This litmus test partially explains why Brown may have been reluctant to embrace "African" as an institutional identity and instead selected the American Theatre. Brown was not necessarily ashamed of Africa or aspiring toward whiteness by publicly identifying as American. Rather, Elizabeth Bethel notes that many like-minded nineteenth-century African Americans had formed "a new cultural memory and racial identity" that were "forged by a consciousness of nativity and explicitly American milieux of memory."[15] Consequently, nineteenth-century black intellectuals, including the provocative pamphleteer David Walker, reacted to colonization "plots" by declaring "America" did not mean whites only. African Americans contributed immensely to this young nation, and therefore had just as much right to claim their country.[16] Free blacks who refused to abandon this national project would still be denied full citizenship and systematically divested of rights like the elective franchise, but this land was their land. Bethel argues that well before Du Bois posed the question "Am I American or am I a Negro? Can I be both?," many early national African Americans struggled with this seemingly unresolvable dilemma of African ancestry and American nativity.[17]

Brown decided he could be both American and African. He definitely counted himself among the African Americans who proudly declared the United States their home, and his theater personified that "new cultural memory and racial identity" firmly rooted in North American soil. In this "becoming" phase, Brown contested the "herrenvolk republic" outlined earlier and proved "American" could signify beyond a white particular. But even in the early 1820s, a black theater manager showcasing an all-African company would struggle mightily to reconfigure prevailing conceptions of

"American." Toni Morrison states it plainly and painfully when she writes, "American means white, and Africanist people struggle to make the term applicable to themselves with ethnicity and hyphen after hyphen after hyphen."[18] David Walker, William Brown, and other early black voices who defined "America" as their own would ultimately fail to convince their fellow citizens that "American" and whiteness were not synonymous. Nevertheless, Brown and company were determined to dispense with the hyphens, not as an act of assimilation, but as a restatement or rediscovery of "America."[19] The name American Theatre announced Brown's loyalty to this country and staked his claim on a shared future, but, more important, his act of naming reminded a nation who it happened to be.

Prior to announcing his Americanness to Manhattan, Brown had already done the patriotic groundwork to warrant such a title. Beginning in his Minor Theatre phase, he supported native-born playwrights at a time when U.S. dramatists were waging an uphill battle for recognition and productions. Commenting on the state of national drama between 1815 and 1828, Walter Meserve concluded that, as the country became more economically and politically nationalistic, its literature did not follow suit. If anything, the preexistent prejudice against national drama worsened. Opponents or critics of U.S. playwrights advised that if the national theater was patient, suitably talented, native-born writers would eventually emerge.[20] Also, national drama tends to develop with the demand and permission of the larger society, and antitheatrical religious and political leaders in various cities opposed theater on moral grounds.[21] So, in the meantime, critics and theatrical managers reasoned that U.S. drama was really English drama; therefore, U.S. theaters could appropriate English plays as they pleased. Unfortunately, professional domestic dramatists were slow to emerge, and promising writers were reduced to mere dabblers in theatrics.

One prolific closet dramatist was the ever present, always vigilant M. M. Noah. Ironically, this increasingly satiric and dismissive newspaper editor would become Brown's preferred national dramatist. In November 1821, at his initial Village theater, Brown advertised a production of Noah's stage Indian drama *She Would Be a Soldier; or The Plains of Chippewa* (1819). William Coleman, editor at the *Evening Post*, heralded the upcoming production: "Encourage to American genius—We perceive by handbills which are posted up on the corners of the streets, that this evening there is to be performed by a company of colored gentleman and ladies, at the corner of Mercer and Bleecker streets, the American drama of *She Would be a Soldier, or the Plains of Chippewa*, written by Mordecai Manassah Noah, Esquire."[22] Brown further demonstrated that his commitment to "American genius" was not a fleeting or cynical gesture by staging Noah's gothic melodrama *Fortress of Sorrento* three months later, in January 1822. The *Spectator* also commended Brown for showcasing an American-born dramatist: "We are glad to find also, that they are so patriotic as to give preference to the productions of our own country."[23] This same article noted how Brown's performers "wander through the gardens of imagination in both hemispheres, and cull the choice flowers, no matter whether they bud upon the banks of Avon, or bloom upon those of the majestic Hudson." Of course, Noah could not compete with "Brother William," but as an act of patriotism, or perhaps in reaction to Price's Shakespeare ban, Brown elevated and celebrated this local artist.

Brown's interest in national artistic production extended beyond drama into the fine arts. At the abbreviated Hampton's Hotel residency, Brown supplemented his Shakespearean productions by displaying at the close of each evening's performance "a grand historic Painting representing Fear, Horror Despair, &c." A bill of January 1822 announced that for a separate admission price of one shilling, "[t]hose who may feel anxious to patronize American Taste and Genius, will be pleased to remain after the curtain is dropped, and take tickets."[24] Brown's broadly defined "American Taste and Genius" now included not only U.S. actors in domestic plays but a historic painting by a homegrown visual artist. As a theatrical producer turned curator, he promoted a multifaceted, cross-medium vision of U.S. art that any patriotic fan of native artistry could support. The next logical steps were for Brown to construct and announce his American Theatre, devoted to such nationalistic impulses.

After the Shakespeare arrests of January 1822 forced Brown back to the Village, the African American manager began constructing a larger theater to accommodate and promote his inclusive national vision. Dr. McCune Smith reported how Brown earned enough revenue from his pleasure garden and theatrical ventures to construct a completely new theater "of wood, roughly built, and having capacity for an audience of three to four hundred."[25] Previously Brown had rented spaces in the Village and on the West Side, but Eighth Ward tax assessments for 1823 listed him as the owner-occupant of an "African Theatre" at 1215 Mercer Street. Tax assessment records for 1822 reveal that this Mercer Street property formerly belonged to Samuel Broadhurst and consisted of a vacant lot.[26] Apparently, Brown purchased the lot at Mercer and Houston Streets and constructed his second Greenwich Village theater from the ground up.

Brown heralded the official opening of his "roughly built" theater in July 1822 with the following card-size advertisement published in, of all places, Noah's *National Advocate*: "AMERICAN THEATRE, Mr. Brown, most respectfully informs his friends and the public, that he has spared neither pains or expense in erecting a Theatre in Mercer-st. opposite the one mile stone, for the purpose of giving rational amusements, and on Tuesday wishes that patronage he has in former times received from a generous audience."[27] Brown's brief yet well-executed July announcement deployed three shrewd marketing strategies to establish the most inclusive, unlimited, and unproblematic institutional identity. First, he mentioned "one mile stone," a well-known marker that indicated his location exactly one mile from City Hall; by including this landmark, he made his remote Village theater easier for lower Manhattanites to find. Second, he called his productions "rational amusements" to counter objections from the city's antitheatrical religious and political leaders who believed theater ruined young people. Finally, because this new theater was larger than his previous spaces, Brown could no longer afford to market exclusively to people of color and risk alienating white patrons. He hoped to maintain the "generous audience" from his garden and upstairs theater, but he also needed to attract more whites to fill three hundred to four hundred seats. Therefore, Brown astutely appealed to "friends and the public" with "friends" signifying his loyal Afro–New Yorker supporters and the "public" referring to all Manhattan theatergoers.

Almost immediately, Euro–New York aggressively denied Brown this institutional identity and his African-inclusive vision for the United States. On the same page with Brown's July 22 announcement, Noah printed the following reaction or clarification: "Mr. Brown opened his Theatre in Mercer-street. The corps dramatique is composed of ladies and gentlemen of color, who commence with concerts. It is rather hazardous to open the African Theatre with the Thermometer at 85."[28] Noah felt obligated to warn Manhattan that Brown's venture had not magically mutated into an "American" institution overnight but was still "African" and different. Avoiding the name American Theatre altogether, he highlighted racial difference by referring to the venture as the "African Theatre" and quipping that the "heat" generated by blacks on a summer evening could be quite combustible. If newspaper readers did not catch Noah's humorous warning, they could read it the very next day when the *New York American* reprinted his comments nearly word for word.[29] In addition, a satirist named Simon Snipe rejected Brown's self-proclaimed American Theatre. He opened his collection of observational humor, *Sports of New York*, with the following: "During the months of the prevailing Fever, last year, I was determined to spend a leisure evening at the American, or in plainer words, Negro Theatre."[30] Snipe, like Noah, decided Brown's "American Theatre" was misleading and felt it his duty to alert potential patrons to the true nature of this African establishment.

For a glimpse inside the newly christened and openly contested American Theatre, we must rely on the accounts of two Euro–New Yorkers, the satirist Simon Snipe and a *Spectator* correspondent named Twaites; both writers attended the American Theatre in the summer of 1822. Like Noah, these writers fancied themselves humorists and adopted fairly sarcastic attitudes toward Brown's company; therefore, one must read against their jesting agendas to recover any facts. Snipe described the building as "tolerable well built house, and particularly well suited for the warm weather, as it let breeze in plentifully between the crevices of the boards."[31] In his wry way, Snipe supported McCune Smith's claim that the new theater was a "roughly built" structure. Twaites provided more structural details in his August 1822 *Spectator* article titled "Theatrical Extraordinary." Twaites first remarked on the theater's inconspicuous exterior: "When I discovered the chaste simplicity of its *front*, I began to suspect the nature of its building; but when I read 'Box' and 'Pit,' over two little holes through its 'wooden walls,' I could no longer mistake its character. It was one of the many Theatres that adorn, and ornament, and improve, and interest, and amuse, and edify our city." Due to the unassuming front, Twaites did not initially realize the building housed a theater, until he noticed the signs indicating a box and a pit. Once inside, he discovered a gallery, which he described "as well conceived, though not quite so happily executed. Understanding that it was to contain 'the gods,' the architects had got it so near the roof that the divinities were obliged to sit out the evening in their curls, as there was not room for either hats or bonnets."[32] Brown's balcony was situated painfully close to the ceiling, and consequently his cramped gallery was not the most comfortable location for these "gods." But more seats translated into more revenues.

After earlier experiments with one large seating area and a controversial partition, Brown now created three seating sections to accommodate the varied classes, castes, and races attending his American Theatre. Modeled after nineteenth-century British theaters, most U.S. theater interiors were configured along a hierarchical three-tiered system consisting of boxes, a pit, and a gallery. Early national audiences were commonly referred to as "the town" because theatrical performances were the rare contexts in which lower-class laborers, middle-class clerks or artisans, and upper-class merchants occupied the same space. In this tripartite configuration, the upper classes occupied the boxes, the middling classes the pit, and the lower or working classes the gallery. Theater managers adopted this hierarchy to assert upper-class authority and separate "the refined and the vulgar."[33]

Given that Brown's raucous element was not restricted to his gallery but liberally distributed throughout "the town," it was logistically impossible for Brown to separate the "vulgar" from the "refined." Customarily, the lower-class galleries accommodated the most volatile or "vulgar" patrons, who were known for hurling projectiles at actors, and Brown's gallery was no different. Snipe recounted how in the middle of one dance number, an unfortunate performer "was assailed with a heavy shower of peas, that came from the gallery."[34] The gallery was not the sole source of disorder in this American Theatre, for in the pit—the middle-class ground-floor section closest to the stage—both Twaites and Snipe discovered an extremely raucous mass of humanity that exerted a frightening degree of control over the proceedings. Twaites characterized this middling section as more uncontrollable than the gallery, with "sounds of critical damnation" emanating from the pernicious pit throughout the evening.

This American Theatre also adopted a three-tiered hierarchical arrangement as part of Brown's continuing campaign to integrate, peacefully if possible, "laughter-loving clerks" and "ladies and gentlemen of color." To Brown's credit, one interracial oasis did flourish: the boxes. Traditionally, box seats were reserved for upper-class patrons, who often arrived better dressed and definitely better behaved than other members of "the town." Twaites, whom I assume to be white, arrived early and purchased a seat in Brown's boxes, or more accurately his "box." Twaites commented that manager Brown did not partition his boxes into private units, like the Park and other theaters, but instead created one large box—a distinct arrangement that encouraged a more communal and sociable atmosphere among the "refined" patrons. Twaites assumed a seat next to two "very sallow looking young ladies" who had also arrived early. "Sallow" ladies can read as mulatto women or ladies of color, and because they were unescorted, early, and seated in boxes, it could also read as ladies of the evening. The inhabitants of this integrated oasis refrained from tossing chestnuts and verbally abusing actors, and from his relatively placid perch, Twaites enjoyed his evening. At least in his massive box, Brown successfully integrated Manhattan, but by no coincidence, he accomplished the difficult task of peaceful desegregation in the most elitist section of his establishment.

Brown also expanded his integrationist project by creating an interracial orchestra. Snipe recalled a mini-orchestra of three musicians the night he attended, and he seemed excited by the diversity onstage: "The Orchestra consisted of three instruments of music, a violin—clarionet—and a bass fiddle; which instruments were performed on by two white men and one black one!"[35] Snipe's exclamation mark was understandable because, for the first time in a Manhattan theater, Euro– and Afro–New Yorkers were performing together. So, in his undivided box and his orchestra, Brown had achieved some semblance of interracial harmony. Or had he? Twaites described the mini-orchestra as four musicians, one for each part or section, and at his sarcastic best, he offered this hilarious appraisal of their musical prowess: "I will merely add, in order to give some idea of the skill of the musicians, that although the violin player unfortunately snapp'd a string in the middle of a solo, the best ear could not distinguish any difference in the air." Broken strings or fully strung, Twaites regretted hearing all he heard from this disharmonious foursome.

As for the rest of the "town," Simon Snipe exposed the limited success of this social engineering. He encountered a "variegated audience" dispersed throughout Brown's American Theatre, consisting of "white, black, copper-colored, and light brown" theatergoers. Apparently whites were no longer segregated or protected behind a partition; in fact, at this American Theatre, Snipe recalled a "corner of the Pit, partitioned off for 'the gemmen and ladies of color.'"[36] If we accept Snipe's observation, Euro–New Yorkers were now such a dominant presence in Brown's pit that a significantly decreased Afro–New Yorker contingent was forced to occupy a "corner" of the main floor. Brown's remote location had apparently reduced his original "colored gentry" base, and his American Theatre was now overwhelmingly populated, at least in the powerful pit, by white leisure seekers. This increased cadre of "laughter-loving clerks," who attended for the "sport," represented an economic boon for Brown, but these patrons created a disruptive and dangerous climate for his actors and other audience members.

A precariously integrated pit and gallery assailed the company with "razzes" and radishes and began to dominate the productions. During the brief hotel residency discussed in Chapter 2, this audience-actor byplay had proved colorful yet manageable. Hotel patrons imposed on the Shakespearean productions, but the facile performers were comfortable enough to develop an improvisational rapport with their guests. By contrast, the larger and majority-white American Theatre audiences pushed the symbiotic relationship in a more derisive direction. Many New Yorkers were now attending to ridicule a curiosity rather than admire an earnest company of black Shakespeareans, thus making the presentation of any dramatic or major material precarious and even impossible. American Theatre patrons, from the pit and gallery, talked, ignored, or shouted Shakespeare off the stage. When the company attempted to perform Shakespeare's *Othello*, Snipe noted that "although the audience still was restless and noisy I could now and then hear a sentence."[37] Manager Brown stopped the production, which was being ignored, and did not deliver a speech instructing the boisterous group on proper theatrical "behavior" but instead placated the crowd by announcing they would abort *Othello* in favor of songs and dances.

With ridiculing rowdies now outnumbering admiring fans, Brown's integrationist experiment became a cacophonous disaster of vocal pit crews, armed gallery gods, and even retaliating actors. Although the crowd quieted down considerably during the lighter, minor fare, Snipe described how one rhythmically challenged female dancer triggered a fresh chorus of hissing from the pit, and one pit rascal, whom Snipe described as a "Negro," threw a potato at the dancer, striking her on the chin. Frustrated and rattled, this not-so-demure female dancer hurled the potato back into that pernicious pit. Apparently, black patrons were now making "sport" of this company as well, and black actors were snapping under the pressure. Unconcerned with Brown's social experiments and his inclusive appropriation of "American," the most vocal and active audience members were undermining the performances and literally dictating productions. Such practices were not uncommon for early national theater. Washington Irving, through his famous alter ego Jonathan Oldstyle, claimed, "The good folks of the gallery have all the trouble of ordering the music. . . . The mode by which they issue their mandates is stamping, hissing, roaring, whistling."[38]

Brown acquiesced to his vociferous patrons, but he was reluctant to acknowledge or air his audience difficulties publicly. The manager published an advertisement in the *National Advocate* of August 9 claiming, "[I]t is with pleasure that he announces that his theater has been attended with a respectable audience."[39] Some respectable Afro– and Euro–New Yorkers did remain in Brown's refined box, but his pit and gallery ranged from rude to obstructive and would soon turn violent, resulting in a riot in August 1822, fomented by a mob of white ruffians.

That riot—a subject for a later chapter—forced Brown to adopt a more realistic and cautious attitude toward his audience difficulties. Before the riot, Brown had offered three distinct seating areas to separate the "refined" and the "vulgar," but he neglected to charge three different admission prices. Beginning with a postriot, Hewlett benefit in March 1823, Brown instituted a three-tiered pricing system, charging fifty cents for a box seat, thirty-seven and one-half cents for a pit seat, and twenty-five cents for a gallery seat. Ideally, three distinct prices would further separate the raucous element in the pit and gallery from the harmonious black and white gentry in the box. In addition, Brown implemented security measures, as the March benefit bill announced: "Proper persons will attend to maintain Order."[40] If the three-tiered pricing structure did not keep the rabble from the royalty, perhaps a private security guard might discourage a repeat of the August 1822 riot.

The second pamphlet authored by Simon Snipe gives some indication of the effectiveness of the three-tiered pricing system and the security guard. Snipe attended Hewlett's March 1823 benefit and recorded his impressions in an 1824 edition of *Sports of New York*. Always the versatile satirist, Snipe recounted the evening from the perspective of a concerned black patron: "White folks all got on the stage—wonder where the officer was, was just going to speak to 'em myself, when out come Hewlett to sing; and by the great cow tail, he sung a tarnal sight better than some of the white folks there, that join'd in the chorus! . . . White folks had all the fun to 'emselves now. Some on 'em begin to dance, box, whistle, sing, and the dickens knows what all."[41] Snipe utilized this fictitious black spectator to expose three disturbing realities about Brown's social experiment. First, differentiated ticket prices did not have a significant impact because two sections, the pit and gallery, were already equally unrestrained, a problem that a higher admission price could never solve. Second, the "proper persons" were woefully inadequate, nowhere to be found when needed, and therefore this American Theatre remained a precarious place for the black performers and patrons. Snipe may have crafted a black character for comic effect, but his dismayed black persona captured the increasingly unfriendly tenor of these entertainments. Finally, Snipe distinctly characterized the American Theatre as a playground for Euro–New Yorkers who literally dictated what transpired onstage. In the first *Sports*, he described white patrons who loudly voiced their displeasure when subjected to allegedly "major" dramatic offerings and demanded "minor" theatrical material. By the second *Sports*, whites not only continued to disrupt Brown's program with their demands but now displaced Hewlett's performance and entertained themselves.

As for Hewlett and the acting company who had to endure this precariously integrated audience, the most significant personnel change from the Minor to the American Theatre was the loss of S. Welsh, who was replaced by Williams, a skilled singer and dancer. Noah may have been impressed by the vigor of Welsh's highly inventive Lady Ann, but Simon Snipe was underwhelmed by Williams's histrionics. In the first *Sports of New York*, Snipe attributed the crowd's general hostility to her poor preparation. He remarked that when Williams appeared as Desdemona, it was clear the actor "had not studied her part thoroughly," and the audience objected to seeing Shakespeare's tragedies "transformed into mimic burlesques."[42] The pit and gallery voiced their displeasure by pummeling the ill-prepared and seemingly disrespectful performers with chestnuts, peas, and apple cores.

Brown's new leading lady was a "colored" beauty, ideal for "minor" or "illegitimate" entertainment. Obviously underprepared and untrained to handle Shakespeare or other demanding dramatic pieces, Williams impressed Snipe as an attractive "copper-colored" woman who would definitely please Afro–New Yorker patrons. One would imagine she pleased white patrons as well, in particular, a visiting Simon Snipe. In his *Spectator* report, Twaites concurred that the lovely Williams's talents lay not in the dramatic or "major" arena but in the musical or "minor" realm. He witnessed the same ill-prepared actress and recounted how, after missing a cue, "[s]he soon appeared, and some *fine* singing flowed from her pouting lips." Beyond her lovely voice and visage, Williams was also Brown's most gifted and hardest-working dancer, and both Snipe and Twaites highlighted her committed hornpiping.[43] Despite some trouble with an orchestra member who played too quickly, Snipe wrote that "she really danced it well too for I must give praise where it is due."[44] Twaites described Williams as "a young lady, who danced with a vigor seldom surpassed," and claimed that when she finished dancing she "was loudly applauded." A drastic change from Welsh's disidentifying stage European, Williams was an accomplished singer and dedicated hornpiper; in short, she was better suited for the "illegitimate" musical theater that his audience demanded.

Williams proved the perfect leading lady for Brown's "minor" American experiment, and despite his aspirations toward something more legitimate, James Hewlett remained the anchor of this literally besieged American Theatre company. During one scene in which Williams forgot her entrance cue and kept the audience waiting, Twaites remarked that it was Hewlett "who stepped behind the scenes, and, we presume gave Mrs. Williams a hint that her presence was necessary at the window." In the face of flying chestnuts and missed entrances, Hewlett remained the would-be professional, working to keep an amateur troupe honest and a restless audience at bay. Comedian Twaites quipped that "most of the actors did not know their parts," but added that this fault was "borrowed from the Park Theatre," which suffered from the same deficiency.

Simon Snipe was more critical of the company, especially of Hewlett, who, he claimed, provided the pernicious pit with ample material to ridicule. Like his leading lady, Hewlett demonstrated that his singing ability was his greatest asset, but according to Snipe, his educational and linguistic deficiencies rendered the earnest black performer laughable. Over the course of that evening in the summer of 1822, Hewlett sang a popular ballad, "Is There a Heart That Ever Lov'd," and Snipe claimed that "[w]hen this song was finished peals of laughter came from all parts of the house, some laughed, perhaps, because it was sung well; others because it was an excellent song, but the principle part of the audience laughed at the pronunciation."[45] The unrelenting satirist conceded that some patrons appreciated Hewlett's vocal talents and others enjoyed the much beloved ballad, but he concluded that Hewlett's mispronunciations provided the primary source of amusement. Snipe even recreated Hewlett's rendition of "Is There a Heart" using a highly exaggerated black dialect to translate the lyric into "Is dare a heart dat nebber lub'd." Snipe's derisive intentions are obvious; however, Martin Delany's previously discussed remarks on Hewlett's linguistic deficiencies lend credence to Snipe's unflattering characterization.

From the unruly audiences to the unprepared actors, Brown's Minor Theatre, now American Theatre, had "become" an inescapably "minor" and potentially dangerous institution. The change in leading ladies, the audience-aborted *Othello* production, and the many dropped or mangled lines signaled an ominous aesthetic redirection from a subversive Minor Theatre originally committed to blending "legitimate" and "illegitimate" texts, to an overwhelmed American Theatre reduced to song and dance. Who was primarily responsible for this raucous counterpublic sphere—a "minor" acting ensemble or uncooperative auditors? True, uninhibited audience participation and intimidation were familiar aspects of nineteenth-century theatergoing, but the chaotic climate in Brown's American Theatre was more than any actor should have had to endure. The insults and missiles flying from the pit and gallery made it virtually impossible to stage or sustain any remotely sophisticated or serious theatrics. On the other side of this question, Snipe implies that the insubordinate New Yorkers had such regard for *Othello* that they rightfully objected to a "burlesqued" production perpetrated by incompetent actors.

Like the proverbial chicken and egg, one cannot reduce the problems in this symbiotic relationship either to poor acting creating an unruly audience or to an unruly audience producing poor acting. Due to a paucity of "major" as opposed to "minor" talent and those lurking educational deficiencies, Brown's African American company wrestled mightily with dramatic text. Despite Hewlett's commitment and versatility, the troupe was more musically inclined than dramatically adept and thus better suited for pantomimes, melodramas, and musicals than tragedies, dramas, and comedies. The American Theatre audience refused *Othello* because the novelty of black Shakespeare had worn thin; Brown's patrons no longer believed his company capable of staging "legitimate" material, which was better left to "General Price" and his European imports. In what would become a familiar refrain for black performers in the United States, Brown's integrated audience expected, even demanded, songs and dances from an all-African company. However, in spite of audience expectations and the seeming limitations of his company, manager Brown would ultimately define the American Theatre repertoire, and he envisioned dramatic and balletic stage Indians as his most American representations.

Indio- and Euro-Constructed Stage Indians

Stage Indians, constructed by Indians and Europeans, had a profound impact on William Brown's and James Hewlett's creative sensibilities and their vision of a multicultural United States. Many American theater and performance histories neglect to include Native American contributions and concentrate on Euro-constructed stage Indians. But performance artist and scholar Coco Fusco contends that "performance Art in the West" began when "'aboriginal samples' of people from Africa, Asia, and the Americas" were placed on display in the taverns, theaters, pleasure gardens, museums, and zoos of Europe and the New World.[46] Although guilty of native omission, Philip Deloria in *Playing Indian* does note that "throughout a long history of Indian play, native people have been present at the margins, insinuating their way into Euro-American discourse, often attempting to nudge notions of Indianness in directions they found useful."[47] Native Americans, as willing or coerced performers, have contributed directly to the notion of "exterior savagery" in early American entertainment and culture. Opportunistic Europeans and Americans would incorporate that "exterior savagery" into their "interior" as they used seemingly marginal Indian images to shape New World identities and communities.

A moderate review of eighteenth- and nineteenth-century Manhattan newspapers reveals how frequently "tribal" dancers performed Indian identities in pleasure gardens and theaters; Native American chiefs were displayed in Manhattan museums; and entire native deputations displayed themselves in exhibition halls, theater boxes, and even City Hall.[48] Performing natives, or Indio-constructed stage Indians, first surfaced in Manhattan when "exhibited" Indians appeared as audience oddities at the John Street Playhouse. In 1767 the John Street managers graciously extended invitations to nine Cherokee chiefs who were visiting the English colony. Not surprisingly, the chiefs witnessed a production of *Richard III*, a colonial favorite, and according to theater historian William Dunlap, they "regarded the play with attention, but seemed to express nothing but surprise."[49] While their peculiar guests deciphered an equally peculiar Duke of Gloucester, the John Street managers invited curious New Yorkers to watch the natives seated in conspicuous dress boxes strategically located close to the stage. Soon other theater, garden, and circus managers realized that during the slow months, native audience members arrayed in national dress produced revenue. In 1806, with attendance declining at the Park, then-manager William Dunlap advertised the "appearance" of fourteen Indian chiefs in the boxes. At the close of a sluggish 1821 season, Stephen Price invited Indian chiefs from an area called Council Bluffs to witness M. M. Noah's *She Would Be a Soldier*. Heading Park playbills, above the name of the scheduled drama, Price announced that the chiefs would be "appearing" in their national dress.[50]

Consistent with Deloria's claim that native nations desired to influence Indian imaging, the Cherokee chiefs who attended John Street Playhouse in 1767 made a return visit. The contingent was so thoroughly impressed by John Street's "surprising" *Richard III* and so thankful for the gracious invitation that they wished to reciprocate artistically. The following week, the chiefs returned with their warriors and thrilled the John Street patrons with

a "war dance."[51] The decision to reciprocate with a war dance was fitting because the fifth act of Shakespeare's *Richard III* features exciting sword battles between Richard's and Richmond's armies.

Perhaps intentionally, the chiefs introduced a new performance form to
the early national theatrical laboratory. Multiple dancing-native ensembles
would continue to thrill theater and garden audiences with their mixed
repertoire of religious and militaristic practice. Vauxhall Gardens in the remote Greenwich Village became the most consistent venue for "warring"
Indio-constructed stage Indians. In 1807 an Osage Indian ensemble performed a regular diet of "performative" war whoops, war songs, and war
dances, becoming a semipermanent specialty at Vauxhall Gardens. The garden managers were so committed to their native entertainments that they
enlisted the expertise of a Dr. Mitchell to translate the Osage communica-
tions.[52] Vauxhall continued to host dancing troupes into the 1820s, and for
one Fourth of July celebration the managers announced an indigenous entertainment titled *A Trail of Indians*. This special presentation featured an
Indian chief and three "squaws" from Grand River in Ontario, Canada, who
would be performing an Indian war dance accompanied by a war song and
other "native exercises" in "proper costumes."[53]

By far the most celebrated native ensemble to tour Manhattan was a com-
pany of six young braves called "Natives from the West," alternately titled
"Sons of the Forest." They began their artistic assault in December 1824 at
Castle Garden in lower Manhattan and later moved to Hippolyte Barrère's
Chatham Garden Theatre. At both locations, their specialties included "the
Grand War Dance—War Song—Two Chiefs rejoicing after a Victory—The
execution of a prisoner by Scalping—The telling of great exploits after a
battle—Their manner of worship."[54] The dancing braves entertained New
Yorkers eager for personal encounters with an allegedly vanishing culture,
but these "warring" ensembles used these performative opportunities to
project a still thriving people systematically pushed to the margins of the
United States. Through war songs, dances, ritual scalpings, and other religious rites, Indian ensembles delivered metaphoric and literal messages of
cultural and physical survival to their "pale" hosts and expropriators.

Beyond "nudging" notions of Indianness through dress box invasions or
symbolic warrior rites, Native Americans also headlined as curiosities at exhibition halls, museums, and other public spaces. Again adorned in traditional dress and other accoutrements, natives displayed themselves—or, in
most cases, were displayed. In the fluid world of nineteenth-century per-

formance, the line between exhibition and exploitation was easily crossed. Coco Fusco argues that with aboriginal displays in the United States and Europe, "in most cases, the human beings that were exhibited did not choose to be on display."[55] Historian C. Richard King has studied native exhibitions from the latter half of the nineteenth century to the present and agrees that early indigenous exhibitions were blatant examples of Indians being placed on display to celebrate "the Euro-American conquest of North America and their domination and extermination of the first nations of the continent."[56] Fusco also asserts that allegedly authentic versions of "primitive" societies were initially exhibited for entertainment purposes or scientific analysis, but ultimately served as "proof of the natural superiority of European civilization" and "of its ability to exert control over and extract knowledge from the 'primitive' world."[57] Museum versions of Indianness were designed to consume and learn from Indian knowledge while simultaneously demonstrating European dominance. This kind of creation-conquest would prove a popular trope in the Euro-constructed stage Indians created by American and European playwrights and choreographers.

To appreciate the dominant culture's reaction to Indio-constructed Indianness, one only has to consider the many native images crafted by Euro-American and European writers, philosophers, and politicians. As a literary or philosophical concept, the "noble savage" first surfaced in the work of ancient writers like Homer and Virgil and developed further through the work of eighteenth-century French Enlightenment philosopher Jean-Jacques Rousseau.[58] The "noble savage" can be defined as an idealized natural man who is inherently pure and unspoiled by civilization's potentially corruptive influences yet ultimately inferior because he is ruled by antisocial instincts as opposed to reason. U.S. artists constructed mythic Indians to recover a nostalgic "America" forfeited when the young nation matured and rebelled against British oppression. Their self-reflexive natives provided an innocent, less complicated alternative to an increasingly complex, triracial, polyethnic United States.[59] In early national literature, Euro-American writers produced numerous popular novels, such as James Fenimore Cooper's *Pioneers* (1823) and *The Last of the Mohicans* (1826), which romanticized white-Indian relations.[60]

Philip Deloria locates the aforementioned duality of national creation and conquest operating in most Euro-constructed versions of the American "noble savage." He claims that America defined itself with and against this natural man: "Savage Indians served Americans as oppositional figures against whom one might imagine a civilized national self. Coded as freedom, however, wild Indianness proved equally attractive, setting up a 'have-the-cake-and-eat-it-too' dialectic of simultaneous desire and repulsion."[61] Theoretically, the Indian represented both an uncivilized "exterior savage" antithetical to an ordered society and an unfettered "savage" who personified freedom in its purest form. Deloria elaborates on the unfettered "savage"'s critical function for the latest Americans: "If one emphasizes the noble aspect as Rousseau did, pure and natural Indians serve to critique Western society. Putting more weight on savagery justifies (and perhaps requires) a campaign to eliminate barbarism. Two interlocked traditions: one of self-criticism, the other of conquest. They balance perfectly, forming one of the foundations underpinning the equally intertwined history of European colonialism and the European Enlightenment."[62] The "natural" critics imparted "primitive" secrets about individual freedom and fulfillment, and their unspoiled model triggered an intense collective introspection that helped to produce an enlightened New World imagined community, an exemplary republic that surpassed Old World polities and the primordial communities created by the very same Indians. But national self-critique and creation were soon followed by conquest. No matter how pure or wise "exterior savages" appeared to be, their barbaric surrender to destructive natural instincts excluded them from this enlightened "American" project. Despite inspiring Euro-Americans toward a deeper understanding of their better selves, Indians were unworthy and marked for expropriation. Early national artists constructed "noble savages," what Deloria terms "interior Indianness," to replace the real "exterior savages" pushed to the margins.

For the stage, European and U.S. playwrights wrote tragedies and melodramas featuring honorable but predictable "noble savages" as the central characters. Euro-American playwright Robert Rogers created one of the earliest distinctly North American stage Indian chiefs in *Ponteach; or the Savage of America* (1766), a tragedy that dramatizes the long-standing conflict between Chief Ponteach and corrupt European colonists in the Northwest. Not fooled by their outward signs of civility, the inherently wise Ponteach exposes the Europeans as deceitful hypocrites who routinely take advantage of unsuspecting Indians. He first scolds the Europeans for their deceitful tendencies and then wages a fierce battle against the pale intruders, which ends in his defeat and the loss of two sons. At the tragedy's close, a conquered Ponteach disappears into the wilderness, much like Rogers's drama, which never actually appeared onstage.[63] Nevertheless, the creation-conquest duality represented by Rogers's critical yet conquered "noble savage" resurfaced in other stage Indian dramas like Richard Sheridan's *Pizarro* (1799), M. M. Noah's *She Would Be a Soldier* (1819), and even William Brown's *Drama of King Shotaway*.

European and U.S. theatrical artists, especially choreographers, featured the female complement to the "noble savage," the *belle sauvage*, in ballets, musicals, ballad operas, and pantomimes. A definitive example of this native heroine can be found in British playwright George Colman Jr.'s ballad opera *Inkle and Yarico* (1787). Loosely based on a real native woman, Colman's opera unfolds on Barbados, where Yarico, a stunningly beautiful Indian maiden, rescues an English slaver named Inkle, with whom she instantly falls in love. Deloria's creation-conquest duality is manifested in this musical because after Yarico rescues Inkle and abandons her family to devote her life to him, the white stranger reciprocates by selling the devoted heroine into slavery. Of course, as a "minor" entertainment immune to tragic endings, Yarico's love and innate goodness ultimately reform her wayward lover and inspire him to renounce his slaving ways. Based on Colman's model, the prototypical *belle sauvage* is a trusting and physically appealing native heroine who falls for a European stranger.[64]

Unlike her male counterparts, the *belle sauvage* is never literally defeated by the new arrivals but is culturally conquered and assimilated into European society. Colman constructs an interior-exterior dichotomy first by describing the natives as "black as a peppercorn" while drawing Yarico as a fair-complexioned Indian. An engraving included in the Inchbald edition of the opera depicts Yarico with "fine" European features and her personal servant Womski with a flat nose and other African features.[65] Also, in terms of language Colman has the "interior" Yarico speak perfect English, and her "exterior" kinsmen communicate in an exaggerated pidgin English. In essence, Yarico, the exceptional native, is allowed inside civilization, whereas her people, the "exterior savages," remain physically and culturally outside the Euro-Caribbean community.

With "exterior savages" dropping in for staged declarations of war, native curiosities exhibiting in museums, and non-Indian dramatists, composers, and choreographers crafting tragedies, melodramas, musicals, pantomimes, ballad operas, and ballets, Manhattan's theatrical landscape was immersed in a stage Indian "vogue" with profound implications for national development.[66] Aesthetically, the nation's theatrical laboratories produced "noble savages" who served as both didactic symbols and unassimilable outsiders, and *belle sauvages*, who represented equally heroic, visually pleasing, and exceptional native maidens. Politically, each Euro-constructed stage Indian reminded Euro-America of the core values, such as freedom and individuality, on which the nation was allegedly founded. However, Euro-Americans also crafted stage Indian dramas to justify destroying or relocating Indians as part of their manifest destiny.[67] This entire theatrical and extratheatrical stage Indian fascination paralleled important developments in Indio-European relations, including the War of 1812 and the Indian Removal Act of 1830. After decades of warring with native populations and "unofficially" pushing "exterior savages" west, in 1830 the nation officially adopted the Indian Removal Act, which relocated first Americans into territories west of the Mississippi. During this period of geographic expansion, "playing Indian" was not merely a theatrical novelty but a powerful form of propaganda fostering national unity.

Deloria's theory of "interior" versus "exterior" Indianness summarizes the complex connections among real Indians, Euro-constructed stage Indians, national expansion, and American identity: "[I]nterior Indians . . . proved crucial in letting one oppose the English and be American. Complete incorporation of this particular form of Indian was impossible, however, as long as its savage twin existed at the edge of expanding national borders. The exterior savage Other assured Americans of their own civilized nature, and more important, justified the dispossession of real Indians."[68] For early national Americans, the "interior Indians" provided an indispensable critique of white colonial deficiencies and a cultural disconnection from Mother England that ultimately made an "American" identity possible. Despite this cultural and national work of "playing Indian," Euro-America still needed to address the lingering threat of "exterior savages," and this imagined community solved that problem on metaphoric and literal levels simultaneously. Metaphorically, as a kind of performative answer to Indian performers who restaged their war dances in pleasure gardens, the latest Americans constructed and then consumed their self-reflexive, "interior" native heroes and heroines as acts of conquest. Embedded in Robert Rogers's *Ponteach* or George Colman Jr.'s *Inkle and Yarico* is the belief that Euro-Americans would eventually upstage the first Americans and assume the awesome mantle of supremely civilized and enlightened New World citizens. Literally, European colonists and later Euro-American settlers expanded the borders of their imagined community and in the process dispossessed and decimated "exterior" Indianness. For European arrivals, and perhaps African arrivals like Brown and Hewlett, "playing Indian" in the theatrical laboratory was simply a preamble or rehearsal for real native displacement and potential Indian erasure.

Staging Native Americas

Euro-constructed stage Indians represented the dominant form of "interior Indianness" in the early 1820s, but Euro-Americans and Europeans were not the only participants in these performative acts of creation and conquest. William Brown and James Hewlett incorporated the rich resources of Indio-constructed performance; explored the indigenous histories of North America, South America, and the Caribbean; and produced European and Euro-American drama. Accustomed to hybridity and combinations, these New World Africans merged Euro-constructed "interior Indians" with Indio-constructed "exterior savages" to produce highly inventive Afro-constructed stage Indians that reinforced and diverged from convention. Hewlett's and Brown's Afro-Indian combinations demonstrated a greater engagement with and sensitivity to multiple Native Americas than those of any other early national theatrical artists. During Brown's Minor and American Theatre phases, the company staged Richard Sheridan's adapted *Pizarro*, a European-authored stage Indian tragedy; M. M. Noah's *She Would Be a Soldier*, a Euro-American stage Indian drama; two original stage Indian ballets choreographed by James Hewlett; and finally, Brown's original Afro-Indian insurrectionary piece, *The Drama of King Shotaway*.

Augustus Von Kotzebue's *Pizarro* (1799), which was translated and revised for the English stage by Richard Sheridan, was one of the most produced stage Indian dramas in the early national United States. During the first three decades of the nineteenth century, *Pizarro* appeared on the New York stage three or four times each season.[69] As a neophyte theatrical producer, Brown recognized the popularity and economic profitability of this particular piece and staged all or part of *Pizarro* on four separate occasions. *Pizarro* dramatizes the Spanish invasion of Peru led by a corrupt general named Pizarro. In the piece, Rolla, a historical native rebel, functions as the classic "noble savage" who counters the invasion with a force of reportedly twelve thousand Peruvian Indians. Although the play bears the name of the Spanish general, the tragedy unequivocally belongs to Rolla, and as a testament to his theatrical attractiveness, most established and aspiring stars, including Aldridge and Hewlett, featured this Peruvian hero in their repertoire. At some point during the inaugural season of 1821 in the Village, Ira Aldridge joined the company and played this stage Indian hero.[70] Also, for his benefit bills of January 1822 and March 1823, Hewlett featured Rolla scenes from *Pizarro*. The native chief is supported by the play's European hero, a Spanish soldier named Alonzo, who joins the Peruvian cause after deciding, with the help of a Spanish priest named Bartolome De Las Casas, that the Europeans are waging an unjust war.[71] Not surprisingly, Rolla dies valiantly, and Alonzo must lead the Peruvians to victory. In the play's rhetorical conclusion, Alonzo proves he has learned from the martyred native by promising to return home with a message — specifically De Las Casas's message — that Spain's genocidal actions were deplorable.

Although *Pizarro* can be read as a pro-native, anticolonial stage Indian drama, the tragedy perpetuates conventional Euro-constructed natives, especially the *belle sauvage*, and Brown's productions reinscribed an anglicized Indian heroine. According to the plot, Rolla is enamored of a fair-skinned Peruvian beauty named Cora, but in the tradition of Colman's Yarico, this native maiden rejects her native suitor and falls for Alonzo, the conscientious Spanish hero. Commenting on his debut performance as Rolla, Aldridge recalled that the company's "gentle Cora was very black, requiring no small quantity of whiting, yellow ochre, and vermillion to bring her cheek to the hues of roses and lilies."[72] Given the timing of this production and the paucity of female actors, S. Welsh probably performed Cora in this "whiting" or whiteface. In a September 1821 review, Noah described Welsh as "sable," which suggests a darker African American.[73] Aldridge explained the company decided to "lighten" the dark actress because it wanted to create "such a face as Sheridan describes in the text."[74] By remaining faithful to Sheridan's translation and lightening Welsh, Brown reinforced Colman's belief that an Indian maid coveted by a white soldier needed to be Europeanized. Brown may have applied the "whiting, yellow ochre, and vermillion" to please his growing cadre of white patrons, yet one wonders if the remaining Afro–New Yorker patrons required such extensive anglicization. James Hewlett, as a choreographer, would eventually challenge this European standard of native beauty with his first stage Indian ballet.

Continuing the tradition of dramatic "noble savages," M. M. Noah penned one of the most popular American stage Indian dramas, *She Would Be a Soldier*, loosely based on the Battle of Chippewa, which took place during the War of 1812. In June 1819 the Park Theatre premiered this patriotic piece, which was well received and continued to attract full and enthusiastic houses.[75] Like Rolla, Ponteach, and other "interior" natives, Noah's stage Indian, simply called Indian Chief, is the "natural man" who shames morally compromised whites. Biographer Jonathan Sarna argues that Noah's version of the "noble savage" surpassed earlier indigenous heroes, especially those created by American writers, because Noah's chief was "brave enough to criticize the white man's encroachments and educated enough to speak perfectly standard English."[76] In the play's climactic scene, American forces have captured the Indian Chief, and the General extends his friendship; however, the unrepentant native rejects the olive branch in these words:

> Your friend? Call back the times which we passed in liberty and happiness, when in the tranquil enjoyment of unrestrained freedom we roved through our forests, and only knew the bears as our enemy; call back our council fires, our fathers and pious priests; call back our brothers, wives and children, which cruel white men have destroyed — Your friend? You came with the silver smile of peace, and we received you into our cabins; we hunted for you, toiled for you; our wives and daughters cherished and protected you; but when your numbers increased, you rose like wolves upon us, fired our dwellings, drove off our cattle, sent us in tribes to the wilderness, to seek for shelter; and now you ask me, while naked and a prisoner, to be your friend![77]

The Indian Chief's treatise on European deception perpetrated in the name of friendship is so passionate and accurate that the General does not even attempt to deny the charges. Other Euro-constructed stage Indians were only allowed to look fierce and sagacious while they stumbled through rudimentary recitations in pidgin English, but Noah crafted a most articulate stage Indian.[78]

Ever the patriot, Noah concludes the drama on a note of imperialistic compromise. After the chief declines the offer of friendship and the General nonetheless spares his life, the suddenly repentant native meekly reconsiders and extends his Euro-American neighbors a second chance at friendship. The General promises that whites will remain within their territory, and the Indian Chief receives a "belt of wampum" as a peace offering. Although Noah's "noble savage" is allowed to continue living, Deloria's creation-conquest duality still applies. The Indian Chief's poignant rhetoric provides the requisite self-criticism, but the paltry peace offering of "wampum" symbolizes Euro-America's conquest of "inferior" and easily placated indigenous nations.

Undaunted by Noah's sardonic attacks on his institution, Brown, a shrewd manager, appropriated this stellar "noble savage" and produced Noah's national drama in early December 1821.[79] Before Brown even announced the American Theatre, this production of *She Would Be a Soldier* established his commitment to homegrown playwrights. Artistically, the drama was a perfect fit for Brown's company because it offered a humorous yet patriotic account of the War of 1812, a romance in the midst of battle, and a direct challenge to Euro-America through a loquacious native chief. Indian Chief only appears in the final act, but as a testament to the exceptional character Noah created and Manhattan's stage Indian vogue, many lead actors elected to perform this small role. One of the Park's best performers, Maywood, created the role in the original production of June 1819 and encored the role in a revival in mid-December 1821.[80] Hewlett preferred lead characters, but the chief's passionate speech, in standard English, would have piqued his rhetorical appetites. Brown closed his first season with Noah's ode to Indio-European compromise, but the next season he revisited the "noble savage" with a tragic Afro-Indian uninterested in compromise.

Before Brown debuted his original drama, however, the company produced the first ballet choreographed by an African American. Consistent with Brown's integrationist and multicultural "American" project, that ballet featured Native Americans. A playbill of October 1, 1821, for the first Village theater, reprinted in Odell's *Annals of the New York Stage*, indicates that James Hewlett's *Pantomime Asama* premiered on September 24, 1821.[81] Hewlett's pantomime avoided the conventional Euro-obsessed *belle sauvage* by choreographing a romance between two Indian characters, Asama and Asana. He was not the first American choreographer to diverge from the customary Euro-Indian romantic pairing. Another stage Indian ballet, *Orai and Otago; or Indian Love*, premiered at the Park a year earlier and featured an Indian-Indian love affair.[82] Hewlett not only altered the typical romantic coupling, but he also subverted the Euro-centric fantasy of the *belle sauvage*. The playbill for October 1 announced that Hewlett danced the role of Asama and Welsh danced the part of Asana; Afro–New Yorkers finally had their "sable" *belle sauvage*.

Prior to Hewlett's ballet, an Afro-Indian beauty was unheard of because English writers like George Colman Jr. were incapable of imagining such a genetic and cultural amalgam. In the Old and New Worlds, English political figures and artists had a difficult time envisioning or accepting an Afro-Indian character because they viewed Africans as uncultured vessels in need of guidance, but regarded Indians as highly cultured beings.[83] Most dramatists socialized by English society, including Euro-American writers, could not truthfully dramatize a character who was part African and part Indian because they could not reconcile such seeming opposites. Furthermore, English or Euro-American audiences may well have been reluctant to acknowledge publicly the beauty of an Afro-tinged *belle sauvage*.

James Hewlett did not share Colman's limitations as to what constituted a desirable *belle sauvage* and envisioned a darker indigenous beauty. Finally free of Cora's whiteface, Welsh proved an African-inflected Indian heroine could succeed. According to the October 1 playbill, Brown's integrated clientele so delighted in this Afro-Indian Asana and the piece was received with such "unbounded applause" at the September 24 premiere that the company revived *Pantomime Asama* a week later. That this alternative Afro-Indian *belle sauvage* and Sheridan's Europeanized Peruvian Cora could co-exist in the same repertoire was not surprising given the conventional yet unconventional manager Brown and his contrarian Africanist aesthetic that accommodates but never resolves difference.

Hewlett's *Pantomime Asama* may have introduced the concept of an Afro-Indian beauty and advanced the idea of Indian-Indian love, but other non-Indian choreographers crafted stage Indian ballets that simply perpetuated the Indio-European couplings of conventional *belle sauvage* theatricals. Stephen Price and Edmund Simpson commissioned a French choreographer named Monsieur Labasse from the "Academie de Musique" in Paris to create a piece exclusively for the Park Theatre. Labasse's much anticipated *La Belle Péruvienne* premiered in March 1822, and Noah's *National Advocate* published a lengthy prospectus for the action of this three-act stage Indian ballet.[84] Labasse's choreography used the male-female duet and the Indio-European romantic trope to affirm the superiority of European society over Indian culture. His duets explored how an unsophisticated, "natural" beauty can acquire grace and deportment under the proper tutelage of a civilized European. The *Evening Post*'s theater critic William Coleman marveled at a second-act duet in which the white stranger, danced by Labasse, teaches the Indian maiden how to dance like a proper European lady.[85] Ostensibly, Labasse was preparing his New World subject, the "exterior savage," for her entrance into a more refined Old World society. By contrast, Hewlett's *Pantomime Asama* eschewed the typical *belle sauvage* journey from "exterior Indianness" to European acceptance; instead, he explored the potential for romantic relations within a native community in the Americas.

Ironically, this spectacle of a *belle sauvage* dancing with any male — African, Indian, or European — demonstrated how far non-Indian choreographers like Hewlett had strayed from indigenous performance. The aforementioned Cherokee warriors or "Natives from the West" rarely integrated the sexes onstage, as these "braves" tended to perform solo dances and same-sex duets in their recreations of purely masculine warfare. Olaudah Equiano, an African slave and steward, witnessed Indian dances on the Mosquito Shore of Jamaica and noted that "the males danced by themselves, and the females also by themselves."[86] This does not mean female natives, such as the three "squaws" from Ontario, were barred from public displays but simply that Indian dancers in Euro-American spaces practiced a form of gender segregation.

Although both Hewlett and Labasse imposed male-female couplings on native aesthetics, the two choreographers still managed to incorporate elements of Indio-constructed dance, specifically competitive duets between male warriors. In the opening scene of Labasse's ballet, rival Red and Black chiefs compete for the affections of an uninterested Indian princess through various physical contests: a foot race, a wrestling match, a grand combat with tomahawks and shields. Labasse borrowed this concept of dancing rival chiefs from troupes like "Natives of the West," and his appropriation inspired other non-Indian choreographers to do the same. In June 1823 Vauxhall Gardens staged a grand ballet titled *Indian Heroine; or the Rival Chiefs*, which starred Mina, an Indian princess; Miami, one rival chief; and another unnamed rival chief. This ballet featured competitive dances between the two rival chiefs and was so well attended that Vauxhall managers repeated the piece the very next evening.[87]

During the final days of William Brown's managerial career, James Hewlett premiered his second Afro-constructed stage Indian ballet, *Balililon*, which featured this rival-chiefs motif. Odell reprinted the following description from a June 1823 playbill: "The ballet of Balililon 'for the first time' was acted by Hewlett, Bates, Jackson, and Miss Lavatt. The ballet included a Grand combat between the Prince (Hewlett) and the Chieftain (Bates), an Indian war dance by the Prince, and the Grand Battle of the Susquehannah."[88] Hewlett's second effort deemphasized the romantic storyline featured so prominently in his first and concentrated on competitive duets between the Prince and Chieftain along with a solo war dance performed by the Prince. This strictly male composition departed from Euro-constructed Indian conventions and embraced the native dance practices of the militaristic visiting ensembles.

On the warfare theme, Hewlett's second ballet also tapped into Native American military exploits to restage the Grand Battle of the Susquehannah. Unlike Labasse and other non-Indian choreographers, Hewlett grounded his latest ballet within the history of a specific native people. The Susquehannock, also known as the Conestoga, originally lived along the Susquehannah River, which ran through Maryland, Delaware, and Pennsylvania. According to Captain John Smith, the Susquehannock were an imposing nation of seven-foot-tall warriors with booming voices who engaged in a series of battles with white colonial militias.[89] From the description of *Balililon*, it would appear Hewlett's grand battle resurrected and reconstructed a more militant Native American past that reminded Euro-America of Indian ferocity.

Similar to Hewlett's historic second ballet, Brown's dramatic first declined to address an African American past or present and instead dramatized another oppressed people in the Americas, specifically the Afro-Indian Caribs on the island of St. Vincent. In January 1822 he premiered *Shotaway; or the Insurrection of the Caribs of St. Domingo* as the first defiant artistic action of his seemingly acquiescent Minor Theatre.[90] For his equally defiant benefit nights in June 1823, Brown revived his original stage Indian drama under the new title *The Drama of King Shotaway*. On the playbill, Brown also announced that *Shotaway* was "founded on facts taken from the Insurrection of the Caravs in the island of St. Vincent." Theater historian Samuel Hay maintains Brown was a Garifuna, or an Afro-Indian Carib from St. Vincent, and was essentially staging his own history. Hay probably reached such a conclusion because the 1823 playbill also stated that Brown wrote the drama from "firsthand experience."[91] As a ship's steward, Brown may have witnessed the 1795 uprising, but I doubt he was born on St. Vincent because when he premiered the play in 1822, he mistakenly placed this insurrection on the island of St. Domingo—or Santo Domingo—not St. Vincent. If Brown was born on St. Vincent, he would surely know the difference between Santo Domingo and his home island.

Brown's black dramatic first is not extant, so we will never know how he restaged the native uprising of 1795. Of course, a missing manuscript has not deterred scholars and artists from speculating about Brown's motives for writing the drama. Samuel Hay contends that Brown penned *Shotaway* for explicitly political reasons after municipal authorities closed his Shakespearean productions. As discussed in the previous chapter, however, an *Evening Post* article revealed that Brown had been planning his dramatic debut before the specious arrests, and the forced closing simply delayed his first benefit night as a playwright. Carlyle Brown's history play, *The African Company Presents Richard the Third*, claims that William Brown wrote *Shotaway* to prove black people could dramatize their own stories.[92] Carlyle Brown's explanation may be closer to the truth, and William Brown may have written *Shotaway* in reaction to a contemporaneous drama about a Caribbean uprising. In November 1819 the Park Theatre staged English playwright Horace Twiss's *The Carib Chief*.[93] Twiss's five-act drama chronicles an insurrection led by two chiefs, Maloch and Omreah, on the island of Dominica. Caribbean natives, or Caribs, join forces to repel French invaders with assistance from English troops stationed at Guadeloupe. Twiss's scenario replicates many details of the St. Vincent insurrection of 1795 but with one major difference: in St. Vincent, English troops were the enemy and French forces were Carib allies. *The Carib Chief* probably inspired Brown to author his version of a Carib uprising against the English, which he allegedly could do from "firsthand experience."

Because Brown never published any of his plays, we must rely on "official" histories written by eighteenth- and nineteenth-century English colonists and modern scholars to piece together the people and events of the failed native insurrection.[94] As for Carib origins, both modern scholars and "official" histories agree that in 1635 Spanish slave ships headed for Santo Domingo were shipwrecked off the coast of St. Vincent. Surviving slaves took refuge among the native Caribs, and after decades of intermixture a new group, part Indian and part African, which English officials labeled "Black Caribs," emerged. In addition, some modern scholars claim that slaves from nearby Barbados and St. Lucia regularly escaped to St. Vincent and intermingled with the Afro-Indian Caribs. The island served as a haven for shipwrecked or escaped Africans, until English colonists seized complete control and established slavery as a viable economic institution.

As a European possession, St. Vincent changed hands repeatedly between French and English colonial empires until the Treaty of Paris in 1765 established England as the primary European presence. Initial relations between Caribs and English colonists were highly volatile, but following a full-scale English-Carib war and a series of small skirmishes, the warring factions signed the Treaty of 1773, which demarcated mutually agreed upon property boundaries. English officials negotiated this peace with two Carib leaders, Chief Joseph Chatoyer (Shotaway) and his brother DuValle. After signing the treaty, the two indigenous leaders enjoyed seemingly cordial relations with their English neighbors. In his two "official" reports on St. Vincent, Sir William Young placed Shotaway and DuValle as frequent guests at the homes of English gentlemen. He also claimed that the brothers received several generous gifts from whites, like a silver-mounted broadsword that Shotaway would later use in the 1795 insurrection against the English.

Theater historian Errol Hill surmises that, given the extensive slave population in early nineteenth-century America, William Brown's *Drama of King Shotaway* could be interpreted as "a vivid anti-slavery statement."[95] Yet Carib history tells a different story. Under English rule, African slavery flourished on St. Vincent, and modern scholars and "official" histories agree that Shotaway and DuValle were prosperous slave owners. Sir William Young recalled that English planters provided loans to Shotaway and DuValle, and with those funds, the brothers purchased nine African slaves and built a thriving cotton plantation.[96] In fact, over time, "African" became synonymous with slavery and debasement, which prompted many Afro-Indian "Black Caribs" to begin denying their African ancestry. True, the play "could be interpreted" as antislavery but only if Brown's version suppressed potentially inflammatory details like Carib slave ownership. And it is highly doubtful that Brown would have dramatized Afro-Indians who denied their Africanness and enslaved Africans, especially considering the African American manager needed to reconstruct this history in a manner least offensive to his loyal Afro–New Yorker patrons.

In spite of Shotaway's and DuValle's rapport with English colonists and their initiation into African slaveholding, land disputes between Carib and English communities intensified, and by March 1795 the tension escalated into a second English-Carib war. Simultaneously, Victor Hugues, French governor of Guadeloupe, was actively planting seeds of insurrection on British-held islands, including St. Lucia, Grenada, and Dominica. In the name of the French Revolution, Hugues enticed the Caribs of St. Vincent to join the international campaign for liberty, equality, and fraternity. St. Vincent's English governor feared that Hugues might be succeeding; therefore, when French forces captured Grenada, the governor declared martial law and called the militia. According to Garifuna folklore, Shotaway was still reluctant to declare war and join the French Revolution because during the first English-Carib war, French troops initially supported but later abandoned the Caribs. Island legend claims that one of Shotaway's wives openly questioned his manhood with this direct challenge: "They are destroying our efforts and you don't even have the courage to go to war against them; give me your pants and put on my skirt that I might go fight." This pointed spousal rebuke allegedly motivated the Carib chief, and when the English governor invited Shotaway to reaffirm the Treaty of 1773, he sent back the equally legendary reply: "It is too late, it might have been sent sooner."[97]

Reportedly, Shotaway made other legendary pronouncements during the 1795 insurrection that would have attracted a neophyte dramatist like Brown and an aspiring actor like Hewlett. Sir William Young published the following speech recovered from a battlefield near Dorchester Hill, an address that Shotaway allegedly delivered to Carib soldiers and French forces:

> Where is the Frenchmen who will not join his brothers, at a moment when the voice of liberty is heard by them? Let us unite, citizens and brothers, round the colours flying in this island; and let us hasten to cooperate to that great piece of work which has been already commenced so gloriously. But should any timorous men still exist, should any Frenchman be held back through fear, we do hereby declare to them, in the name of the law, that those who will not be assembled with us in the course of the day, shall be deemed traitors to the country, and treated as enemies. We do swear that both fire and sword shall be employed against them, that we are going to burn their estates, and that we will murder their wives and children, in order to annihilate their race.[98]

References to brotherhood and liberty reveal Shotaway's familiarity with the rhetoric of the French Revolution. The Garifuna placed a premium on oratory skills, and as a result of their extensive interactions with French colonists, many Carib leaders were proficient in French.[99] Interestingly, the speech also echoes the themes of Robert Burns's Scottish national anthem, "Scots, wha hae wi' Wallace bled," which recreated Robert Bruce's stirring speech to the Scots before the famous Battle of Bannockburn, also against the English.

More than rousing rhetoric, the hero of any tragedy needs a fatal flaw, and as a historical actor and insurrectionary leader, Shotaway had that requisite imperfection. Garifuna folklore maintains that Shotaway and his followers believed mortal means could never conquer the chief, so not surprisingly this extreme hubris and perceived invincibility sealed his fate. When Carib and French forces confronted the English militia at Dorchester Hill, Shotaway challenged an English officer named Major Leith with his aforementioned silver-mounted broadsword. Being a superior swordsman, Major Leith made quick work of the allegedly invincible Carib chief, a catastrophic development that plummeted the Carib forces into complete disarray. The French abandoned the Caribs after Shotaway's death, but small native bands continued fighting a guerrilla war for nearly two years. The persistent warriors were unsuccessful in demoralizing the enemy, and by March 1798 the English captured and deported approximately 5,080 Carib rebels to Rotatan, now Honduras. Today, the descendants of the former "Black Carib" inhabitants of St. Vincent, or Garifuna, are dispersed throughout Central America, the Caribbean, and North America.

Samuel Hay theorizes that, given the style of his past productions, Brown may have incorporated popular songs that undermined the seriousness of this native history.[100] But Brown was capable of presenting dramatic stage Indians. He had previously staged Sheridan's *Pizarro* on several occasions and produced Noah's *She Would Be a Soldier*, which proved that a passionate and well-spoken native could succeed in Manhattan. Brown's dramatic first may have included a song or two, but with Hewlett assuming the title role, *The Drama of King Shotaway* probably featured a showstopping dramatic monologue similar to the Dorchester Hill speech and "Bruce's Address to His Army." Shotaway's aggressive declaration of war inspired by French revolutionary rhetoric would have resonated with black patrons who anxiously awaited the day when slavery was abolished and blacks were recognized as U.S. citizens.

Furthermore, Brown, his actors, and his integrated audiences could firmly identify with the Caribs' desire to rid themselves of the English and control their own island. The St. Vincent uprising of 1795 recalled the same anti-imperialist and antimonarchical attitudes that fueled the American Revolution. In fact, among the characters listed on the playbill for June 1823, Brown included a General Hunter, named for an actual English officer who figured prominently in the second English-Carib war and in the deportation of the rebels.[101] Hunter was the perfect lightning rod for any anti-British sentiments among Brown's more patriotic supporters. And during this early national period, Brown's *Shotaway* was by no means the only revolutionary saga appearing in Manhattan's theatrical laboratories. Drama historian John Collins contends that Brown's original drama was "indicative of a public interest concerning insurrection."[102] Brown's firsthand account of a Carib uprising against English imperialism capitalized on a popular affection for revolution and reminded America of its insurrectionary heritage.

By writing and restaging this native history, ex-steward Brown was also boasting of his worldly experiences and spreading insurrectionary news from the Caribbean. White and black seamen developed a worldly identity distinct from "land lovers," and when they came ashore, sailors enjoyed boasting of their exotic encounters and, more important, spreading subversive, revolutionary ideas to various New World populations. These maritime activists created and disseminated combinations of fact and rumor to raise the expectations of enslaved communities throughout the Americas. In the late eighteenth century, these white and black maritime workers contributed directly to the emergence of Haiti as a black republic by sharing French Revolution slogans and insurrectionary excitement with slaves on the island of Santo Domingo.[103] Having worked aboard transatlantic passenger packets in the late eighteenth and early nineteenth centuries, William Brown absorbed this boastful and subversive spirit and may have even witnessed an uprising or two. Although the St. Vincent insurrection ultimately failed, his *Drama of King Shotaway* commemorated the national aspirations of a courageous "noble savage" and his Afro-Indian followers. And, as Errol Hill has suggested, one could read Brown's embellished boasting about his Caribbean experiences as an antislavery, or at least anticolonial, dramatic statement.

Euro-constructed Indians, a unique creation of the Americas, was not simply some nineteenth-century version of self-help but signaled the desired erasure of first Americans as performers, politicians, warriors, and New World neighbors. Did Brown and Hewlett's Afro-constructed Indians avoid the duality of creation and conquest? The African American company reinforced the *belle sauvage* standard of beauty by whitening a "sable" Welsh to produce a Cora consistent with Sheridan's version of *Pizarro*. But choreographer Hewlett broke from convention by staging an Indian-Indian love story and introducing an Afro-Indian *belle sauvage*. Like other choreographers, Hewlett forced male-female duets on "native" ballet, but he also emulated the Indio-constructed male dancers who "terrorized" Manhattan and exploited their rich history to create a "war combat" ballet that paid homage to a specific indigenous nation. As a producer in search of increased ticket sales, Brown mounted *Pizarro* and *She Would Be a Soldier*, two popular stage Indian dramas that expropriated the wisdom of the "noble savage" only to leave the "exterior savage" disarmed or dead. But as an ex-steward turned dramatist, Brown also "schooled" Manhattan with his "eyewitness" version of St. Vincent history and his Afro-constructed Indians, who embodied the freedom and dignity to which all New World arrivals aspired. However, Brown's lost drama probably replicated the interlocked duality of creation and conquest; his theatrical reconstruction chronicled a too familiar historical process. The historical subject, Joseph Chatoyer, was the prototypical "interior savage" who initially befriended English gentlemen and benefited from African slavery. Yet, like Indian Chief, Rolla, Ponteach, and other Euro-constructed Indian characters, Chatoyer's usefulness was eventually exhausted and when he turned revolutionary, the Carib chief became an "exterior savage" marked for termination. Whether set to music or played straight, Brown staged the familiar narrative of many Native Americans, a painfully redundant indigenous plot replayed from Peru to St. Vincent to New York, always ending on the same saddening note of ultimate conquest.

William Brown, more than any other New York theater manager, could stake an irrefutable claim on being *the* American theater. Diverging from Benedict Anderson's notion of a limited yet sovereign imagined community, Brown and company believed it possible to be coterminous with all humanity. He produced native-born dramatists, encouraged U.S. artists in various pursuits, integrated his audience and orchestra, and staged the nation's Indian, African, and European cultural heritages. Brown and his versatile star James Hewlett were committed to showcasing a history of the Americas through stage Indian ballets and dramas, Indio-constructed "exterior savages," and Euro-constructed "interior Indianness." The highly original stage Europeans, examined in Chapter 2, literally staged the nation's white ethnic diversity—Scottish, English, and the like—which disturbed Americans like Timothy Dwight. The next chapter on the African Company details how Brown incorporated New World Africans into his expansive notion of "American." As Dwight and other pessimists feared, the harmonious offstage integration of all Americans, regardless of race and ethnicity, was an extremely difficult project for one African American manager to undertake, but still an important cultural campaign to persuade the United States to recognize its triracial foundation and multiethnic possibilities.

Tom and Jerry Meets *Three-Fingered Jack*

THE AFRICAN COMPANY'S BALANCING ACT

THROUGHOUT HIS MANY institutional transformations, Brown tended first to test a new theatrical identity before fully relinquishing the old persona and announcing his latest moniker. During the Minor Theatre phase, Brown cultivated his Americanness by supporting native-born artists, but he only announced that new identity after his second Greenwich Village theater was completed. Likewise, in the midst of his American Theatre period, Brown started "becoming" the African Company by exploring the marketing possibilities of a distinctly racial profile. The one constant during all his identity phases was an Africanist affinity for nurturing "an encounter of opposites."[1] He balanced "minor" illegitimate entertainment with "major" theatrical material, Indio-constructed stage Indians with Euro-constructed varieties, and privileged stage European royalty with less privileged white rebels. His initial pleasure garden and all subsequent theaters epitomized the early national "African" outlined in Chapter 1, that is, "African" understood as a complex convergence of multiple Old World African and European cultural practices and values, a fundamental dynamism that embraces difference, and diasporic hybrid identity constantly in the act of reproduction.

Although the theories of Du Bois, Bhabha, and Hall provide clarity and invest nineteenth-century African Americans with unmatched transgressive potential, I would caution that these twentieth-century notions of identity and culture may have been lost on William Brown. His institutional decisions and production choices suggest that ex-steward Brown did not necessarily perceive American—or European—and African as estranged ends of a cultural binary. Therefore, in August 1822 it was by no means uncharacteristic for Brown to place an advertisement in the *National Advocate* announcing that his American Theatre at Mercer Street would feature a troupe called the African Company.[2] For the first time, Brown publicly embraced an African persona, but in that same public gesture he bridged the seeming opposites of American Theatre and African Company. His African Company debuted with productions of John O'Keefe's *Poor Soldier* (1782), an Irish musical about a soldier returning home from war, and William Blake's *Don Juan* (1795), an English pantomime about the famous Spanish lover.[3] Both afterpieces showcased Brown's signature stage Europeans but were still explicitly "African" because they featured James Hewlett and other African Company members impersonating Irish and Spanish characters. The spectacle of Hewlett singing the role of and identifying with an Irish soldier was undeniably dualistic, and the company's willingness to appropriate such Old World European culture demonstrated a fundamental dynamism that embraces difference.

This chapter on the African Company examines this complicated fourth and final stage in Brown's theatrical "becoming" by focusing on the troupe's more explicitly "African" material. On an institutional level, when it came time to name names and choose between African and American identities, Brown still declared both, and that put the "African" in his African Company. The African American manager never officially advertised his institution as the African Theatre; rather, Euro–New Yorker editors like M. M. Noah and William Coleman of the *Evening Post* employed that title in their various reports.[4] Brown's public avoidance of the name African Theatre and his entire counterpublic expansion of the "American" imaginary should never be read as a rejection of Africanness but understood as a direct challenge to the dominant culture's implicit linkage of "American" and whiteness. I argue that Brown's African Company and stage African productions fully realized and perhaps even reconciled the multiple experiences of early national African Americans. The first section of this chapter introduces Manhattan's timely stage African vogue, which dominated the city's theatrical landscape in the early 1820s and partly motivated Brown's adoption of an African-specific identity. The second section dissects the African Company's fleeting yet dynamic balancing act of comedic and dramatic stage

Africans. On an evening in June 1823, "real blackamoors" appropriated Euro-constructed blackness to communicate the multilayered complexities of African diasporic experience in the Americas.

Manhattan's Stage African Vogue

A decade before the full-scale explosion of blackface minstrelsy and one hundred years before the Harlem Renaissance of the 1920s, early nineteenth-century Manhattan witnessed a pseudorenaissance of musicals, melodramas, tragedies, and pantomimes—most of them British imports—devoted to all things African. Obviously, this theatrical and extratheatrical fascination was consistent with America's crisscrossing, transcultural proclivity for masking, but the vogue was also triggered by mounting discomfort with an ever increasing free black population. Unlike the visiting Native American nations, free Afro–New Yorkers were not limited to single-evening dancing exhibitions or weeklong museum exploitations; rather, they lived, played, worked, and worshiped in close proximity to Euro–New Yorkers. One disturbed white citizen directed a letter to the *Evening Post* that complained of the "yells and screeches" emanating from the African Methodist Episcopal Church and analogized these Afro-Christian services to "savage war dances."[5] Broadway promenaders continued to dominate the sidewalks, and in June 1823 another offended citizen reported to the *Advocate* that he overheard a female member of the "colored gentry" remark how she wished a recent yellow fever outbreak "would kill all the whites" so the blacks could have the sidewalks all to themselves.[6] Concerned citizens believed that such escalating "interior savagery" and insubordination needed immediate attention. With statewide emancipation, as decreed in the 1817 gradual emancipation bill, set for July 1827, the related problems of an increasing free black population and its mounting arrogance could only worsen.[7] Understandably, Euro–New Yorkers coveted more manageable, theatrically constructed Africans, and trekked to Stephen Price's Park Theatre, Mrs. Baldwin's City Theatre, and eventually Mr. Brown's African Company for comfort.

Manhattan's representational immersion in explicitly racial others was deeply rooted in Old World medieval festivals, pageants, and mummer's plays, in which Europeans darkened their faces with the ashy residue of burnt cork to approximate the swarthy complexions of primitive yet provocative Africans and Asians. In the sixteenth century, English actors donned elaborate black masks, gloves, and stockings designed by Inigo Jones to explore "blackness" in court masques written by Ben Jonson. During the Italian Renaissance, a popular, black-masked servant named Harlequin emerged as the undisputed star trickster of Commedia dell'Arte. By the early eighteenth century, two varieties of stage African, dramatic and comedic, were competing for space on an increasingly crowded British stage.[8]

The dramatic, often sentimental, and occasionally heroic Anglo-constructed stage African was featured in tragedies, dramas, and melodramas. Initially, these imagined identities were invested with decidedly sadistic and lascivious characteristics intended to titillate audiences, but as this dramatic type gradually expanded, it developed more noble traits. For instance, after first experimenting with a vengeful and villainous moor named Aaron in *Titus Andronicus* (1589–93), Shakespeare constructed a more heroic stage African in *Othello* (1603). Similar to Euro-constructed stage Indians, this complex Moorish general continued to satiate the European preoccupation with "savage" Africans but also supplied an indirect critique of European society. Literary historian Anthony Barthelemy argues that stage African dramas like *Othello* created "an environment in which willing English audiences could compare their governance, mores, and manners against the non-Christian others."[9] Shakespeare constructed his Othello to test the sincerity of professed Italian mores and manners and, by extension, the morality of his own England.

Subsequent English writers replicated Shakespeare's noble African prototype in various guises. In her novel *The History of the Royal Slave* (1688), Aphra Behn resisted the fascination with lurid blackamoors and fashioned a compassionate history of an enslaved African prince named Oroonoko. Based on an actual African Behn met while living in Surinam, a New World colony, her Oroonoko is the ideal natural man, a model human being, and a resounding indictment of slavery. When this character reached the English stage through Thomas Southerne's *Oroonoko* (1695), however, Behn's antislavery sentiments were discarded. Southerne's version duplicated Shakespeare's combination of barbarism and piety, even down to the European wife, and, predictably, his *Oroonoko* became the most successful post-Shakespearean tragedy.[10]

With the second brand of stage African, slapstick slaves and farcical free blacks unleashed their trickster strategies primarily in comedies, musicals, or pantomimes. In refashioning Behn's novel for the stage, Southerne introduced African slaves proficient in lively songs and dances for comic relief and to recreate Surinam's plantation culture. Isaac Bickerstaff's comic opera

The Padlock (1768) pushed this musically inclined African slave to the next level. Mungo, the indisputable star of *The Padlock*, would become the prototypical plantation flunky who plays the servile buffoon in the presence of his Spanish master but, with a subversive twist, croons an antislavery tune while the master is away. More significant, unlike Southerne's plantation Africans, who communicated in a standard English far too "European" for British audiences, Mungo conversed in a distinctly West Indian pidgin English, thus providing the necessary racial distinction that allowed white audiences to recognize this character as "authentically Negroid." In fact, J. R. Oldfield anoints Mungo the first stage African with a racialized dialect and a "radical transformation" for the black image in British drama.[11] Mungo's speech not only designated him as different and more realistic for English audiences; his dialect also marked this farcical stage African as inferior. Regrettably, this mark of inferiority rapidly extended to actual Africans, African Americans, and Caribbean blacks. As for their political and cultural potential, Europeans often used these extremely malleable caricatures as drinking, singing, and dancing rationales for race-based slavery.

Across the Atlantic, Euro-American dramatists preferred comical enslaved and free stage Africans who ultimately served as humorous endorsements of bondage. Andrew Barton's *The Disappointment; or the Force of Credulity* (1767) features a hapless but wealthy free black named Racoon — more affectionately called "Coony" — who is the unsuspecting target of a confidence scheme. The easily duped Racoon "proves" that freedom and financial windfall are wasted on inherently inferior and naturally gullible free African Americans. In *Triumph of Love; or Happy Reconciliation* (1795), John Murdock imagines a plantation "Negro" named Sambo who is emancipated by his beneficent master but ultimately proves incapable of handling freedom. When saddled with self-determination, Sambo immediately devolves into drunkenness and disorderly conduct, prompting one white character to remark: "[S]o much for liberating those people. The greatest number of them, after they are set free, become vicious."[12] With the proliferation of race-based slavery in England, its colonies, and former possessions, Mungo and his New World comic cousins provided exotic theatrical alternatives for eager audiences and supplied political justifications for the slaveholding class. Seemingly contented slaves immersed in music and bumbling free blacks perpetually mired in turmoil reassured Europeans and Euro-Americans that plantation owners enslaved uncivilized Africans on the most reasonable and perhaps humane grounds. For early national Manhattanites in dire need of governable blackness, this second variety of stage African supplied the perfect centerpiece for their "Negro" renaissance of the 1820s.

In March 1822 the Park Theatre initiated the stage African vogue with a revival of James Cobb's highly exotic musical *Paul and Virginia* (180?) after a three-year absence from the stage.[13] Cobb's "tropical" entertainment unfolds on a nondescript West Indian island where brutal Spanish masters abuse their slaves while English masters and mistresses treat their African charges with compassion. As a "tropical" spectacle, *Paul and Virginia* boasts lush and alluring scenes, such as a climactic Caribbean hurricane executed onstage. Given such elaborate scenic demands, this musical was expensive to mount; nevertheless, *Paul and Virginia* was worth the significant expense because the piece guaranteed large audiences and substantial revenues. Over the 1822 season, the Park Theatre staged the lucrative *Paul and Virginia* an impressive four times in a two-month span. A survey of New York theater advertisements for the early 1820s reveals that Cobb's Caribbean musical was easily the most-produced stage African play on the New York theatrical scene.[14]

Baldwin, a former Park Theatre company member, and her upstart City Theatre officially entered the vogue in late December 1822 by staging its version of *Paul and Virginia*. But considering her company performed in a private house, it is doubtful that this staging matched the scenic opulence of Price's Park productions. In that same week, Baldwin followed Cobb's musical with William McCready's domestic comedy *The Irishman in London; or the Happy African* (179?).[15] For the City Theatre production, Baldwin traversed gender and racial lines to assume the role of Cubba, a show-stealing trickster. Musicologist Dale Cockrell lauds McCready's comedy for artfully linking his two main characters, Cubba, the irrepressible "Happy African," and Murdoch, a "wild" stage Irishman, through their shared love of drink and debauchery.[16] This comedic marriage was definitely appropriate because nineteenth-century travel journals, newspapers, and popular illustrations often depicted both African Americans and Irish Americans as continually inebriated subhumans.[17]

The Park Theatre welcomed the new year of 1823 by countering Baldwin's cross-gendered, cross-racial Cubba with a New Year's Day revival of John Fawcett's *Obi; or Three-Finger'd Jack* (1800). Price and Simpson remounted this seriopantomime after an absence of seven years from the New York stage.[18] Traditionally, a seriopantomime merges farcical elements with more dramatic or romantic themes, and Fawcett's *Obi* commingles musically inclined slaves with a legendary bandit named Three-Fingered Jack or Jack Mansong.[19] Baldwin responded to the Park's seriopantomime of January 1 with a comparatively lighter pantomime, William Bates's *Harlequin Mungo; or A Peep into the Tower* (1788), which features Harlequin, one of the earliest characters to appropriate the mask of blackness.[20] Also located on a Caribbean island, Bates's pantomime stars a slave prototypically named Mungo who, after being magically transformed into Harlequin, pursues a forbidden romantic relationship with his master's daughter. In February, Baldwin's City Theatre remounted *Harlequin Mungo*, which meant that their initial dalliance with cross-racial romance received significant public approval. Also in February, the female manager revived Bickerstaff's *Padlock* starring Mungo, the original plantation flunky ultimately responsible for this entire revival.[21]

Thus far Price's Park Theatre and Baldwin's City Theatre featured primarily docile and comforting slaves—with the occasional appearance of a three-fingered bandit—from picturesque West Indian islands. But, as bold departures from tropical musicals and pantomimes, Price and Simpson mounted a series of more ambitious stage African dramas. In March 1823 the Park revisited Shakespeare's archetypal *Othello*, by far the most popular stage African play in the eighteenth- and nineteenth-century United States.[22] The next month, the Park revived George Colman Jr.'s lesser known yet appealing melodrama, *The Africans; or War, Love, and Duty* (180?), starring British comedian Charles Mathews as a comical "white slave" named Augustus Mug. Colman based his melodrama on a French short story, "Selico: An African Tale," about a Fulani family in turmoil.[23] When the play debuted in January 1810, New Yorkers overwhelmingly supported the melodrama, but critics declared *Africans* an "empty spectacle." One critic dismissed the play as "unnatural, laboured, and distressing in itself; and it derives no relief from the phizzes of its black and yellow heroes and heroines."[24] The reviewer could not envision or accept African heroes and heroines, but Colman and transatlantic audiences could. Ironically, Colman could craft a Fulani hero for *Africans* but was incapable of creating an aesthetically pleasing Afro-Indian for *Inkle and Yarico*.

To complete this miniseries of dramatic stage Africanness, in early May 1823 the Park revived another sentimental English import, Thomas Morton's *The Slave; or The Triumph of Generosity* (1817).[25] Morton capitalized on the most popular post-Shakespearean tragedy by transforming Southerne's *Oroonoko* into a musical. His version of Behn's "royal slave," now named Gambia, is a heroic stage African who protects his English masters during a slave insurrection and is rewarded with emancipation. When the Park Theatre premiered *The Slave* in November 1817, critics savaged the musical, but, like *Africans*, the production succeeded at the box office. One critic declared the musical "a disagreeable piece; too much in opposition to the prejudices of education, as to plot; and too poorly written to furnish any renumeration to our feelings."[26] Similar to the disbelieving reviewer of *Africans*, this critic doubted that "real" Africans behaved like Gambia, and he dismissed the musical and its lead character as pure dramatic invention. For some critics, African "noble savages" such as Shakespeare's Othello, Colman's Selico, or Morton's Gambia failed to register as "authentically Negroid." And despite the initially positive public receptions of *Africans* and *The Slave*, those dramatic treatments would fade, while the more humorous commodifications of blackness became the preferred stage Africans among Manhattan managers, audiences, and artists.

Euro–New Yorkers ultimately favored bumbling free blacks and plantation drunkards over the sentimental alternatives because they desired a reprieve from the painfully "real" and insubordinate free African Americans dominating Broadway. Blackface minstrelsy and its comic stage African precursors flourished because these forms were comforting experiences for Euro-Americans in an otherwise turbulent nineteenth-century America.[27] Faced with the incredible challenge of reconciling a growing free black population with a multiethnic "herrenvolk republic" predicated on whiteness, early national Euro-Americans craved user-friendly African Americans. Escapist stage African musicals countered the daily newspaper reports of an escalating "Negro problem" and eased Euro–New York's collective imagination.

As further explanation for this Euro-American preference for risible stage Africans, historian Nathan Huggins asserts that whites crafted humorous black caricatures, not fully grounded in African American culture and experience, to serve as the antithesis of a suitable national identity. At a foundational moment, when Euro-America worked to define itself as fiercely individual and upwardly mobile, the theatrical laboratories offered hapless blackface buffoons as the models of how not to behave.[28] True, dramatic "natural men," like Othello or Oroonoko, had the potential to expose national hypocrisies, but Euro-Americans already had their stage Indians supplying that psychic service. This humorous strain of commodified blackness and its blackface progeny would serve as anti-American. Such inebriated, childlike, and highly sexualized black dramatic identities thoroughly unconcerned with any work ethic, Protestant or otherwise, served as escapist antiexamples or fantasy diversions for a Euro-America committed to moral fitness. Huggins further claims that Euro-America's inebriated and infantile alter egos helped to clarify and defend distinctly northern and southern political positions. Contented and dependent Sambos assured southern slave owners that their besieged institution was not entirely evil but in many respects philanthropic. Similarly, incompetent free Coons confirmed for white northern paternalists, like the New York Manumission Society, that their organizations were essential for saving transitional free blacks from the almshouse or penitentiary. Ultimately, stage Africans minimized mounting concerns over all aspects of the "Negro problem" and allowed Euro-Americans to feel better about themselves, their social policies, and their institutions. Over the next one hundred years, in the national laboratories, white performers refashioned Barton's ineptly urban Racoon and McCready's deliciously drunk Cubba into free and untamed early blackface characters like Zip Coon and Jim Dandy. Likewise, Bickerstaff's ribald Mungo and John Murdock's ridiculous Sambo earned new leases on their theatrical lives via the plantation Sambos who dominated later phases of blackface minstrelsy.

Expanding on Huggins's initial theories, a host of blackface minstrel revisionists have further examined Euro-America's self-defining engagement with commodified Africans. Specifically, Dale Cockrell, W. T. Lhamon Jr., and Eric Lott have extended their minstrel studies to extratheatrical nineteenth-century social rituals, like Pinkster and Callithumpian Bands, to reveal an intense investment in Africanness well beyond the conventional stage. These misrule festivals, in which blacks and whites performed multiple "masks" of blackness, created a receptive climate for Manhattan's stage African vogue and fueled the subsequent century-long national fascination with minstrelsy. Blacking up offstage all but ensured public interest in a similar theatrical activity. To a significant degree, blacks contributed to this offstage construction of Africanness through the Afro-Dutch festival of Pinkster and the African American commemoration of Thanksgiving Day.

Pinkster in New York State was originally a weeklong Dutch religious holiday but rapidly developed into an Afro-Dutch festival once magnanimous Dutch masters, especially around Albany, allowed their African bondsmen to participate.[29] An Angolan-born slave named King Charley, his drum, and his African dancers quickly became the principal attractions at Pinkster.

Sterling Stuckey contends that as this African Pinkster king and his performers became the main curiosities, "respectable" Euro–New Yorkers went from being central participants in a Christian festival to spectators at pseudoreligious African rites.[30] The most controversial African addition was the Toto or Totau dance, a "provocative" ring dance performed in honor of the Angolan deity Totau, who was embodied in the New World by the Angolan King Charley. Pinkster's religious dance resembled the calenda, in which a man and a woman shuffle back and forth inside a ring, dancing precariously close without touching and isolating most of their sensual movement in the hip and pelvic areas.[31] Once the couple dances to exhaustion, a fresh pair from the ring of clapping dancers relieves them and Totau continues. Eyewitnesses remarked that with reinforcements the rites could become an all-night affair.

In fact, an anonymous Pinkster memoir claimed the Totau dance promoted a morally relaxed atmosphere marked by potentially offensive interracial interactions. This memoir recalled that "the blacks and a certain class of whites, together with the children of all countries and colours, begin to assemble on Pinkster Hill" to participate in "a kind of chaos of sin and folly, of misery and fun." Whites participated heartily in the bacchanal, and this disapproving eyewitness reported "a beastly black" and a "beastly white" could be seen "sleeping and wallowing in the mud or dirt."[32] Far from an exclusively African ritual, the Totau ritual with its "wallowing" dancers reveals an interracial version of performed Africanness that massaged white and black New Yorkers into uninhibited revelry. The enticing back-and-forth of the Totau was having such a liberating effect that Albany's Common Council banned Pinkster in 1811. The council cited "boisterous rioting and drunkenness" as the primary reason, but Totau's sexual allure and reports of cross-racial bonding surely influenced the council's decision.

Even after Albany banned Pinkster, New Jersey and New York blacks continued to congregate in Manhattan for less elaborate Pinkster rites. Without benefit of a deified King Charley or Totau-inspired celebrants, Euro– and Afro–New Yorkers gathered at Catherine Slip on the East River to hawk produce and perform a range of dances. These annual gatherings soon developed into weekly dance competitions. Euro– and Afro–New Yorkers flocked to witness cadres of market dancers vying to dominate the Slip, and similar to Albany's Pinkster, an African-centered performance space emerged.[33] Catherine Market became an urban nexus of interracial American culture where racial opposites interacted and exchanged performative conventions.[34] Euro–New Yorkers eventually participated in the dance competitions, even appropriating some of the complicated black dance steps, and as Shane White suggests, these cross-cultural interactions motivated white performers toward minstrelsy.[35] Without question, the Catherine Market dances increased interest in performed blackness, fueled the vogue, and eased some of the escalating racial tension.

Pinkster in Manhattan and Albany popularized black dancers and invited whites into African-dominated performative contexts, but Euro-Americans also cultivated their own blackface masking rituals. Throughout the early 1800s, in urban centers such as Philadelphia and New York, Callithumpian Bands of working-class whites engaged in racially marked saturnalias on New Year's Day.[36] For this classic inversion ritual, Euro-Americans dressed in outlandish costumes, applied chimney soot or grease paint, and engaged in acts of mischief. With an unruly air, the blackened bands paraded through city streets demanding food and drink from their social superiors and tussling with their social inferiors, black citizens in particular. In what has become a familiar refrain for minstrel revisionists, Dale Cockrell claims that these "demons of disorder" did not intend to denigrate African Americans with their black masks but indulged in nonracial representations of an available other to discover their working-class selves. He further argues that participation in this blackface festival prepared working-class whites to embrace minstrelsy as skilled performers and thoroughly involved audiences.[37] The fact that some Euro–New Yorkers "sooted" up in their free time reveals yet another reason for the considerable white interest in stage Africans.

Although a strictly African American event, Thanksgiving Day represents another significant African-inflected social ritual that potentially fueled the stage African vogue of the 1820s. Celebrated on New Year's Day with the Callithumpian rites, Thanksgiving Day was a comparatively more serious and sober annual observance memorializing the U.S. ban of the international slave trade. On January 1, 1808, Afro–New Yorkers Peter Williams Jr. and Henry Sipkins delivered the first Thanksgiving Day sermons at the AMEZ Church on Leonard Street. These sermons recalled Africa's glorious past, recounted the injustices endured under American slavery, and assessed Afro-America's current condition and future prospects.[38] Following the addresses, someone read the Congressional Act of Abolition, which officially announced America's withdrawal from the international slave trade effective January 1, 1808. Historians Leonard Sweet and Geneviève Fabre contend that, from this first observance to the beginning of the Civil War,

Thanksgiving Day commemorations provided rapidly assimilating free blacks with a much needed pause to reflect on their African origins and the legacy of slavery. Fabre argues that this event, with its addresses and other declarations, effectively trained African Americans for the day when they could participate in civic affairs as first-class citizens.[39] By helping free blacks make the transition from dependent slaves to free individuals, Thanksgiving Day celebrations could counteract the dominant perception that the "American Negro" was ill-prepared for or unappreciative of emancipation. And as far as the 1820s vogue, this black holiday contributed another racialized ritual to Manhattan's confluence of African-centered social performance, which in turn heightened interest in theatrical blackness.

Therefore, with Afro–New Yorkers commemorating the end of the slave trade in the daylight hours and working-class Euro–New Yorkers assembling Callithumpian Bands for their evening revels, it comes as no surprise that New Year's Day was the ideal date for theater managers to showcase their stage Africans. The Park Theatre premiered George Colman Jr.'s *The Africans* on January 1, 1810, and revived John Fawcett's *Obi; or Three-Finger'd Jack* on January 1, 1823. Colman's play was the perfect choice for January 1 because the melodrama realistically depicted the sadistic West African slave trade. Also, by staging *Africans*, Price and Simpson may have attempted, in their unique way, to acknowledge Afro–New York's Thanksgiving Day and the Congressional Act of Abolition. Or perhaps Park management wished to pay its respects to working-class Callithumpian Bands and hoped to attract those enthusiastic revelers to the theater. By no coincidence, when the Park premiered *Africans* on January 1, 1810, the theater drew a massive house and earned seventeen hundred dollars, the largest one-night receipts since the doors opened in 1798.[40] Conditioned by Pinkster dances, Callithumpian Bands, and Thanksgiving Day, New Yorkers were primed to consume stage Africans, even in a slave trade melodrama. Colman's antislavery stage African heroes may have earned the Park Theatre a lucrative payday in the early 1810s, but by the 1820s the African vogue and ancillary social rituals — except Thanksgiving Day — were firmly grounded in that other strain of blackness, the ridiculous, occasionally raucous, but ultimately comforting stage African.

Sensuous Totau celebrants, enterprising market dancers, and mischievous Callithumpian Bands all served as liberating fantasies or freeing vehicles for Euro-Americans in search of a misplaced folk "self," which brings us back to Nathan Huggins's astute assessment of Euro-America's investment in performed blackness. In the early 1820s, a major double standard was driving the national fascination with blackness, stage Africans, and blackface minstrelsy. In essence, the theatrical laboratories could easily degenerate into closed shops because "low status" groups, like Native and African Americans, were often denied representational control in the dominant culture. But the "high status" group was completely free to draw from "the lower group's cultural pool," and consequently the appropriated culture of the dispossessed groups became the dominant group's "folk art."[41] This double standard explains why blackface minstrelsy became a national sensation, and whiteface minstrelsy, controlled by African Americans, remains a hidden performance tradition.

As discussed in the previous chapter, Indianness provided a significant "cultural pool" for Euro-Americans in search of an original, unspoiled, "folk" America. But fiercely somber Euro-constructed stage Indians rarely delivered comic release. Therefore, outrageous Mungoesque stage Africans, and late-night Callithumpian misrulers—all unconcerned with European propriety or decorum—were enlisted to allow white audiences and performers much needed access to vicarious thrills and forbidden "folk" pleasures. David Roediger extends and reconceptualizes Huggins's fantasy notion by claiming that Euro-Americans came to identify "whiteness" with industrialization and progress, whereas "blackness" personified the preindustrial joys that white America had to forsake as the nation matured. Freewheeling, uninhibited stage Africans now represented the "natural," uncivilized self that working-class, and some middle-class, whites secretly wished to rediscover.[42] Callithumpian Bands, Pinkster, stage African musicals, and eventually minstrel shows provided contexts for recovering the sinful pleasures sadly left behind. Such were the genesis and social implications of a stage African vogue that, before minstrelsy's ascendance, transformed blackness into a desirable and marketable cultural commodity.

Stage African Balancing Act: *Tom and Jerry* and *Obi*

William Brown was reluctant to embrace a limiting racial identity and to perform primarily stage African material, but, by June 1823, he would appreciate the popularity of African-inflected productions enough to join this festival of relatively safe commodified blackness. After the riot of August 1822 closed his establishment for several months, Brown's American Theatre finally reemerged in March 1823 for a benefit performance by James Hewlett that featured strictly European ballads and comedic sketches.[43] Two months later, a playbill for June 7, 1823, announced that Brown's African Company would be appearing at the neutral "Theatre, in Mercer Street," not the American Theatre or the African Theatre.[44] For his first full-scale stage African evening, Brown selected "minor" or "illegitimate" musical material featuring black characters. He opened with William Moncrieff's *Tom and Jerry; or Life in London* (1826), a wildly popular British extravaganza that boasted two showstopping, dancing stage Africans. Brown closed the evening with John Fawcett's seriopantomime, *Obi; or Three-Finger'd Jack* (1800), which dramatizes the famous Afro-Jamaican bandit Jack Mansong. When Brown staged explicitly "African" productions, his company marketed a rare product that other theaters could not — or would not — duplicate: an ensemble of black performers impersonating popular black caricatures.

Manager Brown was forced to embark on this latest stage of his identity journey without the ample services of his star attraction and most versatile performer. The playbill for the March 1823 benefit announced Hewlett's departure from the company: "Positively the last Night! Mr Hewlett At the particular solicitations of a number of his friends, is induced once more, before his departure for the Southward, to make his appearance in this city."[45] While Hewlett pursued a solo career, Brown employed three actors to replace him. The male-lead triumvirate consisted of Mr. Bates and Mr. Jackson, who both joined the company during the Hampton's Hotel residency, and Mr. Williams, a newcomer who would assume major roles in both *Tom and Jerry* and *Obi*. Brown also replaced his female lead, Williams, with an actress named Johnson who, in the tradition of S. Welsh, performed both male and female roles in *Tom and Jerry*. To people these more spectacular and scenically demanding stage African musicals, Brown also expanded his African Company with supporting actors and assembled his largest ensemble to date.

The most intriguing and momentous addition was an actor named Mr. Smith, a white stage veteran who played a constable in Moncrieff's *Tom and Jerry* and an auctioneer in a slave market scene that Brown appended to this musical. George Odell's *Annals of the New York Stage* includes only one white actor named Mr. Smith, a southern-born thespian who made his New York debut in August 1787 and appeared in primarily comic roles.[46] By 1823 Smith would have been on the New York stage for roughly thirty-six years, which would certainly qualify him as a veteran actor. Earlier, Simon Snipe reported that Brown hired white musicians, a major sign of racial progress if not artistic advancement, but Smith's appearance with the African Company marked another major milestone, as this previously all-African company became the first integrated acting company in Manhattan, if not the United States. Mr. Smith's conspicuous Euro-American presence surely had a profound impact on the troupe's chemistry, its range of representation, and, of course, the audience's reception. I would argue that Brown's simultaneous decisions to cultivate a racially specific profile like the African Company and to integrate his black ensemble were consistent with his modus operandi. This subtle or even ironic duality reflected the fundamental dynamism and encounter of opposites that characterized Africanist or diasporic performance in the Americas. Brown's consistently Africanist institution incorporated but never resolved differences; therefore, his African Company could embrace a white member and still claim a more than geographic or biological connection to African culture. Brown would need these Africanist values as he attempted to market this African Company in an increasingly competitive theatrical market that had recently fallen in love with Euro-constructed stage Africans.

William Moncrieff's *Tom and Jerry; or Life in London*, the first piece on the playbill of June 7, was not an exclusively African musical but rather a melodious tour of London featuring a pair of hilarious Afro-Brits. This musical extravaganza originally debuted at the Adelphi Theatre, a minor London theater, during the winter of 1823 and enjoyed an extended run.[47] Moncrieff adapted the piece from Pierce Egan's popular novel *Life in London; or The Day and Night Scenes of Jerry Hawthorn, Esq. and His Elegant Friend Corinthian Tom in Their Rambles and Sprees through the Metropolis* (1821). The novel and the musical follow an urbane Tom and his country cousin Jerry as they embark on a frenetic tour of London's high and low culture. Throughout their rambles, Tom and Jerry's suspicious girlfriends, Kate and Sue, clandestinely follow their roving beaux, expecting to corner them in some indiscretion. As for the high culture, the cousins visit fashionable establishments like Almack's, an upper-crust dance hall in the West End that hosts elite quadrille dances and elaborate masquerade balls. In terms of low culture, a character named Bob Logic guides Tom and Jerry through London's seedier side, represented by the Holy Land slums of the East End. While exploring this disreputable terrain, our heroes wander into a tiny tavern named Mr. Mace's Crib at All Max—a play on the upscale Almack's in the West End. Egan describes Mace's clientele as a mixture of lascars, blacks, jack-tars, coal havers, dustmen, women of color, and a few "remnants of once fine girls."[48]

Moncrieff's musical reached the Park Theatre in early March 1823, and New York's *Albion*, an Anglophile weekly, was greatly impressed with act 3, scene 3, in which Logic, Tom, and Jerry visit Mace's Crib.[49] Dusty Bob, a "Negro" coal whipper, and African Sal, a "Negro" prostitute, are two regulars at this motley tavern, and they steal the show with their infamous "Comic Pas Deux." Toward the scene's close, Tom suggests to Dusty Bob and African Sal, "Come, start off, my rum ones! the double shuffle," and gathering his meaning, the "Negroes" begin their dance: "Accompanied by Rosin, on his cracked Cremona, and Jerry on a pair of Tongs, to the Air—'Jack's alive.'" In the course of the "pas deux," when encored, Sal, by way of variance, and in the fullness of her spirits, keeps twirling about; at the same time, going around the stage, Bob runs after her, with his hat in his hand, crying "Sarah! vy, Sarah, ant you vell? &c."[50] Based on Moncrieff's text, the "double shuffle" and the stage African "Comic Pas Deux" were intended to be "low" culture dances contrasted against the elegant minuet and waltz later performed by a society couple, "Mr. and Mrs. Lightfoot," at Almack's in the West End.

During the American Theatre phase, Brown's all-African ensemble, especially the leading lady Williams, established a reputation as crowd-pleasing, orchestra-defying hornpipers; therefore, this twirling, double-shuffling duet was ideally suited to the company's talents. But Manhattan's critical reception of Dusty Bob and African Sal's comic dance was as mixed as the divergent opinions on Pinkster's Totau dance in upstate New York. The *Albion* reviewer remarked the dance was "quite in *keeping*," meaning the reviewer believed the spirited twirling was completely appropriate for an East End establishment. Yet another critic from the *New York Mirror, and Ladies' Literary Gazette* expressed great offense at the "blackened" *pas de deux*: "Dusty Bob and the Negro wench, in their *characteristic* dance, gave existence to a sensation in many bosoms for which there is no name but *disgust*."[51] This reviewer also declared this dance "characteristic" or "in keeping" for a "Negro" couple from the Holy Land slums, but not in a remotely positive sense. He abhorred Moncrieff's "minor" musical and claimed that *Tom and Jerry* remained on the Manhattan stage because the public demanded the piece, and managers were "duty bound" to revive it incessantly. When the Park eventually performed *Tom and Jerry* with the "disgusting" stage African dance deleted, this prudish critic announced, "We were pleased to find that the *waltzing* was entirely *cut out*," and further praised Park managers for working toward "the correction of public taste and morals" by removing Dusty Bob and African Sal's lurid gyrations.

Brown's *Tom and Jerry* ignored the *New York Mirror*'s "moralizing" and retained the allegedly "offensive" stage African waltz. On the playbill for June 7, he prominently advertised Dusty Bob and African Sal as two central characters supplying the "African" in his African Company. Although dancing was nothing new for the company—Hewlett had choreographed stage Indian ballets and Williams had executed English hornpipes—African Sal and Dusty Bob marked the first time Brown's performers danced as distinctly African characters. The African Company's portrayals of African Sal and Dusty Bob were markedly different from the Euro-American versions. Price and Hippolyte Barrère, who both produced *Tom and Jerry* several times, never featured real black actors in these roles but instead employed white actors in blackface and wooly wigs.[52] Brown's black talent executed Moncrieff's "Comic Pas Deux" without those counterfeit costumes, offering an intriguing alternative for New Yorkers in search of the "genuine" article.

If the intimate gyrations of this highly sexual dance were not disturbing enough, Brown's production pushed the morality meter even further. Replicating the original Adelphi Theatre production, Brown cast a man, Mr. Jackson, as the prostitute African Sal. It is possible that the Park production cast the musical in a similar same-sex fashion, which, in addition to the pair's unrestrained Africanness, might have triggered the *New York Mirror* critic's disgust. As an ex-seaman Brown surely had some experience with the East End, and by casting a man, he may have intended a sardonic commentary on the attractiveness of East End sex workers. More likely, by having a black man impersonate African Sal, he sharpened the comedic effect of the scene, though a female impersonator would definitely diminish the heterosexual excitement of the *pas de deux*. Alternatively, two twirling, double-shuffling men could have produced a thoroughly satisfying homoerotic spectacle for certain members of Brown's audience.[53]

As he titillated with a "grotesquely" African and latently homoerotic *pas de deux*, Brown skillfully infused political commentary into London's low culture, transforming Moncrieff's seemingly harmless musical extravaganza into a subversive indictment of slavery and the slave trade. He balanced the indecent machinations of the infamous same-sex "Negro" couple with a highly sentimental original scene titled "Life in Limbo—Life in Love, Vango Range in Charleston, on the Slave Market." Similar to his comments concerning the problematic partition in the rear of that first Village theater, George Odell condemned this appended slave market scene as "pathetic" largely because a black company was depicting slavery onstage.[54] Distracted by the race of the performers, Odell failed to consider the historical conditions and theatrical precedents potentially driving Brown's addition. After seventeenth-century British merchants gained a foothold in this international commerce in Africans, the empire established the infamous Royal African Company to control a rapidly expanding industry.[55] Brown's creation and presentation of a figuratively enslaved African Company unwittingly or perhaps intentionally bridged the theatrical and "real" worlds of an early national United States still struggling with this devastating institution. One could assume that Brown appropriated the name African Company to confront lingering issues of human bondage, but, regardless, the racially specific name and additional scene complicated this latest institutional phase.

Brown was by no means the first playwright to stage a slave market scene from a sympathetic or sensational perspective. By the late 1700s the human trade was a major theme in European and Euro-American poetry, novels, and dramas, with most of this literature depicting slavery as an evil industry that decimated families. To present their antislavery case with the greatest force, white playwrights even constructed melodramas in which despotic Asians and Africans enslaved Europeans.[56] Two plays revived during the stage African vogue, William Bates's *Harlequin Mungo* and Colman's *Africans*, feature vastly different slave market scenes that might have influenced Brown's original addition. The opening scene of Bates's *Harlequin Mungo* portrays a West Indian slave market as an absurdly ridiculous flesh market where an English mistress can purchase a stout slave to protect her from her husband, and a judge can acquire a slave to decipher his law books.[57] By endowing slaves with unrealistic physical agency and unsuspected mental capacity, Bates artfully subverts or reverses the conventional master-slave relationship. Also through these sardonic reversals, Bates invests commodified Africans — the slaves and the roles — with personalities and individual potential well beyond their debased conditions. As a contrast, Colman's *Africans* conjures a decidedly more severe or perhaps realistic slave market. In act 2, scene 3, Colman familiarizes audiences with the West African slave trade by placing faces on black and white slavers, specifically West African generals who are gathering their prisoners-of-war to sell at auction. He also establishes the accuracy of his market scene by including a line about the necessity of working quickly because the British Parliament recently passed a bill banning English involvement in this pernicious trade.[58]

For his tour through "Vango Range" in Charleston, South Carolina, Brown combined the comic spectacle of Bates's West Indian auction with the stark realism of Colman's West African slave market, a balance of seeming opposites. According to the playbill for June 7, the entire African Company appeared as slaves in this appended scene, and the spectacle of a predominantly black ensemble arrayed in shackles was possibly a ridiculous sight, verging on pathetic, as Odell claims. However, a scene titled "Life in Limbo—Life in Love" suggests more sentimental intentions; it implies a scene in which Africans confront the potential loss of family and identity as they are sold into bondage. Beyond the initial shock or even aversion of seeing real Africans chained, an affective slave market scene could generate great sympathy or empathy in black and white patrons, especially among slaves or ex-slaves in attendance.

Alternatively, the jarring realism of a slave trade scene could have produced intensely negative emotions in Brown's integrated audience. According to the bill for June 7, the auctioneer in the Vango Range scene was played by Mr. Smith, the white veteran actor who integrated the African Company. The specter of a Euro-American performer auctioning slaves away from loved ones might have stimulated feelings of guilt and indignation among white patrons and intensified feelings of anger and resentment among blacks. Incredibly, the same Mr. Smith appeared as a London watchman in another *Tom and Jerry* scene titled "Life in the Dark," in which he applied the billy club to Dusty Bob, the "Negro" coal whipper. In one evening, Mr. Smith was recruited to assume multiple nineteenth-century incarnations of "the brutalizing man," but this kind of extreme representational tension was typical for Brown's Euro-constructed and Indio-constructed stage Indians, as well as his royal and common stage Europeans. Now in this uncensored production of Moncrieff's musical, the African Company embraced Dusty Bob and African Sal's controversial *pas de deux* but balanced those lighter and looser stage Africans with the harshly realistic and emotionally affective spectacle of a white human being selling black human beings. Whatever the audience's emotional reaction to this balance of laughable and sentimental Africanness, Brown was building on the theatrical precedents of earlier enslavement scenes, and his appended scene heightened the emotional intensity of Moncrieff's musical extravaganza.

Dramaturgically, Brown imposed this slave market on Moncrieff's London-based musical tour, but transporting *Tom and Jerry* to Charleston was historically appropriate, given America's continued involvement in the trade. In spite of various federal and state laws prohibiting international and intra-national slave trading, in June 1823 South Carolina and other southern port cities continued to support prosperous markets specializing in human beings. From his steward days, Brown surely knew something of these markets, and his "Vango Range" recalled Charleston's actual Vendue Range, a popular antebellum market on that city's waterfront that featured auctioneers or "vendue masters" who brokered many items, including slaves.[59] America's ongoing, internal slave trade was not restricted to the South. Despite a state law in 1788 that banned the trade in New York State, Manhattan remained a safe harbor for foreign and national ships carrying human cargo. According to James Rawley's history of the transatlantic slave trade, as late as 1862 one newspaper observed that "the City of New York has been of late the principal port in the world for this infamous commerce."[60] Given New York's status as principal port for this illegal industry, it seems fitting that Brown exploited the topical nature of Moncrieff's musical to expose the continued presence of the trade in the northern and southern United States. Perhaps New Yorkers were not prepared for this kind of metatheatrical depth and African contrariety, but ready or not, the conclusion to the June 7 performance pushed this stage African balancing act even further.

Given the popularity of island-based stage African musicals and Brown's maritime experience in the Caribbean, it was an obvious choice for the ex-steward to close his stage African evening with a lavish, tropical seriopantomime like John Fawcett's *Obi; or Three-Finger'd Jack*. As mentioned earlier, nineteenth-century pantomimes tended to be light dramatic stories set to music and performed without spoken text; a seriopantomime, however, implies that the subject matter—in this case, Jack Mansong—is more dramatic than comedic. Fawcett's seriopantomime premiered in July 1800 at the Haymarket Theatre, a minor London theater, and later played at Covent Garden, a major house.[61] Jack Mansong was a self-emancipated slave turned revolutionary who plotted to massacre the white colonists and free the slaves of Jamaica.[62] English authorities uncovered the conspiracy and hired a detachment of five hundred Afro-Jamaican soldiers to track and defeat Jack's insurrectionary forces. During a confrontation, Jack lost two fingers on one hand, thus earning the legendary nickname "Three-Fingered Jack." Following his failed insurrection, Jack escaped into the mountains and continued to terrorize the island as an internationally renowned highway bandit. In reaction to his terrorizing, the Jamaican Assembly offered a bounty for Jack's head, and by 1781 a search party finally killed the elusive thief.

Although Fawcett features the sinister free Afro-Jamaican in his serio-pantomime, most of the characters are pleasant, musically inclined Afro-Jamaican slaves. With a balance of risible and serious stage Africans already incorporated into the text, *Obi* was the ideal vehicle for Brown to test the limits of his stage African balancing act. In several distinct ways, Fawcett differentiates the "good" Afro-Jamaicans, or contented slaves, from the "bad" Afro-Jamaicans, or Three-Fingered Jack and his menacing associates. Fawcett first creates distance between the two varieties of stage Africans through the duets and solo songs that are so integral to pantomime as a form, because it is primarily through music that we hear characters communicate. The contented slaves and their kind masters intone beautiful melodies while Jack never utters a note; he is a conspicuously silent menace. In fact, at one point, Jack becomes intoxicated and strums his banjo, but he absolutely refuses to sing; instead he forces Rosa, the Planter's daughter whom he has kidnaped, to serenade him.[63] Never hearing the bandit's voice creates an intriguing, mysterious character, but his lyrical silence makes Jack an isolated, inaccessible dramatic figure.

As for the musical communication of Fawcett's "good" Afro-Jamaicans, their melodies generally project well-adjusted slaves, but the verses also artfully disclose master-slave tensions beneath the placid plantation transcript. To open the pantomime, two slaves sing this duet:

> The white man comes, and brings his gold—
>> The slaver meet him on the Bay—
> And oh, poor negro then be sold,
>> From home poor negro sails away.
> Oh, it be very very sad to see
>> Poor negro child and father part—
> But if white man kind massa be,
>> He heal the wound in negro's heart.[64]

Their lyrics expose feelings of familial separation and geographic displacement similar to those Brown explored in his original slave market scene, "Life in Limbo—Life in Love." However, the duet also suggests a "kind" master can assist his slaves in healing their wounded hearts. Following the duet, a slave chorus adds clear conditions for their pro-master sentiment:

> We love massa — we love mass, when he good,
>   No lay stick on negro's back —
> We love much kouskous he give for food,
>   And save us from Three-finger'd Jack.

These "good" slaves acknowledge their master's role as provider and protector from the "bad" Jack, but they only love him conditionally. They love him "when" and "if" he is good; presumably they are not enthralled with "massa" when he is despotic or arbitrary. Fawcett subtly foregrounds this important distinction and he musically weaves in similar relational complexities throughout.

Fawcett's seriopantomime further distinguishes between "good" and "bad" Africans, or "interior" and "exterior" blackness, through onstage representations of two distinctly Afro-Jamaican cultural practices: Obeah and Jonkonnu. "Bad" Jack terrorizes "good" Africans and their masters through a cabalistic art known as Obeah — or "obi." Historian Orlando Patterson characterizes Obeah, which is closely related to the African deity Onbaios, as "a type of sorcery which largely involved harming others, at the request of clients, by the use of charms, poisons, and shadow catching."[65] In act 1, scene 3, Fawcett depicts a murky cave where an "old decrepit" and "grotesquely" dressed "Obi Woman" refills Jack's magical "obi horn," which the bandit believes can render him invincible in any confrontation.[66] The "good" slaves also believe in Jack's Obeah-aided prowess. When an overseer demands that the slaves murder the bandit on sight, a reluctant chorus replies:

> We kill when we come near him —
> But no swear loud, for when we bawl,
> Three-Finger'd Jack hear us.[67]

The slaves hesitate because they are convinced that Jack's Obeah has made him omniscient. English traveler R. C. Dallas claimed that "a prejudice in favour of the magic of Obeah prevailed," and even when converted and baptized, Afro-Jamaicans continued to believe in the powers of this sorcery. Dallas also maintained that if English colonists had introduced Christianity — or "white obi" — with greater vigor, Obeah would have ceased to ensnare or frighten slaves.[68]

The "serio" in Fawcett's pantomime is predicated on the dramatic conviction that these divergent religious systems are incompatible and must ultimately collide.[69] Before that inevitable showdown, the "good" Africans Sam and Quashee are christened by a priest, and Quashee feels bold enough to assure his worried wife: "Me laugh at Obi charm—Qaushee strong hearted."[70] To conclude his seriopantomime, Fawcett stages the Obeah-Christianity standoff, describing how "Quashee crossed his forehead, and tells him he has been christened. Jack is daunted, and lets his gun fall."[71] Quashee's newfound confidence in the face of Obeah and Jack's cowardice when challenged by "white obi" confirms R. C. Dallas's position that Christianity could triumph over African magic in the Afro-Jamaican mind.[72]

Fawcett balanced the ominous cave and dark Obeah rites with Jonkonnu, an open-air, master-sanctioned Afro-Jamaican festival celebrated by "good" slaves around Christmas.[73] Act 1, scene 6, is devoted to this "Negro Ball" in which Fawcett introduces "Jonkanoo (the Master of the Ceremonies)."[74] Jonkonnu's primary attraction was this Afro-Jamaican king of the festivities who guided a band of merry followers from house to house collecting tributes, and, in exchange for cash, the king and entourage performed for their hosts. Fawcett's version of the raucous Afro-Jamaican fete opens with a solo by the Jonkonnu master:

> We negro men and women meet,
> And dance and sing, and drink and eat,
> With a yam foo—with a yam foo!
> And when we come to negro ball,
> One funny big man be massa of all—
> 'Tis merry Jonkanoo.

The "one funny big man" alludes to the fact that the Jonkonnu king occasionally paraded from house to house on stilts, thus heightening his stature. This "Master of Ceremonies" boasts that he is "massa of all," but his followers astutely temper his ambitious claim:

> Massa he poor negro treat,
> Give grand ball, and Jonkanoo.

The Jonkonnu celebrants remind their fearless leader that the real "massa," the English planter, is the one financing this jubilant gathering of "good" Afro-Jamaicans. Speaking of the master, before Fawcett's "Jonkanoo" officially begins, the Planter, Overseer, and Clergyman enter to bless Sam and Quashee, and after blessing and arming the volunteers, Fawcett's magnanimous Euro-Jamaicans exit the stage, leaving the slaves to their ball. This momentary marriage of Afro-Jamaican festival and Christian ritual implies that the master class endorsed Jonkonnu as a favorable African-inflected cultural practice.

On a broader, political level, Fawcett's "good" and "bad" Afro-Jamaicans represent opposing ends of the nineteenth-century slavery debate. The praise-singing, servile stage Africans personify the pro-slavery position, whereas Jack's self-emancipated presence embodies antislavery sentiment. Of course, we never hear what Jack has to say about slavery or his insurrectionary past, but his ability to exist outside the plantation system proves that enslavement is not the only option for Afro-Jamaicans. Even among the seemingly "good" Africans, Fawcett challenges the assumption that slaves are contented and indifferent to freedom. In act 1, scene 5, a colonial official reads this proclamation before a group of slaves: "Reward for killing Three-Finger'd Jack! One Hundred Guineas, and Freedom to any Slave who brings in the Head of Three-Finger'd Jack!"[75] The announcement especially motivates Sam and Quashee, two slaves who will become the heroes of this pantomime, and they are genuinely excited by one word: "At length Quashee and Sam come look at it on opposite sides — seem as if animated by the same feeling — point particularly to the word 'Freedom,' then to their *Wives and Children*. They each take up a little *Black Child*, and kiss it very affectionately, and swear to perform the great task." Pro-master melodies may romanticize plantation life, but Quashee and Sam do not agree to hunt this three-fingered bandit as a defense of slavery or the master class. They are motivated by freedom and are willing to risk their lives to secure emancipation for themselves and their families. In the end, the pro-slavery position appears to prevail as the "good" blacks kill a very "bad" Jack and parade his severed head and disfigured hand onstage, but the freedom-focused agenda of an allegedly contented Sam and Quashee cannot be overlooked. Undoubtedly, Sam and Quashee's motivations for hunting and killing the infamous bandit were not lost on Brown's African Company or his remaining African American supporters.

As an ex-steward who sojourned throughout the Caribbean, Brown doubtless had some knowledge of Afro-Jamaica's "good" and "bad" cultural practices. Brown's *Obi* production projected the ominous aura of the "bad" Jack Mansong and his Obeah by casting Mr. Bates as the Afro-Jamaican bandit. Snipe's second edition of *Sports* remembered Bates as "a terrible big ugly looking black man,"[76] which suggests he was the perfect intimidating actor to project Fawcett's silent but sinister villain. As for the "good" Jonkonnu rites, Brown relied on the capable feet and voices of his musically talented, if dramatically challenged, African Company to titillate and delight Manhattan audiences. Yet, one has to wonder whether Brown's production of Fawcett's subtly challenging script further aggravated or eased the minds of Euro–New Yorkers preoccupied with their insubordinate free blacks. Given the power of this representational laboratory, pro-master and festive Jonkonnu stage Afro-Jamaicans, executed by actual black actors, could reassure Euro–New Yorkers that African Americans remained containable and were not social, political, or religious threats. Some whites, unable or unwilling to separate the staged image from reality, may have been convinced by this spectacle of black actors performing amusing, generally docile "colored" caricatures that this is how flesh-and-bone blacks believed and behaved.

Real-life, daily-reported national developments, however, complicated the audience reception of Brown's *Obi* production. In his dissertation on American drama and the antislavery movement, John Collins argues that Fawcett's seriopantomime resurfaced on the American theatrical scene whenever insurrections were in the news. *Obi* had its American premiere in Philadelphia during the 1802–3 season, and Collins claims that the piece was extremely popular due to the "interest engendered by the St. Domingo and Gabriel Prosser insurrections."[77] He also contends that American theaters rediscovered Fawcett's seriopantomime in 1823 due to excessive media coverage of a slave conspiracy uncovered in Charleston, South Carolina, specifically Denmark Vesey's aborted uprising during the summer of 1822.[78] The dual goals of the Vesey-led plot were to free all slaves in the area and kill all whites, but the ambitious plan never materialized because authorities discovered the intrigues through a slave informant. Vesey, his lieutenants, and followers were all arrested, and when the news broke nationally, the Charleston rebels became instant media stars.

From July to September 1822, New York newspapers obsessed over the Vesey conspiracy, publishing equal amounts of fact and fiction.[79] The *Spectator* offered the most extensive and dramatic coverage of the plot and court proceedings, routinely devoting its front page—usually reserved for paid advertisements—to the Charleston affair. Unlike other papers, the *Spectator* reprinted information straight from various "official" trial records circulating around the nation. Equivalent to an 1820s Court TV, these reprinted records transported the reader directly into the courtroom to hear the sordid particulars of the failed uprising.[80] Noah's *Advocate* published the most alarmist coverage with editorials warning Euro–New Yorkers that if they continued to indulge their "Negro" population, they could have another Charleston. He cautioned readers that blacks "are a much more shrewd and intelligent race of people than is generally imagined."[81] The insurrectionary plot in Charleston generated popular interest in Fawcett's seriopantomime featuring an Afro-Jamaican bandit, but in a media-saturated, post-Vesey frenzy, Brown's *Obi* production probably exacerbated rather than eased white paranoia. An imposing, "terrible big ugly looking black," Mr. Bates performing Fawcett's intensely silent "bad" Jack could send shivers through any disquieted Euro–New Yorker.

But more than physical menace, this African Company was dramatically defiant. This "shrewd" and "intelligent" collection of African American artists presumed control of multiple and often divergent theatrical meanings — in this case, stage African roles initially written for white actors. In earlier productions, the black company disputed Euro-America's stranglehold on cultural representations of Indianness and Europeanness and commanded the symbolic controls traditionally off-limits to "low status" groups. On June 7, the African Company's reinterpretations of stage Afro-Jamaicans and Afro-Brits undermined white performers in similar roles and signaled this company's complete mastery of commodified blackness. Brown exploited the balance of "good" and "bad" Afro-Jamaicans in Fawcett's *Obi* and adapted Moncrieff's *Tom and Jerry* to stage a same-sex comic *pas de deux* alongside a slave market reconstruction. Both productions established that the African Company—now featuring one white actor—could coexist with difference and unresolved dualities. With an aborted black insurrection in the news, Brown's company of black chambermaids, stewards, waiters, and former slaves could expose and intensify the simmering tensions beneath the public transcript and reveal the agency in seemingly innocuous comedic Africans and increasingly insubordinate real Afro–New Yorkers. Much like King Charley's unquestioned dominance at Pinkster, the African Company's representational authority was a partly enjoyable and partly disconcerting experience for Euro–New York.

According to available records, Brown declined to continue his stage African balancing act beyond this singular evening, which seems a curious choice, given that his predominantly white patrons preferred "illegitimate" musicals and pantomimes. During the American Theatre phase, audiences vociferously demanded fewer declaiming blacks and more dancing blacks — less Othello, more Mungo. Comedic stage Africans offered the perfect solution for placating "laughter-loving clerks" and increasing revenues, and theoretically Brown's unmatched productions featuring black performers—literally the "real" thing—should have crowned him the undisputed champion of the city's momentary stage African renaissance. Sadly, manager Brown's campaign to "out-African" white companies never translated into increased patrons or income, and by late June 1823 he would be facing retirement. Fawcett's already perplexing seriopantomime combined with Brown's penchant for blending disparate strains of stage Africans resulted in too many unreconcilable versions of blackness for Euro–New York to digest. Also, by its very essence, a multifaceted company of early national black artists disproved, rather than endorsed, the general assumption of African American inferiority. Brown's institution, never limited to stage Africans like Mungo or Othello, symbolized black cultural and social progress and therefore represented a direct challenge to white supremacy.

From the start, Brown's "becoming" was never separatist, unashamedly integrationist, and always reflective of progressive New World African values. One might question the accuracy of associating an allegedly limited African identity with inclusion, but if we return to the concept of "African" in the early nineteenth century, we can appreciate the association. Sidney Mintz and Richard Price assert that heterogeneous African cultures in the Americas were marked by their "openness to ideas and usages from other cultural traditions." By combining that appreciation for cultural difference with a "stress on personal style," African American cultures fostered "a fundamental dynamism" that remained open to change, elaboration, and creativity.[82] That fundamental dynamism and acceptance of difference were present in all four institutional phases or identity shifts examined in this history. Such values—not some newspaper editor's commentary or a paid advertisement—made Brown's institution African, and being African in the early national United States meant appropriating and refashioning all available culture practices.

In the final analysis, Brown's Africanist and well-intentioned social and theatrical experiments fell victim to poor timing. He was constructing inclusive and integrated entertainments at a moment when Euro–New Yorkers resolved to exclude—or at least marginalize—blacks from the national imaginary. As Euro-America accelerated toward a racially restricted "herrenvolk republic," and many African Americans responded with an understandably protective separatism, white theater managers like Price and Baldwin still exhibited that thoroughly American propensity for racial appropriation in their production choices. The immediate issue for manager Brown was the extent to which he would be allowed to participate publicly, along with Baldwin and Price, in the connected processes of masking and national imagining. Brown's experiment with a "real" African Company failed to unseat Price's and Baldwin's blacked-up counterfeits, because it was never necessary for whites to witness "real" Africans performing stage Africans. Blackface minstrelsy would soon make it painfully evident that white audiences preferred their commodified blackness delivered by white performers.

In Fear of His Opposition

EURO–NEW YORK REACTS

ACCORDING TO LEGEND, in the aftermath of the summer riot of 1822, Brown posted a placard declaring, "White people do not know how to behave at entertainments designed for ladies and gentlemen of colour."[1] This alleged acerbic reaction to the riot seems risky even for an audacious entrepreneur like William Brown. If he dared to hang such an incendiary sign, one wonders how effective Brown would have been in sustaining the white patronage that had become so crucial to his theatrical solvency. Because we lack documentation and doubt Brown ever hung such an antiwhite banner, why has the legend of the sign survived into the twentieth century? Frantz Fanon claims, "[W]hen a story flourishes in the heart of a folklore, it is because in one way or another it expresses an aspect of 'the spirit of the group.'"[2] Twentieth-century African American historians like Langston Hughes, William Weatherby, Roi Ottley, and Loften Mitchell reprinted versions of the sign because they believed it possible or at least plausible that Brown would take such a defiant position. These writers perpetuated the legend because it spoke to their theatrical and historical communities as a statement of overt social and artistic resistance indicative of the more combative "spirit" exhibited by "New Negroes" of the 1930s and 1960s.

In the context of 1820s Manhattan, those "New Negroes" were yet to emerge; nevertheless, the imagined placard does reveal some truths, or at least half-truths, about Brown's entertainments. As for half-truth, the alleged sign suggests that Brown designed his entertainments specifically for persons of color, which is partially correct because he did create a garden to serve dispossessed black leisure seekers. Furthermore, Brown's innovative whiteface minstrels, stage Europeans, and stage Afro-Indians were all firmly rooted in the political desires, communal concerns, and artistic aspirations of Afro–New York. However, as this study has demonstrated, with each institutional phase from African Grove to American Theatre, manager Brown embraced, integrated, and represented all New Yorkers, not "colored" citizens exclusively. He even extended a hand to his initial herald and eventual detractor M. M. Noah. As for undeniable truth, the legendary placard perceptively accuses whites of being ill-prepared to accept entertainments designed *by* "ladies and gentlemen of colour." Beyond one or two curious evenings of blackened Shakespeare, whites refused to allow African Americans unmediated access to serious theatrical representation. White theatergoers, attracted to novelty and enamored with staged difference, initially greeted an all-African company with great interest, and in the early months of his theatrical career, Brown benefited financially from his profile as a "curious" counterpublic sphere. But the generous patronage of culturally "touring" white clerks, sailors, and circus workers had limits.

Finally, the most accusatory portion of the sign, "white people do not know how to behave," would have implied that Manhattan's "colored gentry" deemed itself socially superior to whites. As noted earlier, English visitors Frances Trollope and Charles Mathews found blacks to be better behaved than their white counterparts. Truthfully, Broadway's black promenaders and Brown's garden "dandys and dandizettes" did indulge in a range of superior attitudes, and their elite posturing was partly responsible for rising antiblack antagonisms. Although the placard remains an unsubstantiated legend, there is ample evidence to prove whites misbehaved quite often, quite effectively, and quite creatively during all four theatrical phases.

The primary contention of this chapter is that whites did not know how to behave when confronted with black progress as epitomized by Brown's entertainments. Effectively bombarding this African American company in waves of aggression, white political, cultural, physical, and metaphorical attacks divested these black artists of their much coveted artistic agency. The first wave was a political assault that embroiled Brown's Minor Theatre in a statewide constitutional debate. Manhattan politicos feared that Afro–New Yorkers were exercising the elective franchise too freely, so they launched a legislative offensive to construct color-coded suffrage limitations and used

Brown's theater as a convenient and highly visible scapegoat. The next wave, an intricate cultural assault, targeted the company's dual performance tradition of whiteface minstrelsy and stage Europeans. In the press, Euro–New Yorkers demanded that the "colored gentry" dominating public spaces on Sundays be contained by any means necessary, while in the theater world Stephen Price launched a theatrical crusade against black Shakespeareans. The third wave of white misconduct was a partly racially motivated, partly competitive physical assault executed primarily by circus workers and their associates. The fourth and final attack materialized as a multipronged, international, metaphorical assault—blackface minstrelsy—which delivered the most damaging and fatal blows to these entertainments designed for ladies and gentlemen of color.

Political Assault: Constitutional Convention of 1821

After initially dismissing the African Grove's whiteface minstrelsy as empty mimicry, M. M. Noah, newspaper editor and Republican operative, quickly realized the inherent dangers to the racial order when African Americans "masked" or "trained" for future possibilities. Samuel Hay was the first historian to examine how Noah's coverage of the "African Theatre" transformed African American thespians into political boogeymen, frightened white citizens, and marshaled opposition to black suffrage.[3] For political background, in the summer of 1821, New York State politics operated under the illusion of a two-party system, but one party clearly dominated the political scene.[4] The reigning Republican Party billed itself as the state's populist option because its base consisted of artisans, small upstate farmers, and a growing class of poor Irish immigrants. New York's once potent, but now profoundly ineffectual, other party, the Federalists, continued to embrace the old Dutch aristocracy, moderate-to-wealthy upstate farmers, and Manhattan's wealthiest merchants. Federalists also represented the conservative party, committed to preserving suffrage rights for men of property and opposing any plans to enfranchise poorer citizens, black or white. Although Federalists remained the party of aristocratic Old New York, their Republican opponents branded them the pro-black faction because many party regulars were current or former slave owners. Prominent Federalists John Jay and Alexander Hamilton founded the New York Manumission Society to assist blacks in their transition from slavery to freedom. In fact, a Federalist governor and state assembly passed the gradual emancipation bill of 1817, which legislated the end of slavery statewide by July 4, 1827.

Federalists may have set emancipation in motion, but by the early 1820s Republicans controlled which civil rights, including the elective franchise, would be extended to manumitted Afro–New Yorkers. From the birth of the union, free blacks with a freehold property worth twenty pounds or a rental property valued at forty shillings could vote throughout New York State. With abolition six years away, acutely paranoid Manhattan Republicans feared that propertied black voters were already exerting too much influence on local politics. The populist party claimed that black voters, manipulated by Manhattan Federalists, decided a crucial municipal election in 1813 in favor of the aristocratic party. Republicans feared that, as more blacks were emancipated, they would remain Federalist pawns and continue deciding elections counter to Republican interests. Therefore, when the populist party gained control of the state legislature in 1820, Republicans proposed a state constitutional convention to reevaluate important provisions, including suffrage rights. The agenda was to remove all property requirements for white men, thus creating a new generation of poor Irish Republicans; while they were cultivating this new immigrant voting block, however, the populist party schemed to eliminate many free blacks from the political process. As mentioned, the Federalist Party opposed extending voting privileges to propertyless men, black or white, so it resisted the proposed convention and its allegedly populist objectives. Despite Federalist objections, New York voters decided through a statewide referendum to hold a constitutional convention in August 1821.[5]

As a Republican Party mouthpiece, Noah constantly railed against "Federalist-controlled" black voters, and as early as April 1820 he created a series of satiric yet serious articles accusing Garry Gilbert, New York's voter registrar, of recruiting black voters in dancing cellars and brothels.[6] A month into the convention of 1821, Noah revived the antiblack vote campaign with an article reporting how convention delegates were sixty-three to fifty-nine in favor of striking the word "white" from the new voting legislation, a change that would allow all propertyless men, including blacks, to vote. With Republicans down a few votes, Noah queried: if Euro–New York did not allow "Negroes" to serve as legislators, judges, lawyers, or jurors, why should they be allowed to vote? His editorial also reprinted the statement of a Republican delegate, Colonel Young, who reasoned that because whites did not allow blacks to circulate socially on equal terms, Euro–New York did not want blacks voting on equal terms.[7] Federalist delegates Peter Jay—son of John Jay—and R. Clarke countered Young's logic by arguing that black soldiers who volunteered during the War of 1812 proved to be the most efficient naval fighters and, therefore, earned suffrage rights.[8] To close the September 24 update, Noah published delegate names and how they intended to vote. This decision to "name names" was surely a precarious disclosure for any delegate drifting counter to public sentiment in his district, but Noah was only getting started.

With his side trailing in the suffrage showdown, Noah slyly interjected Brown's institution and all it signified into the center of the legislative battle. The day after his update, Noah positioned Brown's latest *Richard III* as an ominous example of black cultural and political transgression. He warned Manhattan with an introduction to a reprinted playbill: "The following is a copy of a printed play bill of gentleman of colour—They now assemble in groups; and since they have crept in favour with the convention, they are determined to have balls and quadrille parties, establish a forum, solicit a seat in the assembly or in the common council, which if refused, let them look to the elections. They can outvote the whites, as they say. One black gentlemen most respectfully insinuated, that he thought 'as how he mout be put on the grand jury.' "[9] As part of his September 25 warning against Afro–New Yorker determination, Noah highlighted symbols of black economic progress such as "balls and quadrille parties" and, by implication, Brown's theater. But Noah made it clear that these menacing, assembling Afro–New Yorkers were interested in far more than cultural pursuits. In his earliest coverage, Noah claimed that the African Grove chatter was "imitative" and lacked any substantive engagement with international, national, or local politics; now in this introduction, he alerted Euro–New York that gentlemen of color were aspiring politically. The phrase "have crept in favour with the convention" implied that, as reported in his first update of September 24, the pro-black vote faction had sufficient votes to create more black suffragists. Noah even hinted that male Afro–New Yorkers harbored political aspirations far surpassing suffrage and conjured up black "boogeymen" who planned to serve on the Common Council or be appointed to the grand juries, which indicted their fair share of "colored" criminals.

Noah's apocalyptic vision of blacks serving on juries and running for office, not to mention producing *Richard III*, was designed to alter votes among the delegates. Perhaps influenced by Noah's warning, the convention voted seventy-four to thirty-eight to remove property qualifications for white males and to raise them for black males. The newly drafted Constitutional Article Second, Section I, read: "But no man of colour, unless he shall have been for three years a citizen of this state, and for one year next preceding any election, shall be seized and possessed of a freehold estate of the value of two hundred and fifty dollars, over and above all debts and incumbrances charged thereon; and shall have been actually rated, and paid a tax thereon, shall be entitled to vote at such election."[10] This decision to retain property requirements for black citizens essentially required second-class Afro–New Yorkers to serve an apprenticeship period before enjoying the full benefits of equality. Free black males had to achieve middle-class status before they could vote; in other words, they had to be twice as good as the new Irish immigrant voting block.[11] The new article also included a three-year residency requirement because of widely disseminated rumors that increased black suffrage rights would incite a mass migration of election-minded African Americans into the state. This political assault on Afro–New Yorker progress, via Brown's theater, allowed the reigning Republican Party to invent a "white vote" to counteract an allegedly potent black vote. That "white vote" transcended class difference and strengthened a single-race "herrenvolk republic" by guaranteeing the most destitute Irishman his suffrage rights because he was white and by denying the poor black male the same privilege precisely because he was not.[12]

Was the political assault on free blacks and Brown's theater necessary? In other words, how potent were the black voting "boogeymen"? Contrary to Republican concerns, free blacks never played a major role in deciding any municipal or statewide election. Prior to the constitutional convention, in the Manhattan elections of 1819, only 100 Afro–New Yorkers voted, and in the first municipal election after the constitutional changes, 163 blacks exercised their suffrage rights.[13] Based on these numbers, 63 more Afro–New Yorkers voted after the convention, which indicates that Republicans did an inadequate job of completely securing the political borders. Nevertheless, the black voter, it seems, was more mite than monster.

Noah's political assault was a symbolic action waged against a phantom black voting block, but, more important to this study, the Republican operative's calculated introduction to the *Richard III* playbill identified Brown's institution as politically subversive. Ever the perceptive editor, Noah recognized the civic training potential in stage Europeans or extratheatrical white-face minstrels and understood that if Hewlett could play King Richard onstage, he might ultimately believe he could become an alderman offstage. By mere association in Noah's paranoid imagination, this editorial assault equated playmaking and pleasure gardens with explicitly political activities, such as voting and holding office, and reaffirmed the notion that performance in the United States is often about possibility. Republicans may have overestimated the black menace at the ballot box, but Noah acknowledged and now alerted Euro–New York to the performative negations of white supremacy developing at this African American theater. And when Brown relocated his stage Europeans next to the Park Theatre, Stephen Price and municipal authorities would take definitive steps to oppose this significant aesthetic menace.

Cultural Assault: Shakespeare
Closing of 1822

Brown's entertainments, especially whiteface minstrelsy and stage Europeans, contested the cultural supremacy of Euro–New York, generated considerable anxiety among the "high status" group, and attracted unwanted "official" attention. Manhattan's "colored gentry," appareled in "cossack pantaloons" or "cambric dresses," cut a most visible and imposing presence as they strolled along a most public Broadway or lounged within Brown's semiprivate African Grove. Many Euro–New Yorkers fretted publicly that the vigorously displayed "elite" fashions were having a negative affect on Afro–New Yorker behavior. The letter of August 1820, introduced in Chapter 1, complained of black promenaders, or whiteface minstrels, walking defiantly down the thoroughfare, four or five in a row, with cigars dangling from their mouths. Shane and Graham White, who have investigated why "black dandys and dandizettes" and similar African American displays troubled working-class, middle-class, and upper-class whites, contend that "[f]or many whites, a well-dressed black was at least a slightly comic figure, but there was also often, in whites' observations, an underlying sense of disquiet, a fretful complaint at the blurring of what had seemed relatively clearcut racial boundaries."[14] For much of the August 1820 letter, that concerned people-watcher appeared mildly amused by the modish pageant, but he closed with a call for action: "Quere—Ought not some regulation to take place on this subject."[15] But although this gentleman believed that municipal authorities needed to intercede and regulate this weekly behavior, he failed to proffer a plan. Should the city ban "Negroes" walking in rows or forbid blacks from dressing better than whites? Whatever the solution, other distressed citizens shared their personal experiences with Afro–New Yorker insubordination in M. M. Noah's *National Advocate*.[16] Without question, whiteface acts perpetrated on the street or in a pleasure garden blurred boundaries and threatened a civic order predicated on white supremacy.

From another, more conservative perspective, some white and black critics interpreted the ostentatious public displays as proof that the race did not possess the necessary discipline to be emancipated and productive citizens. White moralists interpreted the public exhibitions as a sign of Afro–New York's moral depravity and feared that the uninhibited carousing, particularly in sections like Five Points, might lead the city's white youth into degeneracy.[17] Also, the expensive attire raised questions. How did blacks acquire this costly attire? Did they steal the clothing? If they could indeed afford the high-priced, stylish apparel, that would indicate economic growth in Afro–New York; therefore, thievery provided the more comfortable explanation. Interestingly, African American observers sensed a similar lack of self-control in the promenaders' excessive presentations of their bodies. In July 1827, on the eve of full emancipation, Russwurm and Cornish's *Freedom's Journal* decried the aggressive behavior and disputatious nature of the "fashionable participators in 'the rights of man.'"[18] The black editors also explicitly denounced "Broadway Negroes" directly as "unenlightened" and "wicked" and admitted that these "immoral" creatures engaged in excessive presentations that reflected badly on the race.[19] Both an "underlying sense of disquiet" and doubts concerning Afro-America's ability to handle freedom and moral responsibility were evident in white and black reactions. Yet unlike their white counterparts, Russwurm and Cornish believed that "Broadway Negroes" constituted a small, self-absorbed, but highly visible segment of Afro–New York.[20] They maintained that "unenlightened" dandies misrepresented the race, whereas white editors and concerned citizens viewed the "colored" promenaders as an accurate reflection of an entire race and, more important, a dangerous indulgence that again compromised social boundaries.

Legislation designed to contain extratheatrical promenaders never materialized, but a white theater manager and municipal authorities did launch a cultural offensive to establish "white" theatrical territory and erect more definitive racial boundaries. Not surprisingly, the assault centered on protecting America's most beloved European writer, Brother William Shakespeare. In early January 1822 Noah published an article, "Hung Be the Heavens with Black," which creatively described the cultural assault, or infamous Shakespeare arrests:

> The ebony coloured wags were notified by the Police, that they must announce their last performance, but they, defying public authority, went on and acted nightly. It was at length considered necessary to interpose the arm of authority, and on Monday evening a dozen watchmen made part of the audience. . . . Come, come, said the watch, none of your play acting airs — into the black hole with you. The sable corps were thrust in one green room together, where, for some time, they were loud and theatrical; ever and anon, one would thrust his head through a circular hole to survey the grim visages of the watchmen. Finally, they plead so hard in blank verse, and promised never to act Shakespeare again, that the Police Magistrates released them at a very late hour.[21]

Who exactly was the "arm of authority" arresting these "coloured wags"? Theater scholar Joyce Green MacDonald declares this authority was the "white police power coming to the defense of Shakespeare."[22] Noah reported a dozen magistrates were ordered to arrest the troupe and that the production was closed because it presented a "fire hazard" and "public nuisance."

Noah's editorial competition, William Coleman of the *Evening Post*, expressed skepticism at the arrests: "*The African Theatre*, which has recently made some *noise* in this city, is no longer permitted to be opened for the amusement of the public. It appears, from the Advocate of yesterday morning, that the Police found (*or thought*) it necessary to interfere, and the whole dramatic corps were actually taken to the watch-house."[23] Coleman concedes the "noise," or Brown's boisterous presence on Park Row, but the phrase "or thought" implies Coleman believed the "Police" may have engaged in unwarranted muscle-flexing. Municipal records indicate no indictments or penalties handed down for nuisance or fire hazard, so as the last line of Noah's description insinuates, these arrests were not a legal matter but a cultural confrontation. The company's crime was performing Shakespeare, and the "white police power" did not initiate the arrests but were manipulated by cultural authorities like Stephen Price. Once Price realized that Brown intended to compete with the "Theatre" by usurping Shakespeare, he deployed the dozen watchmen to deliver a definitive message to this African theater.[24] "Coloured wags" were not welcome to partake in Shakespeare's growing cultural cachet, and they were jailed because "Star Giver General" Price deemed it necessary to protect William Shakespeare from Brown's "inappropriate" stage Europeans.

As Jane Moody explains, "[C]ultural objects [the performance of a Shakespeare play, for example] do not occupy fixed positions in a stable hierarchy of cultural relations, but are understood in relation to both institutional structures, and the political and theatrical meanings of particular occasions."[25] In line with that reasoning, my examination of stage Europeans in Chapter 2 argues that Shakespeare did not arrive in the United States as sacred property, meaning the Bard did not occupy a lofty, fixed position in a national hierarchy. And one could argue that the most culturally "American" Shakespeare was practiced by S. Welsh, with her intertextual, dramaturgical revisions and high-low aesthetic fusions. Nevertheless, Price and other cultural authorities considered Brown's stage Europeans demeaning, farcical, and inescapably "minor." Simon Snipe accused the troupe of reducing Shakespeare to mimic burlesques, and Scottish visitor Peter Nielsen claimed that the company murdered "the king's English" in its 1822 production of his national drama, John Home's *Douglas* (1771).[26] Someone had to defend the artistic integrity of European scribes and protect the purity of the English language from slanderous black actors. Noah did his part by keeping a watchful eye on Brown's progress and demonizing a black theater to sway convention votes, but he never called on municipal authorities. Price, the nation's procurer of high culture, infused Shakespeare with such political import that when a company of black amateurs threatened the Bard he felt compelled to involve the "white police power."

Price's cultural assault on "blackened" Shakespeare was part of his broader agenda to institute a more stable aesthetic hierarchy in this country. Lawrence Levine claims that most early Americans did not exhibit elitist or territorial attitudes toward Shakespeare, and that not until the early twentieth century would the Bard become the exclusive property of "polite" classes and "educated portions of society."[27] With U.S. theatrical artists and audiences slow to mature, the "Star Giver General" assumed the awesome responsibility of delivering first-rate Shakespeare, Italian opera, and other elite entertainments to the nation. For Price, elevating national artistic tastes was a critical step in removing a young United States from the shadows of Europe, but as a rampant Anglophile, Price generally turned to Mother England for his cultural cues, especially regarding the "correct" approaches to producing the Bard. Shakespeare scholar Gary Taylor argues that, depending on the historical moment, English theater and its public perceived the Bard in vastly different ways. Taylor found that as early as 1725, Alexander Pope edited and published a literary collection of Shakespeare's plays "which suppressed the theatricality of the plays in favor of their readerliness." Pope argued that the errors in Shakespearean texts were due to the poor memory of actors—in short, "the stage was to blame for obscuring Shakespeare's genius."[28] This English trend toward a more classical, literary, and allegedly accurate Shakespeare had a profound impact on manager Price, and he championed standards for "correct" Shakespeare to the exclusion of U.S. amateurs, black or white. Stephen Price envisioned topflight British stars in "legitimate" Shakespearean productions, and his dogged pursuit of that vision fomented conflicts with Brown's company.

Economically, as well as culturally, the territorial Price had much invested in "literate" Shakespearean tragedies, comedies, and histories properly performed by British stars. When Brown moved to Park Row to stage quintessentially "American" Shakespeare, Price was in the planning stages for a historically accurate production of *Henry the Fourth, Part II*. Scheduled to premiere in February 1822, this major event would feature a shamelessly elaborate and supposedly authentic Henry V coronation complete with more than two hundred actors and equestrians.[29] In the winter of 1822, a monumental Shakespearean showdown was brewing on Park Row: properly staged, historically accurate, thoroughly English-inflected Stephen Price productions versus thoroughly American, popularly minded, amateurishly staged William Brown productions. Consistent with Jane Moody's theory, this massive *Henry the Fourth* was the momentous occasion to which Euro–New York's social elites attached great artistic and cultural significance. Properly produced Shakespeare could generate greater reverence for the Bard—but, more important, it could also help establish Price's much desired cultural hierarchy in the states.

With a much anticipated *Henry the Fourth*—the city's cultural event of the year—in production, the last thing Price needed was a "novel" African American company siphoning customers of various colors. Samuel Hay maintains that the "real reason" Price wanted the Park Row residency terminated was that this "minor" troupe was emptying the Park's gallery.[30] Realistically, Brown's company could hardly rival the major theater in terms of production values or acting talent, but Brown could prove a significant box office competitor because of his audience integration. Instead of segregating

Afro–New Yorkers in a balcony, Brown allowed black and white patrons freedom of movement in his boxes, pit, and gallery. On Park Row, as opposed to the remote Village, Brown could easily attract black patrons trapped in the Park gallery along with inquisitive Euro–New Yorkers constantly in search of the latest trend.

According to Joyce Green MacDonald, Price, Noah, Snipe, and Nielsen were disturbed by stage Europeans for the same reasons whiteface minstrelsy generated disquiet. She writes, "The African Company raid is an early example of the use of Shakespeare as a tool for enforcing cultural and political hegemony. Instead of imperial or colonial power, however, the New York police mounted their defense of Shakespeare on a platform of the cultural authority of whiteness. . . . The danger and transgressive power of black Shakespeare lay in its public contradiction of the supposedly rigid and absolute construction of ideologies of racial difference."[31] MacDonald's "cultural authority of whiteness" is reminiscent of David Roediger's "herrenvolk republicanism"; both ideologies assert Euro-American supremacy and entitlement based solely on color. "Blackened" Shakespeare's true menace rests not in its ruination of a revered writer but rather in its challenge to absolute racial ideologies. If allowed to continue, S. Welsh could have disseminated an aggressively womanist, self-reflexively submissive Lady Ann relatable to Afro– and Euro–New Yorker audiences. Likewise, James Hewlett's Scottish and Irish stage Europeans might have bridged the seeming cultural divides between blacks and similarly dispossessed white ethnic groups. Price and other reactive whites understood how stage Europeans contradicted the comfortable assumptions of white supremacy and challenged racial difference. This transracial, transcultural company was behaving as if it was no different than any group of Americans enamored with Shakespeare's tempting tragedies and charming comedies. If anything, the brief Hampton's Hotel residency sounded the alarm that Euro–New York needed a boundary erected to convince the "coloured wags" that Shakespeare was not their "brother." Backed by municipal authority, Price successfully demarcated once common cultural property and, through imprisonment, taught this troupe that Brother William was yet another white entitlement.

Manager Brown could have avoided these culturally and financially motivated Shakespeare arrests if he had refrained from "public contradictions" of racial ideologies and embraced the conventional differences inherent in stage Africans, particularly the comedic variety. Always the subversive, Brown bypassed the inferior caricatures, and because black Shakespeareans were apparently as threatening as black voters, Euro–New York felt compelled to create and police its cultural borders. Price was more than willing to marshal the city's political forces to protect the integrity of a theatrical icon and defend the logic of a racially divided New York, but did he reach the company in time? Did his police-supported offensive and boundary-defining message eliminate black Shakespeare? As discussed in Chapter 2, black actors had already appropriated "the cultural sanction bestowed by his works,"[32] so it was too late for cultural and political authorities to intercede. Beginning with *Richard III* in the upstairs theater, Taft, Welsh, and eventually Hewlett refused to behave like limited black actors and, instead, behaved as limitless black performers who could transracially inhabit European material from Scottish ballads to Shakespearean tragedies. But available sources also reveal that following the arrests, Brown avoided the Bard with the exception of an aborted *Othello* production in the summer of 1822. Unofficially barred from Shakespeare, the company discovered other stage Europeans—Irish, French, Spanish—in "minor" or "illegitimate" theatrical material, but a physical assault would frustrate those cross-racial explorations as well.

Physical Assault: Summer Riot of 1822

Beyond establishing a cultural hierarchy or escaping the "Negro problem" through exoticized stage Africans, some Euro–New Yorkers deemed it necessary to "check" overindulged blacks and their ambitious institutions physically. Paul Gilje, riot historian, argues that "[i]nstitutions that were a source of pride for blacks were the focal point for attacks by whites," and rioters targeted black churches because "it was as if whites feared the sense of moral equality, even superiority, enjoyed by blacks through regular religious worship."[33] But white aggression against seemingly superior African Americans was never limited to moral institutions; equally prideful black sites, like Brown's economically and culturally menacing American Theatre, became targets.

Overtly antagonistic audience behaviors such as spewing epithets or hurling apple cores were typical for early national theater, but incidents of physical contact with actors were rare, and nearly destroying an entire theater was unheard of. On August 10, 1822, frustrated whites transformed their annoyance with "colored" arrogance into punishing bodily aggression. The *Spectator* recounted, in an article titled "Unmanly Outrage," how white rioters literally undressed the company: "The *actors* and *actresses*, it is said, were fairly stripped like so many squirrels, and their glittering apparel torn in pieces over their heads; the intruders thus completely putting an end to this play for the night."[34] Unlike more passive white observers who wrote letters demanding regulation, these rioters physically contained black Shakespeareans and actively patrolled racial boundaries. In the process, these direct Euro–New Yorkers had a glorious time ripping the "glittering" emblems of black haughtiness to shreds.

By no coincidence, the physical assault centered on the makeshift, occasionally well crafted, but always interesting apparel of Brown's actors. Manhattan editorialists and satirists were obsessed with what these performers wore and how they acquired their clothing. As previously mentioned, in articles on Charles Taft's unfortunate arrests, Noah's *Advocate* and the *New York American* hinted that Taft stole from private homes to support Brown's productions. Understandably, his actions provoked public suspicions of these "African Amusements."[35] It is more likely that the troupe tapped into the network of "coat scourers," or used clothing sellers, which flourished in Afro–New York, especially because James Hewlett himself worked part time as a scourer and a tailor. The anonymous *Spectator* article on Brown's retreat to Greenwich Village claimed the troupe secured "cast-off wardrobes" consisting of "buff galligaskins, and red plush inexpressibles, ermin'd cloaks, and tin-foil trimmings."[36] Snipe's first *Sports* emphasized Iago's "cast-off" attire in *Othello*, noting that he was "dressed in blue satin pantaloons, and a cap, which appeared to have been in the revolutionary war, by the many shapes it now assumed; he wore a kind of roundabout jacket, or an old coat with the skirts turned up." Iago may have appeared in secondhand attire, but Snipe noted Desdemona's costume was "somewhat superior to that of the other performers" and Othello's was "tolerably well adapted to the character."[37]

As for the riot personnel, various classes of Euro–New Yorkers participated in the August 1822 offensive against black arrogance, including seamen, equestrians, and even a constable hired to serve and protect.[38] Middle-to upper-class whites, like Noah and Price, were most preoccupied with Afro–New Yorker cultural activity and were the first to notice blacks promenading along Broadway, keeping their pleasure garden open late, flaunting the name American Theatre, or appropriating Shakespeare without authorization. It is understandable that culturally besieged aristocratic whites wished to see this African venture humbled, but what did lower- or working-class whites stand to gain from a black theater's demise? Lower-class whites, who resided in disadvantaged communities alongside blacks, had more in common with them than wealthy whites. In particular, poor Irish Americans and African Americans labored and socialized together within integrated neighborhoods like Five Points and Greenwich Village.

The political assault on free black voters in 1821 attempted to drive a wedge between potential cross-racial alliances by foregrounding white commonality across class. The constitutional convention promoted a race-based solidarity between lower- and upper-class whites that encouraged both groups to believe the United States was intrinsically white and in need of protection from an encroaching Afro-America. In the early 1820s, however, Euro–New York's cross-class alliance was a tenuous proposition because working-class whites distrusted powerful upper-class whites as much as powerless free blacks.

"Low status" whites had their own rationales for targeting Afro–New Yorkers. Poorer whites attacked African Americans below them in the social order because this group was vulnerable. Barred from juries, militia service, and now the polls, free blacks were logical victims of white working-class aggression.[39] In addition, the consistent social interactions between "low status" whites and blacks could engender either love or hatred, but in an increasingly divisive Manhattan, cross-racial love was a fading possibility. Upper-class whites could often avoid these interracial interactions, but poorer whites continually endured "black dandys and dandizettes" dressing and behaving above their "station." Whether they realized it or not, the poorest Euro–New Yorkers were stationed on the front lines and had to defend the emergent "herrenvolk republic" on a daily basis.

Ironically, manager Brown's integrationist project was partly to "blame" for this physical assault on Afro–New Yorker progress. When whites were not assailing black churches, they were destroying institutions where blacks and whites commingled. David Roediger specifically cites Brown's theater as a location attacked because it was a public space where racial mixture was encouraged.[40] Brown's integrationist project was a courageous and forward-thinking social experiment, but the riot exposed his managerial miscalculation. Brown made the crucial mistake of welcoming any and all Euro–New Yorkers into a theatrical training ground where aspiring blacks rehearsed for citizenship and perhaps theatrical careers.[41] The drama or social tension intensified as Brown attracted more white "laughter-loving clerks" to witness his company of limitless black performers appropriating a range of European theater. Entertainments designed to serve or nurture ladies and gentlemen of color understandably disconcerted many white patrons, and Manhattan's noticeably confident, even arrogant "colored" citizens were by no means the best ambassadors for interracial harmony. Brown did provide Euro–New Yorkers with the option of retreating behind a pit partition, but as their numbers increased, more whites were forced to confront spatial integration. The overwhelming numbers of Euro-American patrons, some of them hostile toward impertinent African Americans, rendered this integrated theater a picture-perfect target for white aggression.

In addition to concentrated apparel paranoia and precarious integration, another factor in the physical assault was the economic competition felt by a circus manager, James West, white circus workers, and the ever present Stephen Price. West's Broadway Circus was located north of Canal Street, between Grand and Howard/Hester Streets just east of Broadway, six blocks south of Brown's theater.[42] He purchased the property in September 1820, and by the summer of 1822 his permanent circus was open every evening except Saturday and Sunday, featuring equestrian acts, tightrope walkers, clowns, musicals, and pantomimes. The *Spectator*'s "Unmanly Outrage" article describes a well-organized attack involving circus performers: "Saturday night, a gang of fifteen or twenty ruffians, among whom was arrested and recognized one or more of the Circus riders, made an attack upon the African Theatre, in Mercer-street, with full intent, as is understood, to break it up root and branch; and the vigour of their operations is reported to have corresponded fully with their purpose. First entering the house by regular tickets, they proceeded, at *quick time*, to extinguish all the lights in the house, and then to demolish and destroy every thing in the shape of furniture, scenery, &c. &c, it contained."[43] The methodical nature of the offensive — purchasing tickets, dimming the house — indicates that the riot was calculated, and that the mob intended to destroy Brown's American Theatre. The article also reported that someone recognized one or more rioters as "Circus riders" or equestrians at the circus, and in a sworn statement, an eyewitness named Mary Dunlop confirmed that "a man named Yeaman attached to the circus was one of the rioters." Brown, personally assaulted in the melee, also filed a couple of statements claiming a group of whites attacked his establishment, and he specifically named three assailants associated with the circus: Peter Hector, James Bellmont, and Augustus West.[44]

Was this Augustus West related to circus manager James West? The record is unclear about such a connection, but working from the court case file and other public records, Paul Gilje and George Thompson Jr. have recovered the addresses and occupations of all the arrested rioters. Gilje was the first to confirm that circus performers and their roommates and relatives constituted a good percentage of the apprehended ruffians. Two perpetrators, James Carnes and William Lawson, were employed as equestrians at West's circus. Gilje also discovered that the Brown-identified Peter Hector worked as a "black at circus," which prompted the riot historian to conclude that Hector was the lone African American ruffian participating in the August assault.[45] But Brown's statements specifically claimed whites—including Hector—attacked his theater. Apparently, Gilje misread Hector's occupation, "black at circus," to mean the assailant was a black person working at the circus, when in reality, Hector was a white dancer employed as a blackface clown at the circus.[46] The Mister Yeaman whom Mary Dunlop recognized and the James Bellmont whom Brown identified both performed at West's circus. Thompson also discovered that Brown incorrectly identified James Bellmont, and it was actually his brother George Bellmont who participated in the riot. James Bellmont was not entirely innocent, and by consulting other records, George Thompson Jr. found that James was indicted in July 1822 for attacking the young actor Ira Aldridge.[47] Apparently, competitive animus between Brown's actors and West's circus performers—including relatives—had been building for nearly a month before the August riot.

Based on the significant circus worker presence in the riot, Gilje concluded that "the people involved in that other low theater disliked the competition the African Grove presented."[48] By August 1822 Brown's American Theatre had "become" a "low theater," committed to "illegitimate" material like pantomimes and musicals, and Manhattan's newest leisure impresario, James West, was now providing competitive company on this "low" or "minor" tier. As the lone leisure options in the upper reaches of Manhattan and with a somewhat shared repertoire, Brown and West were natural rivals. During the summer of 1822, West and Brown both staged John O'Keefe's musical *Poor Soldier* (1782) and William Blake's pantomime *Don Juan; or The Libertine Destroy'd* (1795). Of course, their production approaches were vastly different, with West offering whites in the lead roles of Patrick and Don Juan and Brown featuring black actors as stage Irishmen and stage Spaniards.[49] Regardless, circus workers and their relatives attacked a company that produced similar material and presented direct competition.

The greater economic challenge for West's circus was not Brown's trans-racial Irish or Spanish stage Europeans but the threat that "real Ethiopians" could undermine the marketability of West's counterfeit blackface circus acts. Combined, the July assault and August riot produced six assailants employed by the circus, and four of the perpetrators, Yeaman, Hector, James Bellmont, and another rioter named Charles Lee, all appeared in some version of blackface. As previously mentioned, Peter Hector appeared as a circus "black" or blackface clown. At different points over the summer of 1822, Yeaman, Bellmont, and Lee each headlined in a "grand serious pantomime," *La Perouse*, which featured a prominent "Monkey" character. For the role, the white actors blacked up and sported a furry simian suit.[50] With good reason, West's blackface impersonators worried about job security with flesh-and-bone blacks performing nearby. When it came to representing characters of color, primate or human, Brown presented theatergoers with a choice between a counterfeit product at the circus and the "real thing" six blocks north.

Fortunately for the circus workers, Brown was initially reluctant to explore the artistic and economic potential of stage Africans except for his interrupted production of *Othello*. Also Euro–New Yorkers were rapidly realizing that blacked-up white comedians were preferable to real "Negroes" performing serious or comedic roles. By the late 1820s, blackface circus clowns would emerge as innovators of minstrel specialty acts, prompting music historian Russell Sanjek to designate the American circus the "incubator of the minstrel show."[51] Undoubtedly, West and his circus workers could profit from the American Theatre's demise, but theirs was not the only white theatrical institution invested in this calculated offensive.

Although not directly implicated in the attack, Stephen Price may have encouraged certain circus employers to finish the cultural assault he initiated on Park Row. Park Theatre actor and future circus manager Joe Cowell claimed that Price secretly desired to chase West from Manhattan because a permanent circus was doing "serious injury" to the Park's receipts.[52] Price managed to infiltrate West's circus through a nonthreatening, cooperative approach. The first evidence of a relationship between West and Price surfaced in June 1822, when the Park Theatre advertised an appearance of an elephant recently displayed at the Broadway Circus.[53] Next, in July 1822, the Park company used the circus to remount its ostentatious coronation of Henry V featuring elaborate equestrian acts.[54] By this July production, the circus performers were still technically West's employees, but rioting equestrians like Carnes and Lawson may have moonlighted in Price's circus remounting.

The circus riders and blackface clowns may not have been Price employees at the time of the riot, but the predatory manager soon changed that. During the summer of 1822, New York experienced the worst yellow fever epidemic in municipal history, and many residents and businesses relocated from lower to upper Manhattan to escape the outbreak.[55] Price convinced West to allow his company to move its productions to the Broadway Circus, and Noah even reestablished his *National Advocate* operation in the circus's box office.[56] By late August the Park Theatre and other prominent institutions had transformed these rural margins into the city's commercial and theatrical center, but unfortunately Brown's theater was no longer operational to reap the benefits. With a maliciously ironic flare, Price advertised his circus residency as the "Minor Theatre."[57] Brown had assumed that exact institutional persona earlier in January after Price chased the enterprising African American producer back to the Village, and now Price, with the help of his future circus workers, had again expelled Brown from the center of Manhattan's theatrical landscape. With the American Theatre temporarily disabled and other leisure outlets hampered by the fever outbreak, Price's "Minor Theatre" did excellent business as, again, the only ticket in town.

The *Spectator* reported that although Brown was badly beaten in the riot, he declined to press charges against the perpetrators and instead sought some kind of compromise. Despite this conciliatory position, public prosecutors intended to pursue charges against the white rioters, at least as far as the social climate would allow. In nineteenth-century New York, blacks were permitted to file charges and testify against whites, but convictions were rare, especially when primarily black witnesses testified.[58] Only one indicted rioter, George Bellmont, was found guilty for his assault on Brown, but the Court of General Sessions never sentenced Bellmont. As for his brother James Bellmont, who attacked Ira Aldridge, that circus performer was never even tried.[59] In his memoir, Aldridge lamented: "Of course there was no protection or redress to be obtained from the magistracy (for unhappily, they were whites)."[60] The material damage totaled two hundred dollars and was never recovered, but Brown lost more than money; he lost actors, patrons, and representational control. As a site of riotous misbehavior, a den of disorder, his venture was now saddled with an unsavory and unshakeable reputation, and although Brown did engineer a comeback by March 1823, his interracial experiment was permanently compromised. The sticks and stones of the August 1822 riot by no means destroyed Brown's entertainments, but the metaphorical assaults on the concept of a black theater would deliver the fatal blows.

Metaphorical Assault: Written, Theatrical, Extratheatrical Blackface

As Euro-Americans came to realize they preferred "white niggers" to actual black performers, minstrelsy proved the most effective counter to African American progress, and thus the erasing of the African Company truly began. Ira Aldridge biographers Herbert Marshall and Mildred Stock contend that in June 1823 when U.S. theatrical pioneer Edwin Forrest unveiled "the southern plantation Negro with all his peculiarities of dress, gait, accent, and dialect, and manners," the days of "Negro" theater were numbered.[61] Coincidentally, Brown retired from theatrical producing that very month. Minstrelsy emerged as a "popular entertainment craze" at the very moment that genuine black performers were being driven out of the theatrical laboratories. As discussed earlier, blackface circus workers, precursors to minstrelsy, literally "beat" Brown and company from the stage. Metaphorically, an African American theater could not coexist alongside the white-authored stage "Negroes" crafted by Edwin Forrest, Micah Hawkins, Charles Mathews, T. D. Rice, and other minstrel originators because their white-authored expropriations of blackness obstructed "the visibility of black performers."[62] Minstrelsy would so thoroughly distort the existence and significance of early nineteenth-century black artists that a preeminent black intellectual like James Weldon Johnson dismissed Brown's troupe as "pathetically ridiculous" and remarked that the best African American talent belonged to the minstrel stage.[63]

More than constructing stereotypes to explain the unfamiliar, this nation's earliest blackface practitioners produced a performance tradition based on revealing, but then ridiculing, Afro-America. European and Euro-American expropriations of black imaging began with the dual stage Africans, but eventually multiple U.S. representational outlets produced an incredible variety of blackface performance. Whether manifested in written, theatrical, or extratheatrical forms, minstrelsy constituted a creative yet assertive metaphorical attack on very real symbols of black social, political, cultural, and economic advancement. When white satirists, composers, playwrights, actors, or theatergoers encountered African American soldiers, actors, preachers, voters, or philanthropists, these particular blacks registered as incompatible with preconceived notions of a preindustrial, enslaved, primitive, and inferior blackness. Through distortion, blackface attempted to render these progressive aspects of Afro-America invisible.

Blackface minstrelsy first emerged in satiric newspaper articles, magazine entries, broadsides, and pamphlets designed to exaggerate the physical features, speech patterns, social activities, and political aspirations of African Americans.[64] Several early examples of written minstrelsy appeared as broadsides, which were essentially playbills with texts and illustrations printed on one side of an oversized page. Beginning in the early 1800s, Boston satirists printed a series of "Bobalition"—black dialect for abolition—broadsides, which lampooned the annual July commemoration of abolition in Massachusetts organized by Boston's African Society.[65] These derisive and dismissive broadsides represent the earliest and most consistent examples of black caricature in America. Indirectly, the broadsides also informed Bostonians that African Americans were organizing and observing their own, communally significant commemorations.

Not surprisingly, Brown's entertainments, from African Grove "dandys and dandizettes" to an upstairs *Richard III*, supplied ample material for written minstrel pioneers. Samuel Hay alleges that Noah's early comedic coverage of Brown's "African Amusements" earned him the dubious distinction as the father of blackface minstrelsy. He contends that Noah's humor was effective and widely accepted by his readership because the editor rooted his satiric salvos in easily identifiable symbols of black progress like voters, brazen promenaders, and ex-slaves turned actors.[66] These concrete examples of black advancement resisted the cultural and political logic of a "herrenvolk" Manhattan, so Noah's written minstrelsy reduced black actors and voters to preposterous "facsimiles" of aristocratic white Federalists. A perceptive Noah appreciated the menace inherent in Brown's counterpublic citizenship training sessions, but he also took solace in Taft's tendency to murder the "King's English." Noah's coverage exaggerated and distorted black speech patterns for comedic effect and to mark black actors as inferior, but again, by devoting his pages to the mockery of "African Amusements," Noah generously, if unwittingly, chronicled the emergence of a black cultural institution.

One superb example of written minstrelsy aimed directly at Brown's theater appeared in New York's *St. Tammany's Magazine*, Cornelius Van Winkle's weekly periodical devoted to cultural and political happenings at home and abroad. Van Winkle published an impressive range of topics related to the darker race, including articles on Egypt, obeah, and an African American hero from the War of 1812. In his December 1821 edition, under the heading "Negro Melodies No. III," he printed a lengthy dramatic speech titled "Soliloquy of a Maroon Chief in Jamaica," which was allegedly "lately spoken at the African Theatre."[67] The soliloquy opens:

> Are we the links 'twixt men and monkeys then?
> Or are we all baboons? or not all men?
> O lily-tinctured liars! o'er whom terror
> Hangs her white flag! why need I prove your error?
> Cold is your blood as snow that paints your skin
> And impotent Albinos are your kin.
> Your hue is of the pallid cocoa-nut;
> Ye fear the stains of parent Earth's own smut;
> Ye shun the fiery god who gilds our hides,
> And fills with generous fire life's ruddy tides;
> In graceful curls who crisps our stubborn hair,
> The matted helm which 'gainst our foes we wear,
> Whose warmth prolific fills all heaven and earth,
> Whose lawful child is nature's every birth.
> We, in the image of primeval man,
> Are what our fathers were when life began?

What distinguishes this well-written piece from other minstrel examples is the absence of dialect. At first glance, the soliloquy resembles the rousing stage Indian rhetoric favored by Brown and Hewlett, but closer inspection reveals a subtle exploitation of black physical stereotypes. In the section quoted here, the writer employs clever phrases like "parent Earth's own smut" to reference the "Negro's" dark complexion, and "our stubborn hair" and "the matted helm" to capture the quality of less-than-flaxen African hair. This kind of veiled parody continues throughout the speech as the sharp-witted writer surveys the black body using ingenious and stereotypic descriptors of African lips, noses, feet, brains, and even knees. The author also answers the "monkey versus man" question posed in the opening line by declaring blacks are "the image of primeval man," thus endorsing the popular belief that blacks were barely upright links between monkeys and humans.

Van Winkle neglects to name the soliloquy's author, but the implication is that someone associated with Brown's theater authored this rumination on "primeval man." By stating the piece was lately spoken at "the African Theatre," the cunning publisher led his readers to believe a black actor intoned these lines, but it is highly doubtful that one of Brown's associates wrote or performed this speech. First, the strident antiwhite tone—"lily-tinctured liars"—sounds too openly antagonistic for Brown, given his openness to integration. Second, in December 1821 Brown's audience base was still Afro–New Yorkers, so allowing an actor to recite a litany of sly black insults would have been deadly. Finally, during his first season Brown was not interested in soliloquies by Afro-Jamaican maroons like Jack Mansong but was drawn to the oratory of Indian chiefs and English kings. In truth, the speech's thorough tour of black physiognomy recalls Euro–New York's obsession with black attire, so it is more likely that a white humorist like Simon Snipe juxtaposed the seeming opposites of Africans and theater to produce this minstrel masterpiece.

Other written minstrel publications further burlesqued upwardly mobile Afro–New Yorkers by skillfully conflating their social-climbing activities with the antics of disorderly or criminally minded urban blacks. The underlying assumption in these metaphoric assaults on progressive blacks was that you could remove the "Negro" from Five Points but you could never remove Five Points from the "Negro." A month after Brown's retirement, in July 1823, Noah's *National Advocate* reprinted the first of two anonymous playbills that advertised a series of riotous performances at a fictional "colored" theater. Noah claimed that the playbills were available for purchase on the streets of Manhattan. So, some white humorist or humorists had caught wind of Brown's entertainments, perhaps even attended the performances, and produced these pieces to deride the "ludicrous" concept of a black theater.

Reminiscent of the *St. Tammany's Magazine* soliloquy, the first fictional playbill refrains from dialect, but unlike Van Winkle's minstrel text, the bill incorporates specific white perceptions of Afro–New Yorker theater.[68] The bill announces the opening of a black theater at the intersection of Orange and Cross Streets in the center of Five Points. Ironically, even though Brown had avoided the Points during his brief career, this satirist fictively placed him in the neighborhood that, from the perspective of many Euro–New Yorkers, was the proper or "natural" home for a "Negro" institution. The July playbill further imagined a "natural" black theater by titling the evening's performance a "nuisance in three acts interspersed with a variety of abuse," which capitalized on a popular association of urban "Negroes" with disorder. This staged "nuisance" featured scenes devoted to intoxication, profanity, riot, and "the method of Blockading Side Walks in Seaports." Seemingly, the writer had endured one too many lines of black promenaders or maritime workers dominating Manhattan streets and refusing to "give the wall." And it appears this author may have visited Brown's theater because he conjured an indefatigable hornpipe dancer named "Mrs. Allrags" who, much like Brown's Williams, was the hardest-working hoofer in Manhattan and planned to dance until "one in the morning." Finally, to close the July bill, the writer appended a discerning assessment of the theater's political leanings: "[N]o person admitted who voted in favour of the Missouri bill, or who are in favour of the slave states." Most minstrel material revealed Afro-America as it ridiculed Afro-America, so this bill may have accurately expressed the political disposition of these "African Amusements," but the document primarily intended to expose and deride intimidating and abusive black misbehavior.

The first minstrel playbill was flattering compared with the August 1823 installment, which elevated black theatrical parody to new derisive heights. This follow-up bill metaphorically attacked the possibility of an African American company by indulging in black dialect and by narrating more instances of black criminality. Noah prefaced the second bill with this warning: "Our federal president makers, who are for liberating the slaves of the south, had better pay a visit to these haunts of freemen."[69] As in his political assault on black voters, Noah used the broadside to question the wisdom of emancipating slaves. The second bill begins:

GRAND CONCERT OF DE BOB-LINK SOCIETY[70]
De times hab changed,
But we hab not.

In consequence of *great encouragement* bin had at *skunk* point for dram-tick beformance, de managers will gib grand consert ebery evening dis week.

De public is spectfully formed dat a *new* gumpany of *Africans* habe kommenced *noying* de pop-lace at de above place. De *ladies* and genmen of dis korps are ferior to none in point of *low language* and de *vulgartalons* of some of latter are *first rate*. De enrertainments dat will be brot up consist chiefly in grate woecall powers.

The entire August edition is composed in this difficult-to-decipher dialect, but the author displays some malapropic skills, with inventions like "woe-call" and "vulgartalons," which would become a staple of performed minstrelsy.[71] Also, the phrase "new gumpany of Africans" is a direct and derogatory reference to Brown's momentary African Company. Although one could interpret this flesh-and-blood black theater as a creative outlet and training ground for black citizens and performers, this anonymous artist conceived his "gumpany" as a "vulgar" operation committed to performing "woecall" concerts. This writer, Noah, and many Euro–New Yorkers feared that as slaves were emancipated, they would not improve or "change," but instead, their low-class "enrretainments" would proliferate in areas like Five Points.

Following this introduction, the playbill lists an outrageous assortment of songs scheduled for the "vulgar" concerts, most of which allude to some form of public disorder. Among the imaginative song titles are "Why should we de *watchman* fear / Since when deir call'd dey neber hear"; "If de *marsh-all* should come, how de *neighbours* would laugh / But, as we're *so many*, he only catch half"; "Grand jury man he no get us"; and "Solo on Confinement." The titles are inventive but based in a measure of reality. In all four institutional phases, a persistent problem for Brown was overactive audience participation, which elicited complaints from neighbors, went unchecked by absent watchmen, and resulted in a riot in which only half of the ruffians were arrested. Also, most of the song titles allude specifically to blacks at odds with some aspect of the legal system, including watchmen, marshals, grand juries, the Court of General Sessions, and the penitentiary. Every week, the *Spectator* and the *National Advocate* reprinted the minutes from the Court of General Sessions, which featured a steady diet of blacks charged with various offenses. This opportunistic written minstrel artist shamelessly exploited the widely held association between blackness and criminality for comedic effect.

The song titles are grounded in a combination of racial generalization and urban reality, but distinguishing the legitimacy of the many black arrests from the overriding perception of black criminality is nearly impossible. Historian Leonard Curry maintains that "it was hardly coincidental that the most economically deprived element of the cities' populations tended to commit a disproportionate number of crimes."[72] His research into nineteenth-century criminal records revealed that in most major American cities impoverished blacks were arrested most often for offenses committed outside distinctly "black" areas; when they were arrested, their charges were less likely to be dropped, and if convicted blacks often received harsher sentences than whites. Curry concludes that urban legal systems made it a crime to be black; therefore, one might expect African Americans to develop a cynicism toward the law. Brown's actors expressed their disdain for authority on various levels. On a criminal level, Taft stole cash and cravats to enhance his performances; on a metaphoric level, the company defied cultural authority by producing Shakespeare on Park Row; and on an editorial level, after the August rioters went unpunished, Aldridge blamed this judicial failure on the whites controlling the system.

Even more directed at Brown, the second bill poured salt in the manager's wounds by concluding the fictionalized performance with a full-scale fracas that restaged the 1822 riot:

Finale by big Parrot, companied on de organs of *insult*, base lungs of *curses* and *well toned* pianos of *squizit vulgarity*, wid a *general shout* of *murder* and *watch* by de hole, during which de following *trio* will be sung:

Who de debil care for him?	
He no *offcer*, knock him down.	Woodcock.
Shout aloud, de *riot* hymn,	
We no be in *southern town*.	Whip-poor-will.
Go *H-ll man*, what is't to you?	
Spose he gib you dat new gown.	Jackdaw.
Second	
Dam dat fellow! black his eyes.	
	Caesar Snipe.
What's dat he says? Dere,	
down he goes.	
	Pigeonwing.
Villains! watch! a *citizen* cries	
Some others to his *rescue* flies.	
	Unknown voice.
No watchman here, mob larger grows,	
And we *get off* wid *loud halloes*.	
	Amateurs all.

For the riotous finale, a trio from the "gumpany of Africans" teamed with equally amateurish voices from the crowd to create a tremendous mob scene that obliterated the traditional boundary between actor and audience. This fanciful audience-performer "mob" action resembles many evenings at Brown's theater, and the closing melody about "no watchman" and the "mob" growing larger obviously references Brown's recent travails with obtrusive patrons who behaved as they pleased because no watchmen were present, at least to maintain order.

The second bill capitalizes on the painful details of the August riot but incorrectly designates black actors and audiences as the primary offenders. Beginning with the earliest "laughter-loving clerks" sequestered behind that first partition, white theatergoers were responsible for this theater's chaotic climate. By August 1822 that white rowdiness culminated in an agonizingly real riot featuring white circus ruffians who were later released with "loud halloes" and no prison time. Snipe's second edition of *Sports of New York* (1824), another example of written minstrelsy aimed at the incongruity of a black theater, accurately identified white patrons as the unmanageable element.[73] His partly fictive, partly factual account of the James Hewlett benefit for March 1823 recreated a performance in which rowdy white spectators intervened, sang louder than Hewlett, and successfully hijacked the evening. Trading on more acceptable and appealing racial assumptions, the August playbill recast the ruffians as Afro–New Yorkers and minstrelized these entertainments designed for "ladies and gentlemen" of color into a den of "Negro" disorder.

Written minstrel pioneers were not the only artists to transform, fictionalize, and minstrelize this African institution into a more tolerable and perhaps exciting blackface spectacle. On both sides of the Atlantic, versatile performers from major theaters, minor theaters, and circuses launched the next phase in this metaphorical assault on the African American image. White singers, dancers, and actors appropriated and perfected the rudimentary black dialects, malapropisms, and exaggerated stereotyping of written minstrelsy to become the most recognized and effective minstrel practitioners. Live minstrel artists approximated blacks through blacked-up faces, wooly wigs, "Negro" melodies, and highly physical dances. Minstrel specialty acts differed from stage Africans because those minstrel precursors existed in both comic and dramatic varieties, but blackface favored strictly humorous "colored" subjects. Additionally, stage African playwrights and composers—most of them English—had limited interactions with people of African descent, but blackface pioneers, many of them Irish and working-class, had extensive contact with a range of black talent. White minstrels effectively separated blackness from their black contacts and peddled counterfeit versions of blackness throughout the United States and the world.[74]

The first known, performed minstrel attack on Brown's cabal of black actors did not spring from the fertile imagination of a working-class Euro-American but from a visiting English comedian, Charles Mathews. Mathews was best known for his "at homes," or one-person shows, in which the versatile mimic used humorous monologues, songs, and dances to recreate national or ethnic characters. At the invitation of Stephen Price, in September 1822 Mathews embarked on a theatrical tour of major North American cities. The English comedian agreed to the tour because he wanted to develop a new "at home" about the United States; therefore, while appearing in the various cities, he canvassed for tantalizing characters to populate his latest solo piece. Mathews was most eager to integrate the highly visible and much discussed "American Negro" into his work-in-progress, so he immediately began familiarizing himself with the peculiarities of Afro-America through personal observations of black life and white-authored written minstrelsy. In a letter dated February 23, 1823, Mathews informed a London associate that he was carefully studying the "Negro's" broken English and assured his friend he would soon "be rich in black fun."[75]

Mathews concentrated his comedic eye on burlesquing the "preposterous" notion of blacks performing Shakespeare. His one-man tour de force, *Mr. Mathews's Trip to America*, featured a "Black Tragedian" whom Mathews claimed to have witnessed in an act of "black fun":

Mr. Mathews next informs us that he went to a theatre, called the Niggers' (or Negroes') theatre, where he beholds a black tragedian in the character of Hamlet, and just enters as he is proceeding with the speech, "To be, or not to be? that is the question; whether it is nobler in *de* mind to suffer or tak' up arms against a sea of trouble and by *opossum*, end 'em." No sooner was the word *opossum* out of his mouth, than the audience burst forth, in one general cry "Opossum! opossum!" and the tragedian came forward and informed them that he would sing their favorite melody with greater pleasure; when to please his audience, he gave them

Song.—"*Opossum up a Gum-tree.*"
Opossum up a gum tree,
On de branch him lie;
Opossum up a gum tree,

Him tink no one is by.
Opossum up a gum tree,
Nigger him much bewail;
Opossum up a gum tree,
He pulls him down by the tail.
Opossum, &c.

A malapropic misapprehension of "oppose them" for "opossum" incited this presumably black audience to demand that a "Black Tragedian" perform a "Nigger"-laden version of "Opossum" in the middle of Shakespeare's classic existential monologue. After intoning two more stanzas of the popular melody, the tragedian suddenly discovers another Shakespearean drama: "When he had finished his song he walked up the stage and when he got up the stage he soon came strutting down with, 'Now is the winter of our discontent made glorious summer by the sun of York'; upon which a person in the boxes exclaimed, 'You should play Hamlet, and not King Richard.' 'Yes! yes!' says the man in black; 'but I just thought of New York then, and I couldn't help talking about it.'"[76] Mathews's sardonic fusion of *Hamlet*, *Richard III*, and "Opossum up a Gum Tree" ridiculed this African Company's firm conviction that black actors could honestly interpret any dramatic material, including Shakespeare. This minstrel specialty act reaffirmed the prejudices of Euro-Americans, such as cultural authorities Price and Noah, who believed "Negro" actors, like S. Welsh, could not perform the Bard without regressing into inappropriate melodies. Yet Mathews's minstrel act does partly expose actual performance practice at Brown's Africanist institution. Welsh's womanist Lady Ann did intentionally and artfully synthesize popular music and Shakespeare, uniting the common with the tragic; so in reality, this innovative troupe did cultivate a distinct brand of high-low intertextuality.

Of course, there is ample evidence suggesting that Mathews never attended Brown's theater or witnessed this intertextual "Black Tragedian." First, Mathews's specialty act conjured a majority black audience who called for an allegedly "Negro" air like "Opossum up a Gum Tree." But Brown's actors and integrated patrons preferred English ballads to stage African songs or "Negro" airs; besides, "Opossum" was not a specifically African American melody.[77] Second, musicologist Sam Dennison has examined the three black caricatures featured in *Mr. Mathews's Trip to America* against the comedian's correspondence while in the United States and doubts Mathews encountered these specific personalities. Dennison argues that Mathews was far too elitist to submerge himself in U.S. "folk" culture, let alone an African American theater, and Dennison characterizes the Brit's poorly executed black dialect as more German than "Negroid."[78] This German inflection in Mathews's "black fun" betrays the influence of written minstrel pioneer M. M. Noah. Mathews's line reads like a variation on Noah's line, "Now is de vinter of our discontent, made glorious summer by de son of New York," from his September 1821 assessment of Charles Taft's Richard.[79] Finally, in an open letter published in the *National Advocate*, Hewlett admitted performing privately for Mathews, but the proud and facetious performer denied executing an intertextual fusion of *Hamlet* and "Opossum."[80] The English comedian's inaccurate assumptions about Brown's audience, his cultural elitism, his reliance on written minstrelsy, and Hewlett's denial all indicate that Mr. Mathews never witnessed a possum-infused *Hamlet*.

In reality, the resourceful English comedian did not need to visit New York's "Niggers' Theatre" to realize that black thespians provided the perfect comic contradiction and that this "oppose them" versus "opossum" misapprehension was the perfect malapropism. At the end of a February 1823 letter to an associate, Mathews admitted he had collected several "malaprops" he wanted to work into his new "at home."[81] As a plagiarist, opportunist, and pioneer, Mathews is an excellent example of how blackface minstrelsy can create "black fun" consumers and producers. The English comedian first consumed Euro-America's white supremacy through written minstrel writers like Noah and then fashioned his own critical and imaginative ruminations on the United States' racial dilemma. Mathews carried these learned racial attitudes and appropriated minstrel turns and malaprops, some purely fictive and some rooted in reality, back to London in March 1824, where he premiered his new "at home" in the London Opera House. After a productive sojourn in the "colonies," Mathews's metaphorical assault revealed and ridiculed the idea of a black Shakespearean on two continents; more important, he established a performative paradigm for future blackface minstrels.

Mathews's infectious "Black Tragedian" inspired several of his American cousins to produce similar satiric treatments of black Shakespeare. In 1828 playwright and scenic artist William Dunlap authored a drama entitled *A Trip to Niagara; or Travellers in America*, which featured a stage African named Job Jerryson who works as a waiter in the Catskills and moonlights as the manager of a "Negro Shakespeare Club." Dunlap's frenetic Jerryson reads like a combination of the "wooly-headed" waiter Charles Taft and the atrical manager William Brown. Also in the late 1820s, minstrel pioneer Edwin Forrest crafted a black Shakespearean specialty act, "The Darkey Tragedian, an Ethiopian sketch in one scene," in which an ambitious "Negro" actor implores a theater manager named "Mr. Brown" to allow him to perform *Hamlet* or *Richard III*.[82] This manager plainly mirrors the historical Brown, and the aspiring actor resembles all of Brown's eager black Shakespeareans from Hewlett to Welsh. Thanks to Mathews, English master of "black fun," many subsequent minstrel parodies of African American theater would entertain and soothe generations of enthusiastic transatlantic audiences and simultaneously distort the legacy of an important nineteenth-century African American company.

Coincidentally, not long after Mathews debuted *Trip to America* in London, Ira Aldridge began headlining in Shakespearean productions throughout Great Britain. Audiences familiar with Mathews's latest "at home" assumed that the American-born Aldridge was the "Black Tragedian" the comedian supposedly witnessed and immortalized. A shrewd Aldridge did not discourage such assumptions, because the publicity was priceless; however, once British theater managers and audiences realized that he did not actually perform "Opossum up a Gum Tree" as part of his repertoire, the public demanded he add the "Negro" air. Aldridge first obliged the "particular desire of numerous parties" by performing "Opossum up a Gum Tree" at the Theatre Royal, Bristol, in March 1830.[83] Ten years later, his European admirers would not allow the African American actor to remove the song from his extensive repertoire; in fact, an 1840 Scottish playbill announced that Aldridge would perform a scene from *Mr. Mathews's Trip to America* entitled "To be, or not to be! Hamlet, the Dane! or Opossum Up A Gum Tree."[84] Aldridge later explained in his memoir that he "never attempted the character of Hamlet in my life, and I need not say that the whole of the ludicrous scene so well and so humorously described by Mr. Mathews, never occurred at all."[85] But in a most ironic turn, this very successful black tragedian popularized and profited from a malapropic speciality act that satirized and undermined the very institution that launched his acting career.

Ultimately, this transatlantic, transracial, metaphorical assault on black expressive culture was not limited to the pages of the *National Advocate* and *Freedom's Journal* or the specialty acts of Charles Mathews and Ira Aldridge but also emerged in the American Theatre's very own integrated audience. Unlike today's largely docile theater audiences, nineteenth-century playgoers were active and often uninvited participants in the evening's entertainments. One major reason for this thin boundary between audience and actor was the popularity of extratheatrical parades, festivals, and other social rituals—like Pinkster and the Callithumpians—that conditioned Americans for fully involved masking. Cultural historian Susan G. Davis explains that "disorderly maskings and burlesques were spontaneous performances that encouraged audience participation. Burlesques did not create distance between audience and performers—they reduced it."[86] Many Manhattan leisure seekers, especially "laughter-loving clerks," coveted disorderly burlesques in which they could become active agents in the festivities as opposed to passive auditors.

I have argued that minstrelsy was a metaphoric assault on African American progress, but the August 1822 riot as blackface performance could also be interpreted as an impromptu burlesque for some working-class whites. Apparently, a couple of the misbehaving rioters simply desired to transform, without permission, this counterpublic "colored" theater into their very own makeshift masking ritual. According to Paul Gilje, two maritime workers, not associated with the circus, joined the August riot because they were "out for a good time."[87] Possibly, the sailors first watched the spectacle of circus performers playing strip-the-nearest-"Negro" and then decided to join the irresistible "black fun." After all, with "unpredictable" blacks, who could decipher if the full-scale riot was real or staged, planned or spontaneous?

In early national culture, there were undeniable and deeply ingrained associations between misrule, blackness, and white working-class identity. Blackface minstrel revisionists have linked the minstrel show's explosion to the preexistent popularity of racialized masking rituals rooted in working-class subcultures.[88] As performed minstrelsy emerged in the late 1820s and early 1830s, elite whites read black inferiority in the performances, but working-class minstrel performers and audiences, because of their involvement in Callithumpian Bands and other rituals, understood blackface as a vehicle for challenging respectability and subverting the status quo in favor of a new set of social codes. Minstrel shows and extratheatrical entertainments allowed working-class whites access to a "demonstrative excess" that was lacking in the "new restraint" developing at "legitimate" theaters.[89] Under Price's highbrow leadership and dogged pursuit of cultural hierarchy, Manhattan's pit pranksters and gallery marksmen found their projectile contributions unwelcome at the "legitimate" Park Theatre. Eventually, working-class theaters like the Bowery would provide white males with a thoroughly masculine and unapologetically "rough" semiprivate transcript that remained ideologically opposed to an emergent middle-class tyranny and completely amenable to audience involvement.

Before the Bowery Theatre, Euro–New Yorkers flocked to Brown's counterpublic sphere to develop their distinctly working-class transcript. At base, the "laughter-loving clerks" and other white "demons of disorder" assumed that African Americans would share their passion for spontaneous and unruly burlesque. As mentioned in my Chapter 2 discussion of contentious audience-performer dynamics, Brown's company was well acquainted with the problem of audience expectations. Theater historian David Krasner theorizes these expectations: "In early black theatre, the visibility of 'blackness' onstage was not solely a function of production and performance, but was part of the assumptions of the spectator, whose vision of blackness dictated the way in which cultural images would be shaped during performances. The spectator's authority attempted to force the machinery of projection, identification, and objectification to conform to its expectations."[90] Demonstrative whites carried their desires and notions of blackness into Brown's theatrical experiment and, in a sense, demanded that the company function as their unrestrained, lower-class, "minor" alternative to Price's controlled, middle-class, "major" theater. As documented throughout this study, Brown's white patrons routinely obliterated any notion of a fourth wall and behaved as full-fledged creators of theatrical meaning. On most nights, with a well-placed potato or resounding bellow, Brown's white patrons could transform any remotely dramatic effort into an audience-dominated burlesque. By the end of such a performance, the "laughter-loving clerks" often deserved top billing.

Although far from the clearly delineated "blackness" of Five Points and its cellar subculture, Euro–New Yorkers increasingly regarded Brown's theaters as a cultural getaway where one could witness or indulge in unscripted, unbridled "black fun." Especially when Brown relocated to Greenwich Village, his remote black theater, far from "civilization," seemed the ideal environment for white working-class audiences to escape middle-class puritanism and upper-class gentility and to rediscover preindustrial pleasures, "demonstrative excess," and even anarchy. One can interpret the August 1822 physical assault as a metaphoric offensive against respectability and constraint, and therefore it is conceivable that the two white seamen perceived this riot as a spontaneous, extratheatrical burlesque in need of their contributions.

Ironically, manager Brown not only provided a remote space for whites to produce a most imaginative yet destructive evening of disorder, but the ex-seaman also cultivated a potentially dangerous site of counterpublicity precariously committed to innovation and subversion. Manager Brown was guilty of blurring theatrical and extratheatrical boundaries, particularly with the whiteface minstrel acts and stage Europeans that straddled the thin lines between fantasy and reality, high tragedy and common life. Manhattan's ambitious, versatile, and ambiguous African performers were not above interrupting *Richard III* with "Eveleen's Bower" or playing to an interactive crowd. The American Theatre was also part of that larger struggle to generate "a new set of codes," and Brown's new meanings were best exemplified by an integrated audience, orchestra, acting company, and an overall reclamation or reevaluation of "American."

However, the crucial difference is that Brown's actors wished to finish the subversive performances on their own terms. As a producer and playwright, Brown may have romanticized revolutionaries and rebels of various shades — Shotaway, Wallace, Jack Mansong — but he did so onstage and never expected his Minor or American Theatre to degenerate into an uncontrollably "rough" subculture. Brown's venture could certainly be interpreted as a working-class counterpublic sphere because he catered to waiters, chambermaids, and even slaves, but he was committed to balancing or at least intermingling working-class blacks with genteel dandies. Interestingly, on most evenings at the African Grove those two class-based cultural identities could be located in the same pleasure garden patron. Brown could not control the patrons he attracted or harness their performative ambitions but his advertisements continually targeted ladies and gentlemen, thus proving he had no intention of cultivating a male-dominated working-class subculture. In short, Brown, his performers, and his patrons of color were not consciously fostering the same subculture desired by working-class white leisure seekers. They attended to partake in a refined evening of fantasy, transgression, and training without fear of physical assault.

Brown's entertainments mingled various classes and races offstage and onstage, but unfortunately his "precept of contrariety" invited perilous misrecognitions or divergent interpretations of the performance moment. During the August riot, certain "demons of disorder" misread an Africanist embrace of irregularity as a partiality for misrule and mistook this seemingly chaotic atmosphere as their cue to participate in real mayhem, physical violence, and property damage. The working-class rioters failed, or refused, to appreciate the company's unresolved class oppositions, and sought to participate in an impromptu blackface travesty in which distinctly upper-class pretensions, like the ornate clothing worn by the actors, could be literally stripped from black bodies. The true "danger" was that Euro–New Yorkers could create their brand of "demonstrative excess" against Brown's institutional and aesthetic will. They successfully expropriated a marginal, alternative space fraught with fresh meanings and reconfigured Brown's "polite" yet progressive entertainments designed for ladies and gentlemen into an unrestrained, extratheatrical masking rite and class-conscious playground best suited for an approaching blackface minstrelsy.

Of course, such motivations may have been far from the consciousness of the seamen and circus workers who rioted in Brown's theater, but this speculative explanation rests on one undeniable and ugly truth: Brown's audiences and their expectations ultimately created the public profile for his institution. In the end, just as Noah named Brown's initial "African Grove" pleasure garden, white rioters indelibly marked the final days of Brown's managerial career. Over four eventful phases, this African American manager attempted to control his integrated audiences by erecting a partition in his pernicious pit and experimenting with other security measures to separate potentially unruly whites from refined blacks, but ultimately Brown failed to curb the mayhem. The symbiotic audience-performer relationship disintegrated completely when twenty white ruffians stripped the company of any aesthetic authority. Ruined costumes and bruised bodies aside, the representational silencing of Brown's American Theatre was the most disturbing outcome of what the *Spectator* termed an "unmanly outrage." When the company returned in the spring of 1823, Brown suffered more "demons of disorder" hungry for "demonstrative excess," exemplified by the white patrons during the Hewlett benefit, who, according to Snipe, insisted on outperforming the star attraction. Even after Brown's retirement, the aforementioned fictional playbills of July and August 1823, with their imagined antics of mob rule, continued to brand Manhattan's recently departed black theater as a den of disorder and "Negro" abuse. Sadly, for many leisure-minded Euro–New Yorkers, the unfortunate riot of August 1822 came to symbolize William Brown's theatrical legacy.[91]

The Euro-American aggression, the white misbehaving, commenced when M. M. Noah hyperbolized and demonized Brown's theater into a major threat to the "herrenvolk republic," or at least to Republican dominance. Next, cultural authority Stephen Price joined the offensive against black advancement by identifying black Shakespeareans, along with extratheatrical promenaders, as symbols of class insubordination and racial transgression. These two assaults resulted in freshly erected political and cultural boundaries that severely restricted black male political prospects and virtually excluded this African American company from certain dramatic territory. Still active despite the new borders, Brown's Minor or American Theatre appeared healthier and more arrogant than ever, until economically threatened circus workers, along with friends and family, literally stripped and financially dispossessed the haughty black actors.

Finally, written, performed, and extratheatrical minstrel practitioners, from Charles Mathews to random sailors, finished the job by revealing the endless comedic contradictions embedded in the seeming paradox of a black theater. Their representational salvos were most damaging because a physical assault on black bodies was limited by opportunity and mob energy, but minstrel material could travel effectively through magazines, newspapers, three-dimensional specialty acts, or word of mouth. Brenda Dixon Gottschild astutely characterizes minstrelsy as a "white-engineered construct" that "simultaneously sanctioned white suppression of and agency over the black male body."[92] Returning to the riot, this white suppression culminated when white rowdies forcefully divested black bodies, male and female, of their much coveted artistic agency and inescapably marked Brown's progressive, or at least ambitious, Minor/American/African Theatre as a "den of disorder." As for blackface's ultimate effectiveness in reinscribing white supremacy, Euro-American performers copied, revealed, ridiculed, and replaced African American artists, thus making it easier to fix or limit national notions of "blackness" to drunkenness, thievery, disorderly conduct, sexual licentiousness, and general inferiority. Minstrelsy banished black actors from the national laboratories until the late nineteenth century, when multitalented black performers reemerged as the "real coons" in minstrelsy, vaudeville, and eventually black musicals. But despite significant artistic advances it was already too late—entrenched Euro-constructed minstrels had effectively branded "blackness" and denied African Americans substantive representational control over their public imaging.

To Be — or Not to Be

IF WE ACCEPT THE anonymously authored minstrel playbills, Charles Mathews's intertextual black Shakespearean, and James Weldon Johnson's historical assessment, Brown's legacy was riotous, malapropic, and pathetically ridiculous. Or if we are truly interested in his legacy, we might end with the question: what had William Brown's entertainments truly "become" over this tumultuous, four-stage identity journey? With an almost schizophrenic zeal, Brown's initial pleasure garden had become an Africanist and Americanist artistic institution marked by a fundamental dynamism that was perpetually open to change and reinvention. One could argue that throughout these identity shifts Brown's entertainments were always "becoming" and "remaining" an African Grove appropriating and interrogating white privilege; a Minor Theatre cultivating an illegitimate counterpublic sphere but with major aspirations; an American Theatre revisioning the nation through audience integration and a range of stage Indians; and an African Company balancing all available stage African representations. Brown's legacy was theatrical and extratheatrical performances in which difference was not merely tolerated but fully embraced, actively remodeled, and consistently reproduced.

As an ambitious theatrical manager, Brown never intended for his social and theatrical experiments to be reduced to the mayhem of the August 1822 riot or the January 1822 Shakespeare arrests; therefore, during what appeared to be the final days of his producing career, he sought to remind Manhattan of all that his institution had "become." After committing major funds to new scenery and expanding his acting company for the momentous stage African evening of June 1823, Brown was in serious financial jeopardy.[1] In late June his African Company staged two benefit nights for its beleaguered manager, performances that presumably would decide the fate of these entertainments. The playbill announced: "On June 20 and 21, 1823 at the Theatre, in Mercer Street, In the rear of the 1 Mile Stone, Broadway, The Performers of the African Company have kindly united their services in order to contribute a Benefit to their Manager, Mr. Brown, who, for the first time, throws himself on the liberality of a generous public. Mr. Brown trusts that his unrelinquished exertions to please, will be justly considered by the Gentlemen and Ladies of this City, as on them depends his future support, and they can declare whether he is 'To be — or not to be — That is the question?' "[2] To settle this important question, the company needed to attract a significant crowd, and so it reduced the price of box seats to fifty cents and slashed pit and gallery seats to an all-time low of twenty-five cents. The troupe even discarded the three-tiered pricing system, which had failed miserably at establishing a less chaotic and more congenial climate in the "town." But as with previous productions, the referendum playbills targeted "the Gentlemen and Ladies of this City" and trusted that a more "refined" and "generous public" could peacefully assemble and decide Brown's future.

As for the program on these "To be — or not to be" evenings, Brown and his African Company ignored the city's stage African vogue and his largely white audience's preference for "minor," verging on minstrel, material. The African Company—with one white exception—refused to "please" patrons with strictly songs and dance and, instead, showcased elements from all of Brown's four phases, with a strong emphasis on those most American stage Indians. The referendum performances opened with a revival of Brown's *Drama of King Shotaway* and concluded with the debut of James Hewlett's second, historically rooted stage Indian ballet, *Balililon*. In the middle, the African Company featured the recently retired white veteran actor Smith performing "Collin's Ode on the Passions" and "Simpronius Speech for War." The troupe contrasted those serious recitations with a comic song by Smith and a vigorous hornpipe performed by the "terribly" black and intimidating Bates.[3] Unfortunately, black and white New Yorkers answered "not to be" to this eclectic program and Brown's entire "becoming." They said no to an African-controlled counterpublic sphere, an ever expanding repertoire, the subversively transracial stage Europeans and whiteface minstrels, the uniquely integrated acting company and orchestra, and finally the "variegated audience" that mirrored early national Manhattan.

The previous chapter examined why and how Euro–New Yorkers rejected this truly "American" theater, but to conclude this interpretive history, I consider the elusive black reactions to that white misbehavior and the nation's first African American theater. In this conclusion, I briefly address the extent to which Afro–New Yorkers defended Brown's experiments against white patrons who did not know how to behave at entertainments designed for ladies and gentlemen of varying colors. Then, I consider Brown's protégés and loyal supporters, who perpetuated the legacy of this distinctly African theater as the nation's model theater laboratory. The referendum performances provided Brown with a final opportunity to declare that his legacy was not limited to ridiculous evenings of audience-generated disorder but included rebellious stage Indians, hornpiping African Americans, and serious dramatic recitations. That dynamic combination of performance conventions guided the continued theatrical careers of Brown's progeny James Hewlett and Ira Aldridge.

There are a couple of interesting hypotheses as to why Afro–New Yorkers failed to rescue or publicly defend Brown's institution at this defining moment in late June 1823. Samuel Hay posits that when Brown faced white editorial and physical attacks, blacks did not rush to support him because he alienated Afro–New York. Specifically, Hay contends that black church leaders were noticeably silent during the assaults, and he concludes that this silence marked the first U.S. theater closed "because of collusion between bigoted whites and religious African-Americans."[4] But most religious or moral leaders, black or white, were antitheatrical and therefore loath to defend a theatrical manager. I would agree that unlike other African institutions, specifically churches, Brown failed to establish permanent ties to one area of the city and instead pursued a less-than-ideal nomadic existence, bouncing between the West Side, Park Row, and Greenwich Village. Also, Brown may have initially targeted black stewards and other servants barred from white gardens, but increased prices potentially eliminated many black patrons, and Brown's integrationist project nurtured a broader connection to all New Yorkers.

Minstrel revisionist Eric Lott claims that African Americans did not respond because they lacked the opportunities or outlets to contest publicly the destructive work of blackface minstrelsy in all its forms.[5] However, Afro–New Yorkers, including Brown himself, did react to the political, cultural, physical, and metaphorical assaults on the first African American theater. This "talking back" is simply difficult to recover because nineteenth-century black documents are scarce or not easily recognized. Immediately after the cultural assault or Shakespeare closing, Brown published a Minor Theatre playbill that read: "Mr. B believes it is through the influence of his *brother Managers* of the Park Theatre, that the police interfered. There is no doubt that *in fear of his opposition*, they took measures to quell his rivalry."[6] Brown flatly accused managers Price and Simpson of deploying local magistrates to close his theater. He believed they feared his economic rivalry, thus conceding black Shakespearean productions could flourish on Park Row.

Brown was not the only Afro–New Yorker to accuse Price. In his 1849 memoir, Aldridge recalled that he was preparing to star in *Romeo and Juliet* opposite an "Ethiopian" Juliet, but the production never occurred because "One Stephen Price, a manager of some repute became actually *jealous* of the success of the 'real Ethiopians,' and emissaries were employed to put them down."[7] Aldridge asserted that his "Ethiopian Juliet" was greatly perturbed by the closing and declared that "*nothing but* envy prevented the blacks from putting the whites completely out of countenance." Aldridge and his leading lady were fully confident that a black company could rival imported British stars at the Park Theatre, and after the unwarranted and suspicious arrests, their competitive potential was confirmed.

As for other voices, following the derisive, yet informative, review of *Richard III* in September 1821, Noah acknowledged receiving a "black letter," but he refused to print the item. Presumably, a concerned citizen wrote Noah questioning the review's satirical tone, and in response the editor explained that he was not making merry at the expense of "colored" citizens and that "our criticism on their play was not satire, it actually took place."[8] In August 1823, after the *Advocate* printed the second fictitious playbill, Noah received another letter objecting to those minstrel misrepresentations. This time Noah admitted that the playbill was pure invention, but he went on to state the author "meant no reflection on any individual of respectability."[9] Although Noah seemed to concede that the bill did target Brown's former establishment, he also implied that the retired manager was not an "individual of respectability."

Jonathan Sarna, Noah's biographer, reveals that the sardonic editor's incessant attacks on black voters, actors, and promenaders earned him the dubious distinction as the "blackman's bitterest enemy" in the minds of many Afro–New Yorkers.[10] By March 1827 Samuel Cornish and John B. Russwurm had endured enough of "Major Noah's Negroes"—especially the prostitutes and promenaders — and pledged to defend decent free people of color. In an early issue of *Freedom's Journal*, the two editors summarized the mission of their paper: "Daily slandered, we think that there ought to be some channel of communication between us and the public through which a single voice may be heard in defence of five hundred thousand free people of color."[11] Cornish and Russwurm's agenda was not to defend Brown specifically, but they were definitive in their condemnation of his detractors. In fact, well after the assaults in the summer of 1822, *Freedom's Journal* accused Noah of inciting poor whites against blacks: "Major Noah's efforts to increase the prejudice of the lower orders of society, against our brethren, is exceedingly unkind. The mob wants no leader. Blackguards among the whites, are sufficiently ready to insult decent people of colour. The major ought to have gained experience from the situation of his brethren in other countries, and learned to be more cautious."[12] In this last line, the editors refer to Noah's Jewish heritage, insinuating that a Jewish American should have been more sympathetic to the plight of another minority population. And although the *Journal* understood that "the mob" did not need Noah's encouragement to assault blacks, it believed that the influential editor intentionally agitated existing tensions between the races. Intentionally or unintentionally, Noah's early coverage increased Brown's visibility and alerted white hooligans to this remote Village theater, which contributed to the 1822 "mob" action.

Finally, the most forthright African American reaction comes from Brown's star actor and creative collaborator, James Hewlett, who stepped forward to answer directly and eloquently the metaphoric assault on the concept of a black-operated theater. When Hewlett was informed that Charles Mathews elected to ridicule instead of praise the dramatic capabilities of the "American Negro," this disappointed fellow thespian wrote a letter to, of all places, the *National Advocate*. Noah's brief introduction to this open letter of May 1824 explained that the *Advocate* only consented to publish the item because he believed it might "extract a smile" from his readers.[13] Noah was not publishing this piece as an advocate but as a written minstrel artist intending to entertain.[14] Of course, Hewlett's intentions in sharing the letter were certainly more earnest. This document stands as one of the rare examples of an Afro-American artist "talking back" to the perpetrators of minstrelsy, and in the process, the well-executed letter summarizes and affirms the inclusive agenda and intercultural legacy of Brown's African and American theater.

Hewlett opens the letter by mildly rebuking Mathews for not keeping in touch, thus confirming that the two performers had actually met. He then cuts to the heart of his complaint:

> But, my dear Mathews, in your new entertainment, I lament to say, you have given me cause of complaint. You have, I perceive by the programme of your performance, ridiculed our *African Theatre in Mercer-street* and burlesqued me with the rest of the negro actors, as you are pleased to call us—mimicked our styles—imitated our dialects—laughed at our anomalies—and lampooned, O shame, even our complexions. Was this well for a brother actor?—At your earnest and pressing solicitation, I performed several of my best parts; was perfect to a letter; and although it was a hazardous experiment, I even attempted your celebrated Mail Coach, which met with your unqualified approbation.[15]

Hewlett writes "negro actors, as you are pleased to call us," which suggests he was uncomfortable with the limiting connotations of the phrase "negro actors." Black or white, male or female, Hewlett and Brown believed that competent actors could realize any role. Also, Hewlett was dismayed or disappointed that his "brother actor" requested a private recital and approved the "perfect" material he witnessed, but then undermined that cordial artistic exchange by comedically exploiting "anomalies" like black dialects and phenotypic differences.

A few lines later, Hewlett waxes patriotic and subtly excoriates Mathews's jingoism. He writes: "[W]e were all unmercifully handled and mangled in your new entertainment called a trip among the Yankees." Hewlett objected to what he perceived as attacks not only on African Americans but on Hewlett's entire country, his fellow "Yankees." Along with Brown, Hewlett had vigorously promoted native-born artists, including himself, and a nationalist agenda, so he squarely identified with any and all U.S. characters lampooned or "mangled" in Mathews's caustic assessment of "the colonies." And on the interconnected question of racial and institutional identities, it is noteworthy that in the longer section cited earlier, Hewlett italicizes "African Theatre in Mercer-street." The italics imply that Hewlett, like Brown, did not accept this racially specific title, which the Manhattan media attached to Brown's company, and instead preferred more general or inclusive institutional profiles. In fact, when Hewlett managed the Village theater briefly after Brown's retirement, he chose to advertise as "Theatre, Mercer Street."[16] Hewlett's preference for a less racially marked institutional profile was by no means a rejection or attempted abdication of his African American reality. To the contrary, by defending disparaged "negro actors" and "Yankees," Hewlett simply reaffirmed Brown's integrationist project, which maintained that "African" and "American" were not mutually exclusive identities.

Continuing in a relentlessly respectful tone, Hewlett next chides, even derides, the English comedian for his inability to fathom a black claim on Shakespeare: "I was particularly chagrined at your scenes about the Negro Theatre. Why these reflections on our color, my dear Matthews, so unworthy of your genius and humanity, your justice and generosity? Our immortal bard says, (and he is *our* bard as well as yours, for we are all descendants of the Plantagenets, the white and red rose;) our bard Shakespeare makes sweet Desdemona say, 'I saw Othello's *visage* in his *mind.*'" In this section, Hewlett explains why Mathews failed to appreciate black actors as boundless artists unquestionably suitable for Shakespeare. Mathews could not visualize Othello as the Moor did "in his mind," as an intrepid general marked for greatness, but Desdemona was able to behold her husband as he perceived himself because she looked beyond his visage. As an English elitist who viewed all American actors as inferiors, Mathews would dismiss any "colonist," and especially any African American, who dared appropriate his Bard. Hewlett's letter contested both racial and national prejudice by firmly asserting that "Yankee" theatrical artists had as much claim on Shakespeare as the Brits. Furthermore, his bold declaration that Shakespeare is "our bard," repeated three times, was directed at cultural authority Stephen Price as much as Charles Mathews. After Brown's retirement, Hewlett displayed an intense commitment to "his" Shakespeare, and he perpetuated Brown's legacy of unbounded black actors by performing Shakespearean stage Europeans—and one stage African—from Brooklyn to Trinidad. Over four nights in January 1826, Hewlett transformed a converted Philadelphia schoolroom into the site of a one-man Shakespearean festival, featuring scenes from *Othello*, *Richard III*, *King Lear*, *Hamlet*, *Merchant of Venice*, and *Coriolanus*.[17]

His Yankeeness, Africanness, and Shakespeareanness established, Hewlett concentrated on "Othello's visage" to explain why Mathews failed to appreciate Hewlett's private recitations:

Now, when you were ridiculing the "chief black tragedian," and burlesquing the "real negro melody," was it my "mind," or my "visage," which should have made an impression upon you? Again, my dear

Matthews, our favorite bard makes Othello, certainly an interesting character, speak thus:

"*Haply*, for I am black."

That is as much as to say, 'tis happy that I am black. Here then we see a General proud of his complexion. In our free and happy country, custom and a meridian sun bath made some distinctions and classifications in the order of society relative to complexions, 'tis true, 'tis a pity, and pity 'tis, 'tis true"; but in England, where these anomalous distinctions are unknown, nay, where international marriages and blending of colors are sometimes seen, what warrant can you have for lampooning our complexion?

Hewlett claims that the English comedian failed to acknowledge his "perfect" dramatic interpretations because Mathews could not overcome the complexion, the visage. He realizes that the newly independent United States was preoccupied with race, but he expected a citizen from a country that condones interracial marriages to be less concerned with color. Although Hewlett never expected Mathews to ignore his mulatto complexion completely or "not see color," the aspiring actor did not wish to have his coincidental physical distinction used against him. For Mathews, the color and the dramatic content were ill-matched, irreconcilable, even paradoxical; therefore, "Negro" and Shakespeare remained polar opposites and a malapropic gold mine. By highlighting Mathews's fixation on "anomalous distinctions," Hewlett's letter also indicted Euro-American minstrel artists who exploited exterior or physical differences between the races while failing to appreciate Afro-America's intellectual and artistic capacities.

By no means was this performer of color ashamed of his yellowish tint, and to emphasize that point Hewlett borrowed a line from *Othello*, "haply, for I am black," which he interpreted to mean that the Moorish general recognized the accidental nature of his complexion but still remained proud or "happy" about his complexion. More than 140 years before Stokely Carmichael coined the slogan "Black Power" and James Brown exhorted Afro-America to say it loud, "I'm black and I'm proud," Hewlett essentially proclaimed that nature had made him black, and he gloried in that reality. Notice that when he quotes and explains Shakespeare's prototypical dramatic stage African, Hewlett writes "our favorite bard" for the fourth time, again thumbing his nose at cultural authorities as represented by Mathews, Price, and Noah.

Brown had trained Hewlett quite well. Confronted with Brown's recent demise and the ominous approach of minstrelsy, Hewlett remained Shakespeare's proud representative and a proud black man. As a theatrical producer, Brown allowed African Americans — and the occasional Caucasian — full access to a range of cultural and theatrical representations. He never assumed that a predominantly African troupe should perform strictly stage African material, and Brown's actors flourished under this artistic freedom. In spite of rapidly proliferating theatrical boundaries, Hewlett continued performing roles seemingly at odds with his complexion. By staging all available Americans, Hewlett and his fellow black actors invaded those powerful mimetic laboratories where an early national United States constructed and rehearsed its past, present, and future.

Hewlett fully understood where minstrel gestures like Mathews's imaginative lampooning of darker Americans and his burlesque of an allegedly "real negro melody" were headed. Minstrelsy's metaphorical assault on progressive blacks not only severely undermined Hewlett's professional prospects but also greatly restricted early U.S. theater's range of racial and ethnic representation. Before minstrelsy's emergence, many American artists, not just this black company, disconnected "visages" from culture to construct stage Indians, stage Africans, and stage Europeans. David Roediger makes the excellent argument that minstrelsy may have fostered "astonishing ethnic diversity," yet "this extreme cultural pluralism was at the same time a liquidation of ethnic and regional cultures into blackface, and ultimately into a largely empty whiteness."[18] Minstrel caricatures expanded and overwhelmed the pluralism of Irish, German, and other ethnic characters to create an all-consuming blackface tradition that ultimately defined and serviced white supremacy. But as Hewlett illustrates in his letter, by focusing on his "visage" instead of his "mind" and "perfect" performances, Mathews burlesqued "real negro" actors and rendered them laughable and therefore dismissible. Blackface minstrelsy, in its written and staged varieties, may have facilitated some white encounters with "low status" black culture, but as white artists assumed complete control of racial representation, they simultaneously removed black actors, writers, directors, choreographers, and even audiences from the national workshops. Hewlett's letter demonstrated a profound understanding of that process of expropriation.

To close his frank and prophetic letter, Hewlett offers a few prescient words on the "mind" versus "visage" question, which one of America's most revered human rights leaders would later echo. Hewlett advises Mathews: "In short, you have my entire good wishes; but my dear Matthews, remember when you next ridicule the 'tincture of the skin' not to forget the texture of the mind." When tempted in the future to exploit obvious stereotypes predicated on color, Hewlett writes, Mathews should instead consider the mind, content, and character of his subject; in other words, assess black actors based on how they acquit themselves in their roles, not on popular lore denigrating black features, social behaviors, and mental capacities. Many years later at a Washington, D.C., rally, Martin Luther King Jr. addressed a gathering of racially and religiously diverse Americans with a strikingly similar message. He challenged the United States to value the "content of our character" rather than the color of "our skin"—and if there is any confusion about King's "our," he was referring to all Americans, not simply African Americans. In his letter of May 1824, a frustrated but respectful Hewlett reaffirmed Brown's legacy, which consistently valued content over color and lauded black artists' extraordinarily original capacity to make significant contributions to national culture.

Not finished with Mathews, toward the end of 1824 Hewlett headed for London to stage a personal confrontation with his fellow actor and to further his theatrical career. Regrettably, he accomplished neither goal. Mathews briefly mentions Hewlett in a letter to his wife: "Mr. Hannibal Hewlet has been here, and gave an 'At Home,' and actually applied to Lewis for an engagement. He went to London, as he said, to challenge me, for ridiculing him in a part he never played. I cannot find any body who saw him; but he performed here two or three nights."[19] Hewlett's direct challenge never materialized, and despite Mathews's statement that Hewlett performed in London, no records exist documenting his appearance on the English stage. By the winter of 1825, Hewlett had returned to the states. George Odell claims that Hewlett spent his last theatrical days inhaling exhilarating gas as an "aboriginal ecce homo" at the New York Museum. Odell summarizes Hewlett's museum appearance with these fitting words: "Herein lurks a real tragedy of a negro's thwarted ambition."[20] Theater scholar Barbara Lewis, on the basis of Odell's research, also concludes that Hewlett's career ended as a museum oddity and further pronounces: "James Hewlett could easily serve as an example of the fate of aspiring African Americans, reaching, at an inauspicious time, like dandies aggressively desirous of breaking through the racial boundaries imposed on them in their native land."[21] The aforementioned, rapidly erected cultural boundaries in the United States were proving impassable, a lesson well learned and perhaps accepted by Brown,

Hewlett, and Aldridge. Yet Hewlett refused to concede his career to the historical accident of being born black at this "inauspicious" early national moment and decided to create opportunities and representational freedom in a less culturally restrictive locale.

After his unfortunate appearances as the "aboriginal ecce homo" made it painfully clear that Hewlett would never realize his dream of becoming a respected actor in his native country, Brown's protégé blazed a trail for Port-of-Spain, Trinidad, West Indies. With the rise of minstrelsy in the late 1820s and early 1830s, Hewlett had to escape the United States to reaffirm his commitment to Shakespeare and other components of Brown's legacy. Hewlett headlined at Port-of-Spain's Royal Victoria Theatre roughly from December 13 to December 24, 1837. Speciously billed as "from the Royal Coburg Theatre, London," Hewlett appeared with the permission of the governor of Trinidad and the Board of Cabildo, or the local Port-of-Spain government.[22]

In the boldly contrarian or delicately balanced tradition of Brown's American Theatre, Hewlett's Trinidadian residency combined "minor" and "major" material featuring a triracial range of theatrical characters. Over three evenings, Hewlett performed "major" roles such as Rolla, the rebellious Peruvian stage Indian; Othello, the tragic stage African general; and his favorite, Richard, the sadistic but beguiling stage European. For balance, the already accomplished actor, singer, dancer, and choreographer turned dramatist and composer to create a purely escapist "minor" musical about Port-of-Spain. The *Port of Spain Gazette* announced that this musical would be "a sort of 'Tom and Jerry' affair, light and lively, full of entertainment and fun. It is in him, he knows, and out it must come, and will during the Holidays."[23] Some sixteen years earlier, Brown had adapted Moncrieff's *Tom and Jerry* into a rousing, explorative tour of his current home, Manhattan, and titled the new piece *Tom and Jerry; or Life in New York*; now Hewlett intended to do the same for his newly adopted Port-of-Spain.[24] After the dramatic evenings and the original musical, Hewlett vanished from the historical record.

During the same period, Brown's other protégé, Ira Aldridge, encountered comparatively greater success performing stage Europeans and stage Africans throughout Europe. Aldridge continued and perhaps perfected Brown's stage Europeans with whiteface performances of Shylock, Macbeth, and most notably King Lear in European capitals like St. Petersburg, Russia.[25] Aldridge also transplanted Brown's balancing act of competing stage African images, Othellos opposing Mungos; he continued the signifying practices or artistic "contrariety" cultivated at the always "becoming" Minor/American/African Theatre.

Bernth Lindfors, theater scholar and researcher, has examined the European performances in which Aldridge exploited the two major varieties of Euro-constructed blackness to contest the racial preconceptions of his white patrons. Conditioned by Mathews, Colman, and Bickerstaff, most Europeans anxiously anticipated the images of farcical stage Africans when Aldridge, "the African Roscius," performed at their theater. Invariably, this black headliner disappointed the expectant audience by opening with Othello, a tragic stage African, and closing with Mungo, a comic stage African. As for the effect of this misdirection on the audience, Lindfors writes: "Only now, having already witnessed his polished performance in a serious role, they knew that he was *playing* the fool—in short, that he was acting a part, not manifesting his own innate racial peculiarities. At this point their admiration for Aldridge grew even greater, for they saw that he was a genuine professional capable of successfully sustaining a wide variety of roles in both comedy and tragedy."[26] Lindfors maintains that Aldridge's most intriguing and influential roles were the comedic characters, like the prototypical Mungo, in which he "appeared" to highlight negative African stereotypes. By "playing" African fools in conjunction with African heroes, Aldridge subverted nineteenth-century notions of biologically rooted racial characteristics. The "Signifying Flunkey," as Lindfors aptly describes Aldridge's cultural work, contested the belief that Mungo's dialect was an inherent and inescapable racial peculiarity that marked all blacks as inferior. In short, Brown's most celebrated pupil demonstrated throughout Europe—where stage Africans originated—that these characters were simply roles, not uncomplicated reality. Like all members of Brown's company, Aldridge was trained in a range of representations from foolish to serious, dramatic to comedic, racially white to black—an encounter of opposites or possibilities that might or might not correlate with real life. Yet Brown's training ground also taught Aldridge how to invest seemingly hopeless Euro-constructed Africans with sincere emotions and motivations.

Beyond this stage African balancing act, the most provocative components of Brown's artistic legacy were stage Europeans and whiteface minstrel acts. In the first African Grove, Noah noticed, yet refused to accept, the implications of these whiteface training sessions, but by September 1821 he acknowledged that something was definitely brewing in the remote Greenwich Village and included the dangerous "colored" diversions in his political assault on advancing Afro–New Yorkers. Noah understood that both a black theater and significant African American voters could usher Afro–New Yorkers into the mainstream of Manhattan's cultural and political life. From holding garden councils on the latest machinations of the "mob" to singing Scottish revolutionary anthems before integrated urban audiences, these acts represented important racial crossings. As Afro–New Yorkers celebrated, satirized, and identified with a range of white "others," they bridged the increasing divide between an allegedly debased blackness and a privileged whiteness, and the distinctions between "other" and "self" became negligible. Ultimately, such acts exposed the aspirations of performers like James Hewlett, S. Welsh, or the entire black community, and the dual performance traditions prepared black stewards, domestics, ex-slaves, and slaves for full participation in broader U.S., Caribbean, and European cultures. Beginning with the nation's earliest revolutionaries, "American" identity was rooted in racial and ethnic masking.[27] And for early national blacks, multiple masks of whiteness facilitated a significant transition from dependent slave to free individual or from second-class subject to full-fledged citizen.

Progressive Afro–New Yorkers, such as Brown, eventually converted their masking in expressly theatrical or leisure contexts into concrete political, social, and philanthropic actions. A final legacy of Brown's entertainment was the racial uplift and avenues for broader participation that he provided for an expanding and maturing free black community. In the end, Brown's institutions had "become" a kind of home for Afro–New York, a visible, tangible communal center. Elizabeth Bethel, commenting on free black institutions, writes: "In a world where some were free but others still enslaved these organizations formed the infrastructure of an emerging moral community, organized around two interconnected values: racial unity and racial uplift."[28] With leisure-minded blacks barred from white gardens, Brown interceded in the name of racial unity by creating a garden for his fellow stewards, other free blacks, and slaves. As a theater manager, Brown uplifted Afro–New York by providing a space for an ex-slave like Charles Taft and a Park Place chambermaid like S. Welsh to develop their mimetic potential. Even as the enterprising ex-steward courted whites, he remained as much a part of Afro–New York's nascent infrastructure as African churches and mutual relief societies.

Morality was never Brown's defining principle, but in discussing his venture, Barbara Lewis notes an "aggressive cultural nineteenth-century impetus within the African-American community" that "manifested itself early in the theatre." She argues that "by its very nature, theatre is a collective enterprise, and its presence in a community suggests more than a minimum level of cultural cohesion."[29] Brown's theater did indeed become a site of cultural cohesion for Afro–New Yorkers throughout the city, serving the artistic and social needs of an emergent black community. But beyond cohering Afro–New York, the integrationist agenda of Brown's American Theatre attempted, like no other cultural institution, to unify Manhattan across racial and class lines. More important, the theatrical and extratheatrical transracial appropriations of whiteness, the integrated acting company, and the "variegated" audience actively trained African Americans for broader participation in civic, national, and international affairs.

Even after Brown's retirement from theatrical production, his Greenwich Village institution facilitated Afro–New Yorker involvement in international philanthropy. In his first "African Grove" article, M. M. Noah essentially claimed that international empathy and philanthropy were white entitlements well beyond the grasp of black cooks and chambermaids. But Afro–New Yorkers did extend their political interests and sentiments beyond racial and national borders. In the winter of 1823–24, Manhattan papers published numerous editorials and articles on the long-standing Greek independence struggle against the oppressive Turks, and the dailies also ran many advertisements for Greek balls and other fund-raisers. New York's "colored gentry" planned its own charity ball at Brown's Mercer Street theater on January 1, 1824, to aid the Greek rebels and ran the following announcement in the *Evening Post*: "Gentlemen of color who are desirous of aiding the cause of the Greeks, are invited to attend at the Society Room in Orange street, on Monday next at 7 o'clock, P.M. in order to make arrangements for a Ball, to be given in the Mercer street Theatre on the evening of the 1st of January, (the anniversary of the Abolition Society.) This appeal, it is hoped will be felt with peculiar force on that day, which cannot fail most powerfully to recall the descendants of Africans, the blessings of freedom, and prompt them to unite with their white brethren in resisting the arm of despotism whenever it may be reared."[30] By organizing this ball, Manhattan's "colored" citizens participated in a national fascination and identification with the Greeks, and the phrase "white brethren" implies that blacks could empathize with the Greeks as much as, if not more than, Euro-Americans. The benefit planners assumed that blacks would feel the Greek plight with "peculiar force" on January 1 because that date commemorated the supposed end of U.S. involvement in the international slave trade.

Through a merger of Greek and African American causes, proactive Afro–New Yorkers intended to spend their January 1—usually reserved for Thanksgiving Day—celebrating the abolition of the slave trade and raising relief funds for their "white brethren" across the Atlantic. And this unique Thanksgiving Day–Greek Ball combination event was not the only act of black philanthropy planned for Brown's former theater. A playbill for January 1824 announced James Hewlett's appearance at the Mercer Street theater in a Greek benefit performance.[31] Over three seasons, Brown's productions and social experiments promoted similar intercultural or interracial commonalities, so it is not surprising his theater was used for this kind of international fund-raising. Both Greek fund-raisers demonstrated how central Brown's institution had become to Afro–New York's political and cultural activity, but, more important, they proved that African Americans continued to reach beyond their immediate social circumstances to foster connections with similarly persecuted and oppressed communities.

Today, the name "African Grove," an institutional identity first introduced by Noah, has been recovered and reinvigorated by contemporary African American theater artists and academics. In 1998 playwright August Wilson, in conjunction with Dartmouth College professors Victor Leo Walker II and William W. Cook, created the African Grove Institute for the Arts (AGIA), which is "dedicated to creating, promoting and supporting artistic excellence, advancement, and preservation of Black Theatre and Performing Arts."[32] The AGIA's goals incorporate a central value or tenet of William Brown's legacy, specifically that the national theatrical laboratories work best when all citizens have equal access to the symbolic controls, the modes of representation. Unequal access to representation prevented a working-class subculture like blackface minstrelsy from becoming a genuine site of interracial exchange and reduced that national art form to a demeaning, white supremacist endorsement of "Negro" inferiority.[33]

One could argue that much like this wayward blackface tradition, the original self-other binary that facilitated early national definition was also an outgrowth of unequal access to representational and political resources. Euro-Americans crafted stage Indians and forged a national identity by expropriating native customs and conquering the first Americans. Brown recognized this imbalance of access in the early 1820s and created a garden and theaters where African Americans could contribute to the nation's cultural logic. More recently, theater director George Wolfe and theorist Brenda Dixon Gottschild have concluded that the self-other binary, predicated on racial or cultural territory, is an antiquated, even untenable concept for a contemporary United States. Wolfe explains in a 1994 statement: "[W]e are now at a time in this country when we are all up in each other's Other. There is no 'Other' anymore. We'd like to think that there is. We keep on trying to move out and out into the suburbs or further and further away, but there is no escape anymore. Everybody is up in each other's story."[34] Brown's artists rejected the notion that exclusively white, black, or red material was best suited for certain performers and allowed their African selves to intersect with as many "other" stories as possible. Gottschild views this demolition of the binary as a process of recognition: "When we are able to see the African reflection as the image of our culture, then finally we will behold ourselves fully—as Americans—in the mirror. At that point it will be silly to talk about Africanist presences as 'the Africanist contribution.' That is the outdated language of disenfranchisement, the mindset that implies that the European is something bigger or better into which the African—the Other—is subsumed. But there is no Other, *we* are it."[35] Brown understood the significance of Africans being perceived as Americans, or part of that "we." He intently pursued enfranchisement while providing avenues of equal access to presumptuous African Americans like James Hewlett, Ira Aldridge, and S. Welsh. As the allegedly "low status" group, many Afro–New Yorkers challenged the binary by raiding the center and freely appropriating the culture of the dominant, "high status" group. They experimented in blatantly public labs, from Park Row to Broadway, and with "real Americans" watching, they contested the presumption that whiteness always subsumes or consumes red, black, or brown "others."

As manager of the African Grove, American Theatre, Minor Theatre, and African Company, Brown realized that national possibilities like diversity and enfranchisement did not have to deteriorate into divisiveness or balkanization. But Brown and his collaborators ultimately suffered for this progressive outlook because many Euro-Americans, from Timothy Dwight to the "laughter-loving clerks," were reluctant to accept difference and relinquish control. Brown's initial experiments with audience integration were thwarted by the increased presence of rowdy, misbehaving whites and the unfortunate exodus of "refined" ladies and gentleman of color. And gradually, blackface innovators working in all available representational modes—

print, theatrical, extratheatrical—would bury this model representational workshop beneath a mound of minstrelsy.

Blackface notwithstanding, it is crucial to recover these silenced "other" authors—no matter how seemingly inconsequential and brief their careers—and integrate them into the national narrative, the collective act of imagining the United States. With this project, I have aimed to reinsert William Brown, James Hewlett, S. Welsh, and this instructive African American company back into the complicated process of early national formation and, in the process, to remind some readers how this profoundly diverse country creates and occasionally diminishes itself.

If we decide to revisit and expand our notions of what "American" means and to discard the defensive position that certain cultures can be owned, authenticated, or protected, or that certain populations must remain fixed or essentialized, we can recover Brown's legacy. And if we rediscover his triracial, multiethnic, transcultural performative and managerial practices, more contemporary theater practitioners can cultivate expansive institutions that actively attract and honestly represent an entire nation. With ethnic and cultural explosions and implosions awaiting this country in the twenty-first century, the symbolic controls must be shared, and U.S. theaters—as well as other media outlets—cannot afford to underestimate, ignore, or reject any potential authors and audiences. If we understand that "we are it," the United States can finally retire all those available "others" that have facilitated national definition. The country can rest assured that we have done the work—thanks in large part to "minor" contributors like William Brown—and forged a complex and decidedly heuristic national past, present, and future in the New World.

NOTES

INTRODUCTION

1. *National Advocate*, August 3, 1821, 2.

2. As an unwritten rule, Euro-American pleasure gardens did not admit blacks, but not until 1826 did a white garden, the elite Vauxhall Gardens in Greenwich Village, actually advertise "no admittance to coloured people." See *New York American*, May 4, 1826, 3.

3. Several scholars have contributed to the growing body of primary documentation on William Brown, his institutions, and his performers. Some of these historians-researchers include George Odell, Errol Hill, Samuel Hay, and George A. Thompson Jr. My interpretive history builds on their important research and my own archival investigations of Brown, his company members, nineteenth-century U.S. theater and performance, and early national New York.

4. In particular, Timothy Dwight, essayist, clergyman, and Yale president, envisioned an ethnically diverse, but specifically Caucasian, United States. In volume 3 of his *Travels in New England and New York* (1822), Dwight expounded on the inherent dangers in Manhattan's volatile amalgam of European ethnicities.

5. Different versions of this legendary sign have surfaced in various histories. The sign was first mentioned in a social history of black Manhattan compiled by researchers Roi Ottley and William Weatherby in the 1930s but published in the 1960s. An alternate version of the placard, without the words "of colour," reemerged in a 1960s article on black theater by Langston Hughes. Unfortunately, these secondary sources do not provide a primary source for Brown's bold pronouncement. See Ottley and Weatherby, *Negro in New York*; Langston Hughes, "The Negro and American Entertainment"; and Mitchell, *Black Drama*.

6. Theater historian Samuel Hay made these remarks on Brown's lineage at a National Endowment for the Humanities symposium entitled "Into the Spotlight: A History of African-American Theatre," February 1993. Errol Hill also believes that Brown was a Carib; see his article, "The Revolutionary Tradition in Black Drama."

7. Hall, "Cultural Identity and Diaspora," 394. Stuart Hall's work has been illuminating and foundational, but more recently a group of scholars has offered a postpositivist realist approach to cultural identity that rejects the fixity of identity while also making a strong case for the social location and political implications of experience. See Moya and Hames-Garcia, *Reclaiming Identity*.

8. Gottschild, *Digging the Africanist Presence*, 5.

9. By extratheatrical, I mean popular performances occurring beyond the conventional stage such as outdoor exhibitions, street festivals, and other "social rituals" that provide a cultural work similar to theater. Bruce McConachie's "Towards a Postpositivist Theatre History" (1985) challenged theater historians to investigate "social rituals" that, like theater and drama, "legitimate historical persuasions." In terms of performance in the everyday, anthropologist Erving Goffman, in *The Presentation of Self in Everyday Life* (1959), first used a dramaturgical approach to study how individuals construct and present the "self" in various contexts or frames. In *Schism and Continuity in an African Society* (1957), *Drama, Fields, and Metaphors* (1974), *From Ritual to Theatre* (1982), and other works, Victor Turner developed the concept of "social drama" as a tool for analyzing social relations at critical moments in the life of a society. Turner has connected the "social drama"'s processual form to aesthetic dramas and other cultural performances. Richard Schechner's foundational performance studies work, *Between Theater and Anthropology* (1985), reconnects anthropology with the arts by erasing distinctions between everyday social performance and conventional theatrical practice. Finally, Dale Cockrell's recent study *Demons of Disorder* (1997) offers an exemplary discussion of minstrel theatrics and related extratheatrical social rituals like Callithumpian Bands.

10. On the centrality of theater and mimicry in our early national foundation, see Roach, "The Emergence of the American Actor," and McConachie, *Melodramatic Formations*.

11. Ellison, "Change the Joke," 107.

12. Philip Deloria's cultural study *Playing Indian* (1998) explains the Native American mask in terms of Euro-America's dual pursuits of racial conquest and self-creation. He also concludes that "othering" in America or "wearing the mask" ultimately leads to a self-conscious understanding of the real "me underneath." Deloria's position had been articulated previously by anthropologist Victor Turner, in *From Ritual to Theatre*, where he claims theater or performance has become the domain of "the individual-in-general" or "the real self."

13. Roach, *Cities of the Dead*, 5.

14. Awkward, *Negotiating Difference*, 14.

15. As limiting as racial stereotyping can be, as evident in the irreversible harm blackface minstrelsy has done to African American representation, significant national creation and anxiety can still be uncovered in many examples of racial or transracial "play." Ralph Ellison was one of the first intellectuals to articulate how Euro-America's complex preoccupation with that black-sooted mask was really about whiteness in America; see "Change the Joke." Anticipating more recent blackface minstrel revisionists like Alexander Saxton or Eric Lott, Ellison declared that minstrelsy's extreme popularity was an outgrowth of larger, contradictory, and unresolved Euro-American issues surrounding race. For more revisionist scholarship on minstrelsy, see Wilentz, *Chants Democratic*; Saxton, *The Rise and Fall of the White Republic*; Roediger, *Wages of Whiteness*; Lott, *Love and Theft*; Cockrell, *Demons of Disorder*; Lhamon, *Raising Cain*; and Mahar, *Behind the Burnt Cork Mask*.

16. Mahar, "Black English in Early Blackface Minstrelsy," 19.

17. Bhabha, *Location of Culture*, 74–75.

18. Ibid., 67.

19. Ibid., 70.

20. See Du Bois, *Souls of Black Folk*; Bhabha, *Location of Culture*; and Hall, "Culture, Community, Nation."

21. Gilroy, "'. . . To Be Real,'" 14.

22. Gottschild, *Digging the Africanist Presence*, 13.

CHAPTER ONE

1. Cultural theorist and media critic Richard Dyer's extensive work, especially *White* (1997), provides an indispensable foundation for any consideration of whiteness and representation. Dyer, along with David Roediger, Noel Ignatiev, and Ruth Frankenberg, are some of the major researchers in the growing theoretical field of whiteness studies. These scholars are primarily interested in how whites construct, ignore, or acknowledge whiteness. My discussion is more concerned with how blacks understand, construct, and perform whiteness.

2. In May 1998 the Children Now Foundation of Oakland published a study titled "A Different World: Children's Perceptions of Race and Class in Media." This revealing report examines how children register inequities in the media's portrayal of race and class. One key finding of this report was that "all children agree that the roles of boss, secretary, police officer and doctor in television programs are usually played by White people while the roles of criminal and maid/janitor on television are usually played by African-Americans." Here is just one of many modern examples of media disseminating or reaffirming black and white cultural assumptions. These linkages not only permeate our representational modes but circulate in the painfully more realistic worlds of American classrooms where African American students who ruin curves with high scores or speak "standard" English are often accused of "acting white" and their "blackness" is questioned. Signithia Fordham and John Ogbu have studied this educational dilemma in their article "Black Students' School Success: Coping with the 'Burden of Acting White.'" More recently, John H. McWhorter's *Losing the Race: Self-Sabotage in Black America* (2000) presents a provocative personal and analytical assessment of Afro-America's relationship to whiteness, blackness, and educational achievement.

3. *National Advocate*, August 3, 1821, 2.

4. Molette and Molette, *Black Theatre*, 33.

5. Earl Lewis, "To Turn on a Pivot," 774; Herskovits, *The Myth of the Negro Past*; and Stuckey, *Slave Culture*.

6. Mintz and Price, *The Birth of African-American Culture*.

7. See Du Bois, *Souls of Black Folk*; Bhabha, *Location of Culture*; Hall, "Cultural Identity and Diaspora"; and Gilroy, *The Black Atlantic*.

8. Bethel, *The Roots of African-American Identity*, 117; Stuckey, *Slave Culture*.

9. For information on Manhattan's AMEZ church and other black churches, see

Rush, *A Short Account of the Rise and Progress of the African Methodist Episcopal Church in America*; Browne, *A Brief History of the AMEZ Church*; and Swift, *Black Prophets of Justice*. The background on the African Society comes from Zuille, *Historical Sketch of the New York African Society for Mutual Relief*, and Swan, "John Teasman."

10. Hall, "Cultural Identity and Diaspora," 398.

11. Gilroy, "'. . . To Be Real,'" 14–15.

12. For the blackface minstrelsy revisionists, see note 15 to the Introduction.

13. Cockrell, *Demons of Disorder*, 53.

14. Szwed, "Race and the Embodiment of Culture," 27.

15. Roach, *Cities of the Dead*, 236.

16. Robinson, "Forms of Appearance of Value," 237. For a range of other theoretical positions on passing, see Ginsberg, *Passing and the Fictions of Identity*, and Harper, "Passing for What?"

17. My introduction to "false consciousness" and symbolic hegemony began with Eugene Genovese's *Roll, Jordan, Roll* and later James Scott's *Weapons of the Weak*. Both Genovese and Scott build on Antonio Gramsci's *Selections from the Prison Notebooks*. Scott and Genovese, firmly based in Gramsci, conclude that subordinate groups can break free of this "false consciousness" and become resistant and politically motivated agents.

18. Awkward, *Negotiating Difference*, 181.

19. See Herskovits, *The Myth of the Negro Past*.

20. Trollope, *Domestic Manners*, 309–10; *Memoirs of Charles Mathews*, 3:306. English travel journals are among the most rewarding and misleading primary sources for reconstructing the early national period. As her travel journal attracted readers in the United States, Trollope developed a reputation as a Negrophile. Therefore, one could disqualify her comments as biased; however, Charles Mathews recorded similar impressions during his early 1820s visit, and based on his elitist attitudes and satiric treatment of all Americans, he would never be mistaken for a friend of the "American Negro."

21. Houston Baker, *Modernism and the Harlem Renaissance*, 50.

22. Ibid., 85.

23. Ibid., 85, 114 n60.

24. Gates, *The Signifying Monkey*, 88, 124.

25. The literature on inversion rituals is voluminous, and some significant sources are Max Gluckman's *Rituals of Rebellion in South-East Africa* (1954) and Mikhail Bakhtin's *Rabelais and His World* (1968).

26. Douglass, *Narrative of the Life of Frederick Douglass*, 300.

27. Victor Turner, *From Ritual to Theatre*, 28; Natalie Davis, *Society and Culture in Early Modern France*, 122–23.

28. James Scott, *Domination and the Arts of Resistance*, chap. 1.

29. *Minutes of the Common Council*, 10:566.

30. Today, the term "dandy" carries the connotation of effeminacy or homosexuality, but such was not exclusively the case in early nineteenth-century New York.

31. The first article appeared in the *National Advocate*, February 27, 1824, 2, and the second article in ibid., April 20, 1824, 2.

32. Stansell, *City of Women*, 87–89, 164–65.

33. *National Advocate*, August 3, 1821, 2.

34. Rooted in Isaiah Berlin, Victor Turner defines leisure, a distinctly urban phenomenon, as "freedom from the forced, chronologically regulated rhythms of factory and office and a chance to recuperate and enjoy natural, biological rhythms again"; see Turner, *From Ritual to Theatre*, 36–37. Of course, the same leisure release was coveted by white urbanites, but for Afro–New Yorkers, a most compelling attraction was the explicitly public and rebellious potential of this weekly ritual. Turner also describes leisure as "freedom to transcend social structural limitations" and "freedom to enter, even to generate new symbolic worlds." Far from exemplifying the conservative view of ritual, Manhattan's black promenaders did not stroll to resolve racial tensions but worked to generate a new public transcript.

35. *New York Evening Post*, August 24, 1820, 2.

36. The *Spectator* was a weekly version of the daily *Commercial Advertiser*. All of my references will come from the *Spectator*, which is the more accessible version of the newspaper.

37. In addition, historians Shane White and Graham White have contributed to the discourse on African American urban style through their studies of black balls, parades, and other public displays. The Whites have assessed Manhattan's black promenaders and conclude "black dandys and dandizettes" not only took extreme pride in their well-groomed appearance, but by donning expensive clothing and other accessories, they gave fresh meaning to the "trappings of the elite." Trading on Claude Lévi-Strauss's terminology, Shane White and Graham White characterize these social performers as "bricoleurs" who have invested dominant Euro-American culture with their African past to create a distinctively black hybrid style; see White and White, *Stylin'*, 101. Shane White further argues, reflecting Natalie Zemon Davis's balanced perspective on inverse rituals, that Afro–New York's urban fusion of European and African cultures is too complex to be read simply as accommodation or resistance; see White, *Somewhat More Independent*, 194–99, 202–3. Incorporation of the original form is necessary with any act of revision, and when slaves or second-class black citizens settled into elite white fashions, some deference, accommodation, and even homage was understandable, especially given the primacy of European culture on all levels of U.S. society.

38. *New York Evening Post*, August 24, 1820, 2.

39. James Scott, *Domination and the Arts of Resistance*, 14.

40. Ibid., 8–9.

41. Theater historian Samuel Hay provides a well-researched and plausible assessment of Noah and Brown's relationship in *African-American Theatre*. Hay examines the political and cultural antagonisms embedded in Noah's *National Advocate* coverage and concludes that from day one Noah was intent on sabotaging Brown's endeavor. In fact, Hay contends that Sheriff Noah personally closed the pleasure garden after complaints from Brown's neighbors.

42. See Gilfoyle, *City of Eros.*

43. See Smith, "Ira Aldridge." This article claims that Brown arrived at 38 Thomas Street as early as 1816, but not until 1820 did tax assessment records and *Longworth's American Almanac; a New York City Directory* place William Brown as one of several renters at this address. Also, 1821 tax assessment records show that Brown was one of the rare African American residents; see Thompson, *A Documentary History.* As early as 1795, however, Afro–New Yorkers had created a separate black church, the African Methodist Episcopal Zion Church, at Leonard and Church Streets on the West Side; see Browne, *A Brief History of the AMEZ Church.*

44. Homberger's *Historical Atlas of New York City* includes municipal maps of Five Points, the West Side, City Hospital, City Hall Park, and the rest of 1820 New York City.

45. On the local census, see *National Advocate*, February 16, 1821, 2. For Five Points history, see Anbinder, *Five Points*; Gilje, *The Road to Mobocracy*; and Gilfoyle, *City of Eros.*

46. Shane White has written about cellar entertainments in his history of free Afro–New Yorkers, *Somewhat More Independent*, and Leslie Harris explores this subterranean culture in "Creating the African-American Working Class."

47. *Freedom's Journal*, November 7, 1828.

48. On the naval crew, see Bolster, "'To Feel like a Man,'" 1179. Several transatlantic scholars have partly attributed New World uprisings like the American War for Independence and the Haitian Revolution to the rebellious influences of maritime workers. See Linebaugh, "All the Atlantic Mountains Shook"; Julius Scott, "Common Wind"; Gilroy, *The Black Atlantic*; and Bolster, *Black Jacks.*

49. Smith, "Ira Aldridge," 27. Ashore, stewards were undeniably the nation's "colored gentry," but Dr. McCune Smith may have overstated their importance aboard ship because, although a spirit of interracial comradery pervaded maritime culture, most ships developed racially stratified labor categories. Blacks could serve as sailors or sailmakers on vessels operated by a black sea captain like Paul Cuffee; however, on white ships the primary occupations open to blacks were cooks, personal servants, and stewards. Stewards basically served as glorified house servants to captains or as managers of the ship's service personnel. But despite the racialized job hierarchy on white ships, maritime historian Jeffrey Bolster found that captains often paid their stewards as much as their best sailors; see "'To Feel like a Man,'" 1183. Therefore, the steward was a coveted occupation among African Americans because one could earn a better salary than in most maritime positions open to blacks and a considerably higher wage than in comparable service jobs ashore.

50. See Thompson, *A Documentary History.*

51. Olson, "Social Aspects of Slave Life in New York." As for legal statutes, in 1712 New York City's Common Council passed "An Act for Preventing, Suppressing and Punishing the Conspiracy and Insurrection of Negroes and Other Slaves," which made it illegal for anyone to employ, harbor, conceal, or entertain slaves without their master's permission. Whites caught entertaining slaves without permission were fined five pounds for every night of amusement. Any free "Negro," In-

dian, or mulatto engaged in entertaining a slave without prior permission would forfeit ten pounds for each night. For Brown's sake it was imperative that his enslaved patrons secure permission before attending because as a "Negro" manager, he would have been fined for each slave entertained without a master's blessing. See Kenneth Scott, "The Slave Insurrection in New York in 1712"; Higginbotham, *In the Matter of Color*.

52. *National Advocate*, August 3, 1821, 2.

53. Ibid.

54. Ibid.

55. Two works by Dixon Ryan Fox provide an overview of the Federalist Party, slavery, and Afro–New Yorkers: *The Decline of Aristocracy in the Politics of New York* and "The Negro Vote in Old New York."

56. For physical hostilities between African Americans and Irish Americans, see Gilje, *The Road to Mobocracy*. Also, Levine's *Black Culture and Black Consciousness* examines African American comedy at the expense of Irish Americans.

57. *National Advocate*, August 3, 1821, 2.

58. See Bank, *Theatre Culture in America*, 76–77.

59. *National Advocate*, August 3, 1821, 2.

60. Cultural historian Geneviève Fabre has argued that African American commemorative celebrations, such as Thanksgiving Day, were training sessions for a productive black future in these United States. Thanksgiving Day was an African American holiday commemorating the cessation of American involvement in the international slave trade in January 1808. These annual events indoctrinated African Americans into the rights and responsibilities of being an American citizen and, specifically, citizens with an African past. See Fabre, "African-American Commemorative Celebrations."

61. Lipsitz, *Time Passages*, 16.

62. Ellison, "Change the Joke," 108.

63. Shane White and Graham White make the convincing argument that urban black style became a dominant force in this early national period and continued to have a tremendous impact on fashion trends in subsequent eras. See *Stylin'*.

64. This cautionary article appeared in the *National Advocate*, September 25, 1821, 2.

65. *National Advocate*, September 21, 1821, 2.

CHAPTER TWO

1. *Spectator*, January 16, 1822, 2.

2. Theater historian Michael Booth distinguishes "legitimate" from "illegitimate" pieces by the number of songs in each act and the presence of musical accompaniment to the dramatic action. This information on the British licensing system comes from Connolly, *The Censorship of English Drama*; Booth, *Hiss the Villain*; and Moody, "'Fine Word, Legitimate!'"

3. Moody, "'Fine Word, Legitimate!,'" 225.

4. Ibid., 233–34.

5. For the profound impact of melodrama on nineteenth-century English and American theater, see Michael Booth, *English Melodrama*; Grimsted, *Melodrama Unveiled*; and McConachie, *Melodramatic Formations*.

6. This history of the Park Theatre and Stephen Price is based on T. Allston Brown, *A History of the New York Stage*, vol. 1; Ireland, *Records of the New York Stage*, vol. 1; Wemyss, *Twenty-Six Years of the Life of an Actor and Manager*; Hewitt, "King Stephen of the Park and Drury Lane"; Glenn Hughes, *A History of the American Theatre*; and Lippman, "Stephen Price."

7. *Spectator*, June 14, 1820, 2.

8. In July 1822, more than a year after Brown debuted his company, an equally emboldened female manager named Baldwin—first name not publicized—opened the City Theatre on Warren Street, roughly three blocks from the Park Theatre. Originally a member of the Park's acting company, Baldwin broke with Price's theater over a much publicized salary dispute. According to Joe Cowell, a member of the Park company, Baldwin's theater consisted of eager amateurs and marginal professionals performing plays in a private house. See Cowell, *Thirty Years Passed among the Players*. In addition, on the same day Baldwin's City Theatre opened, Hippolyte Barrère, a French immigrant and confectioner, converted his pleasure garden, Chatham Gardens, into an outdoor canvas theater christened the Pavilion Theatre. See *New York Evening Post*, July 5, 1822, 2.

9. *National Advocate*, September 21, 1821, 2.

10. Ibid. Correcting Noah, George Thompson discovered that Taft actually waited tables at the Shakespeare Hotel, not the City Hotel. See Thompson, *A Documentary History*.

11. *National Advocate*, November 19, 1821, 2. George Thompson has synthesized the information on Taft's emancipation, occupation, and larceny through court records and brief articles published in the *National Advocate* and the *New York American*.

12. *National Advocate*, September 21, 1821, 2; September 25, 1821, 2. The October 1821 playbill is reproduced in Odell, *Annals of the New York Stage*, vol. 3, and Thompson, *A Documentary History*.

13. *National Advocate*, September 21, 1821, 2.

14. See Claudia Johnson, *American Actress*. Traditionally on benefit nights, lead actors or writers received a percentage of ticket sales, and therefore they showcased their best material.

15. *National Advocate*, September 25, 1821, 2.

16. *New York Star*, December 22, 1825, 2; *National Advocate*, December 30, 1825, 2.

17. Thompson has consulted various New York City municipal records and compiled a significant amount of material on Hewlett's theatrical career and other occupations. He found that Hewlett also worked as a tailor and a used clothing seller; see *A Documentary History*.

18. Delany, *Condition, Elevation, Emigration, and Destiny of the Colored People*, 143.

19. Aldridge performed with the troupe until his father, Reverend Daniel Aldridge, forced the young thespian to abandon this indecent profession, but disobeying his father, young Aldridge traveled overseas, where he became a theatrical sensation in western and eastern Europe. Part of the reason Aldridge succeeded on the European stage was his time spent at New York's unique African Free School. From this institution, which served free blacks and newly freed slaves, Aldridge received the kind of basic education that would have significantly benefited Hewlett. For an excellent biography of Aldridge, see Marshall and Stock, *Ira Aldridge*.

20. *New York Star*, December 22, 1825, 2; *National Advocate*, December 30, 1825, 2.

21. Foote, "Crossroad or Settlement?," 130.

22. M. A. Harris, *A Negro History Tour of Manhattan*, 52.

23. *Minutes of the Common Council*, 10:501.

24. *National Advocate*, September 25, 1821, 2.

25. Price's Park followed a seating policy that assigned half its gallery to blacks and the rest to white patrons. Interestingly, white patrons were forbidden to take a seat in the black section of the Park gallery. Historian Toby Widdicombe has recovered and edited an eyewitness account by a foreign visitor who attempted to sit in this black section; see Widdicombe, "New York Theatre in the 1830s."

26. Data on African American incomes in the nineteenth century is difficult to gather, but I base this range on information found in Bolster, "'To Feel like a Man'"; White, *Somewhat More Independent*; and Stott, *Workers in the Metropolis*.

27. *National Advocate*, October 27, 1821, 2.

28. Smith, "Ira Aldridge," 28.

29. Few, if any, Afro–New Yorkers worked as clerks in Manhattan countinghouses or stores, so we can infer that these were white clerks attending the performances.

30. Odell, *Annals of the New York Stage*, 2:36.

31. Gottschild, *Digging the Africanist Presence*, 13.

32. Aldridge, *Memoir and Theatrical Career of Ira Aldridge*, 11. No author is officially listed on this memoir published in 1849, but according to an 1840 playbill for Caledonian Hall, Dingwall, Scotland, Aldridge read from a memoir of his career that he had written himself. I assume this is the same memoir, so throughout this study, I refer to Aldridge as the author. The 1840 playbill can be found in the Ira Aldridge Scrapbook, Folger Shakespeare Library.

33. Thompson includes a January 1822 Hampton's Hotel playbill in *A Documentary History*. Although it is undated, Thompson and I have discussed the bill and suspect this was a January performance based on 1822 newspaper accounts that place Brown's company performing next to the Park Theatre in this month and only this month.

34. *National Advocate*, January 9, 1822, 2.

35. Ibid.

36. *Spectator*, January 16, 1822, 2.

37. *New York Evening Post*, January 10, 1822, 2; *Spectator*, January 16, 1822, 2.

38. During the War of 1812, British forces established a Dartmoor Prison in Plymouth, Massachusetts, and within the prison, black soldiers created dramatic pro-

ductions. They staged popular European dramas like *The Heir at Law*, *Douglas*, and *Romeo and Juliet*, and in some cases painted their faces white to best approximate European complexions. See Bolster, *Black Jacks*.

39. David Krasner's *Resistance, Parody, and Double Consciousness in African American Theatre, 1895–1910* (1997) examines the whiteface performances of the black musical theater pioneer Bob Cole, specifically his vaudeville creation of a white character named Willy Wayside during the 1890s. Nadine George-Graves's recent history, *The Royalty of Negro Vaudeville* (2000), explores how the Whitman Sisters performed whiteness and passed as white ladies onstage and offstage in the early twentieth century.

40. Muñoz, *Disidentifications*, 4.

41. Ibid., 148.

42. Ibid., 109.

43. MacDonald, "Acting Black," 237.

44. Levine, *High Brow, Low Brow*, 20–23.

45. Quoted in Shattuck, *Shakespeare on the American Stage*, 40.

46. The 1830 and 1860 *Richard III* promptbooks are available in the Folger Shakespeare Library's Promptbook Collection. J. C. Cowper was the stage manager at London's Drury Lane Theatre and Manchester's Theatre Royal in the early nineteenth century, and he made voluminous handwritten notes throughout the 1860 promptbook.

47. *National Advocate*, September 21, 1821, 2.

48. All references to *Richard III* come from Inchbald's *British Theatre* (1808). This series published a version popularized by George Frederick Cooke, which replaced Colley Cibber's edition as the *Richard III* preferred by early nineteenth-century actors, including Kean. The Inchbald-Cooke edition differs greatly from modern editions, especially in terms of scene breaks.

49. *National Advocate*, September 21, 1821, 2.

50. Wilentz, *Chants Democratic*, 259.

51. Lott, *Love and Theft*, 28; Cockrell, *Demons of Disorder*, 53.

52. For more on William Wallace and Robert Bruce, consult MacLean's *Scotland: A Concise History* and *Highlanders: A History of the Scottish Clans*; Mitchison's *A History of Scotland*; and Panton and Cowland's *Historical Dictionary of the United Kingdom*, vol. 2.

53. These playbills can be found in Odell, *Annals of the New York Stage*, vol. 3, and Thompson, *A Documentary History*, respectively.

54. Cole, *The Minstrel*, 120–21.

55. Historian Leonard Curry has found that municipal authorities considered some plays, such as Robert Montgomery Bird's *The Gladiator* with its scenes of Roman slave insurrection, too "incendiary" for black ears. See Curry, *The Free Black in Urban America*, 88–91.

56. Lipsitz, *Time Passages*, 16.

57. Carlyle Brown, *The African Company*, 43.

58. *New York Star*, December 22, 1825, 2; *National Advocate*, December 30, 1825, 2.

59. Levine, *High Brow, Low Brow*, 42.

60. hooks, *Ain't I a Woman*, 161.

61. *National Advocate*, September 21, 1821, 2.

62. Sprague, *Shakespeare and the Actors*, 96–97.

63. hooks, *Ain't I a Woman*, 82.

64. Ibid., 71.

65. Stansell, *City of Women*, 218.

66. Levine, *High Brow, Low Brow*, 20–23.

67. *Moore's Irish Melodies*, 42.

68. hooks, *Ain't I a Woman*, 48–49.

69. Not long after bell hooks exposed the various nineteenth-century images of black womanhood, Alice Walker coined the term "womanism," which encapsulates the dual qualities of assertiveness and vulnerability. Walker defines the womanist as "a black feminist or feminist of color. From the black folk expression of mothers to female children, 'You acting womanish,' i.e., like a woman. Usually, referring to outrageous, audacious, courageous or *willful* behavior. Wanting to know more and in greater depth than is considered 'good' for one." See Walker, *In Search of Our Mothers' Gardens*, xi.

70. *Moore's Irish Melodies*, 43.

71. Errol Hill's *Shakespeare in Sable* (1984) chronicles these and other productions.

CHAPTER THREE

1. Anderson, *Imagined Communities*, 6.

2. Ibid., 7.

3. Goodfriend, *Before the Melting Pot*, 6–7. For more on New York diversity during the Dutch, British, and American regimes, see McManus, *A History of Negro Slavery in New York*; James Allen, *The Negro in New York*; Ottley and Weatherby, *Negro in New York*; M. A. Harris, *A Negro History Tour of Manhattan*; Rosenwaike, *Population History of New York City*; Ellis, *New York, State and City*; and Higginbotham, *In the Matter of Color*.

4. Dwight, *Travels in New England and New York*, 3:329–37.

5. The pressure on immigrant populations to assimilate into a normative version of U.S. society existed in this early national period, but the term "melting pot" did not emerge until the early twentieth century. Sollors found, however, that as early as the 1780s "American" was used in national literature as a metaphor for melting; see "National Identity and Ethnic Diversity." Henry Pratt Fairchild was one of the first scholars to contest the "melting pot" concept in his study, *The Melting-Pot Mistake* (1926). He undresses the alleged "melting" as an empty symbol that obscured how Americans actually constructed national culture. The study credited with starting a trend away from the "melting pot" and toward cultural pluralism, multiculturalism, or a "mosaic" metaphor is Nathan Glazer and Daniel Moynihan's *Beyond the Melting Pot* (1963). Interestingly, performance artist Ping Chong argues that an already or always existent multiculturalism in this nation constitutes an "un-

melting pot" of America. See his "Notes for Mumblings and Digressions: Some Thoughts on Being an Artist, Being American, Being a Witness . . ." (1989). More recently, much has been written, in scholarly and broader intellectual communities, on issues of diversity, multiculturalism, and pluralism. Peter McLaren's *Revolutionary Multiculturalism* (1997) argues not for a politics of diversity or liberal pluralism but rather for the decentering of "whiteness." Esteemed fiction writer Ishmael Reed edited a collection of fifty-two essays by various Americans entitled *Multi-America: Essays on Cultural War and Cultural Peace* (1998). These essays offer a wide range of perspectives from an Irish American examining cultural loss caused by assimilation to a Latino writer who illuminates intense racial conflicts between African Americans and Latinos. On the other side of the alleged "culture wars," John J. Miller's study, *The Unmaking of Americans* (1998), argues for a return to the Americanization plan of the early twentieth century and a rehabilitation of the "melting pot." Miller argues that minorities do not need distinct cultural identities and that "divisive" programs like bilingual education and affirmative action keep immigrants out of the American mainstream. By far, the most engaging and accessible history of multiculturalism in America is Ron Takaki's *A Different Mirror* (1993).

6. Anderson, *Imagined Communities*, 6–7.

7. Sollors, "National Identity and Ethnic Diversity," 93.

8. Roediger, *Wages of Whiteness*, 59–60. In addition to Roediger, see Saxton, *The Rise and Fall of the White Republic*, and Theodore Allen, *The Invention of the White Race*. All three studies argue that "whiteness" was constructed as a racial category in the nineteenth century to homogenize the Euro-American national imaginary and thereby resolve or ease Dwight's pluralism paranoia.

9. Axtell, "Colonial America without the Indians," 63.

10. Vermont was the first state to abolish slavery, as early as 1777. In 1799 the New York State legislature passed its first gradual manumission act, which it later amended in 1817. Litwack, *North of Slavery*; Nash, *Forging Freedom*; and White, *Somewhat More Independent*, all discuss the complications of manumission and the difficult process of moving from slave to free person in northern states.

11. Bethel, *The Roots of African-American Identity*, 107.

12. Ibid., 114–15.

13. Thomas, *Rise to Be a People*; Nash, *Forging Freedom*; and Bethel, *The Roots of African-American Identity*.

14. Stuckey, *Slave Culture*, 200–202.

15. Bethel, *The Roots of African-American Identity*, 117.

16. Ernst, "Negro Concepts of Americanism," 208–9.

17. Bethel, *The Roots of African-American Identity*, 82.

18. Morrison, *Playing in the Dark*, 47.

19. For more than a century, historians, sociologists, and anthropologists, starting with Du Bois's *Souls of Black Folk* (1903), have argued that U.S. national culture has been strongly influenced by African cultures. Joseph E. Holloway's edited collection, *Africanisms in American Culture* (1990), offers anthropological studies supporting this position. In *Race Matters* (1993), Cornell West makes his case for the

African Americanization of U.S. popular culture. Finally, Gottschild's *Digging the Africanist Presence in American Performance* (1996) exposes this country's Africanness as manifested in various performance traditions.

20. See Meserve, *An Emerging Entertainment*.

21. An example of antitheatrical attitudes in New York can be found in *An Address, by Several Ministers, in New York, to Their Christian Fellow-Citizens, Dissuading Them from Attending Theatrical Representations*.

22. *New York Evening Post*, November 30, 1821, 2.

23. *Spectator*, January 16, 1822, 2.

24. This rare playbill is reproduced in Thompson, *A Documentary History*.

25. Smith, "Ira Aldridge," 28.

26. George Thompson includes Brown's 1823 tax assessment record for the Mercer Street property in his *A Documentary History*. These documents are available in the New York City Municipal Archives, and are divided by wards.

27. *National Advocate*, July 22, 1822, 2.

28. Ibid.

29. *New York American*, July 23, 1822, 2.

30. Snipe, *Sports of New York* (1823), 3. Snipe published two editions of this *Sports of New York* pamphlet, one published in 1823 and the other in 1824. Portions of the first pamphlet have been reprinted in Odell, *Annals of the New York Stage*, vol. 3, and Thompson, *A Documentary History*.

31. Snipe, *Sports of New York* (1823), 3–4.

32. *Spectator*, August 13, 1822, 2.

33. McConachie, *Melodramatic Formations*, 10–14. For more on early U.S. audience dynamics, see Grimsted, *Melodrama Unveiled*; Bank, *Theatre Culture in America*; McDermott, "The Theatre and Its Audience"; and Gilje, *The Road to Mobocracy*.

34. Snipe, *Sports of New York* (1823), 4.

35. Ibid.

36. Ibid.

37. Ibid., 5.

38. Quoted in Hewitt, *Theatre U.S.A.*, 60.

39. *National Advocate*, August 9, 1822, 3.

40. Thompson includes a reproduction of the benefit playbill in his collection.

41. Snipe, *Sports of New York* (1824), 10–11.

42. Snipe, *Sports of New York* (1823), 6–7.

43. The hornpipe was a European dance that assumed different forms in France, England, Ireland, Scotland, and the United States. In the United States, the hornpipe was a hodgepodge of diverse dance steps like the double shuffle, heel toe, pigeon wing, whirligig, and double Scotch. Premiere U.S. hornpipers also incorporated steps from European popular dances, French ballet, and African American vernacular dance. See Stearns and Stearns, *Jazz Dance*.

44. Snipe, *Sports of New York* (1823), 11.

45. Ibid., 7–9. As for the melody, a British tenor named Philips popularized "Is

There a Heart . . ." throughout America, and the song became especially popular with African American audiences. The song was originally included in Samuel J. Arnold's *The Devil's Bridge; an Opera in Three Acts* (1817), a popular English ballad opera. For the history of the song and the musical, see Wemyss, *Twenty-Six Years of the Life of an Actor and Manager*; Hamm, *Yesterdays*; and Southern, *The Music of Black Americans*.

46. Fusco, "The Other History of Intercultural Performance," 146. For other studies that address indigenous performance, see Meserve, *An Emerging Entertainment*, and Eugene Jones, *Native Americans as Shown on the Stage*.

47. Deloria, *Playing Indian*, 8.

48. In the summer of 1824, a shrewd museum owner, Dr. Scudder, advertised a fierce deputation of "chiefs, squaws, and braves" from the western territories. This deputation of Sanky, Piankashaw, Pahageser-Ioway, Menominee, and Nacato nations arrived in Manhattan after meeting with federal authorities in the District of Columbia. The same deputation also made appearances at the circus and at Manhattan's Common Council in City Hall. See *New York Evening Post*, August 13, 1824, 2; *National Advocate*, August 14, 1824, 2; *Spectator*, August 17, 1824, 1, 3.

49. Dunlap, *History of the American Theatre*, 1:55.

50. *New York Evening Post*, February 14, 1806, 3; *National Advocate*, December 15, 1821, 2.

51. Dunlap, *History of the American Theatre*, 1:55.

52. See Francis, *Old New York*. Unfortunately, Francis does not include Dr. Mitchell's native translations.

53. *New York American*, July 2, 1824, 3. To close *A Trail of Indians*, the native performers appropriated European culture by performing "a Civic Dance" accompanied by violin music. Such instances of Native Americans executing European dance were extremely rare.

54. *National Advocate*, December 10, 1824, 2; *New York Evening Post*, December 15, 1824, 3.

55. Fusco, "The Other History of Intercultural Performance," 147. There were two such publicized incidents from 1820s Manhattan in which Euro-Americans exerted control over the "primitives" and displayed Native Americans against their will. Around Christmas 1820, a Captain Hadlock chaperoned an Esquimaux family — consisting of Chief Koonanux, his wife, and their child — to Manhattan from the polar region of Davis Straits. Captain Hadlock placed the family and its nineteen-foot canoe on display at a Broadway exhibition hall, and in addition he had the chief perform an outdoor water exhibition near Battery Park. Days later, the *New York Evening Post* revealed that Captain Hadlock had kidnaped and displayed this family in Manhattan against its will. Hadlock was arrested and charged, and to acknowledge the wrong perpetuated against the family, New Yorkers raised funds for the family's safe passage back to Davis Straits. See *New York Evening Post*, December 23, 1820, 3; February 3, 1821, 2; February 8, 1821, 2; February 22, 1821, 2. The other questionable exhibition occurred in August 1821 when a Chief Shauwiskanan from the Sock Tribe in Mississippi was displayed at an exhibit hall off Broadway. He ap-

peared under exotic titles such as "the Bowl Boy" and "Double-Jointed Indian," and was advertised as "about eighteen years of age and thirty inches high"; see *National Advocate*, August 15, 1821, 3. An *Evening Post* editorial remarked that some citizens viewed the "Bowl Boy" exhibition as "revolting to the feelings," but the writer assured the public that the chief's deformities were tastefully concealed; see *New York Evening Post*, November 14, 1821, 2. This editorial also noticed "an air of pensive melancholy in his looks," which suggested the chief was displayed against his better judgment, if not his will.

56. King, *Colonial Discourses*, 5.

57. Fusco, "The Other History of Intercultural Performance," 146.

58. See Rousseau's *Discourse on the Origin of Inequality* (1751) and *The Social Contract* (1762) in Masters and Kelly, *The Collected Writings of Rousseau*. Both works offer a sympathetic version of the "noble savage," yet still position European civilization and its "intelligent beings" as superior to nature's "unimaginative animals."

59. Tompkins, *Sensational Designs*, 109–11.

60. Cooper's *Pioneers* is interesting for its range of characters who are either full-blooded Indian, allegedly half-Indian, or so captivated by indigenous culture they have "gone native."

61. Deloria, *Playing Indian*, 3.

62. Ibid., 4.

63. Theater historian Eugene Jones claims that Rogers's heroic tragedy was one of the few, if not only, stage Indian dramas to dramatize but not falsify Native American life. He also suggests that Rogers's sensitivity to native culture and his accurate depiction of colonial relations were key reasons why the play was never produced during this period. See *Native Americans as Shown on the Stage*, 18–19.

64. American dramatist J. N. Barker would reincarnate Colman's definitive native beauty in his operatic melodrama, *The Indian Princess; or La Belle Sauvage* (1808). This operatic melodrama tells the story of Pocahontas, or Matoaka, the famous historical native beauty who fell in love with and married an English colonist named James Rolfe.

65. The engraving can be found on the first page of *Inkle and Yarico* in Inchbald's *British Theatre*, vol. 20 (1808). Theater historian Susan Porter also reveals that white actors traditionally performed Womski and the other island natives in blackface. See *With an Air Debonair*, 162. And according to John Poyer, the actual Yarico was a Carib Indian from the island of Dominica, whom English slavers captured and brought to Barbados. See *The History of Barbados*, 43–45. On islands like Dominica and St. Vincent, Carib Indians were usually genetic combinations of African and Indian races, which explains Womski's dark complexion and African features. For more on African and Indian connections, consult Forbes, *Africans and Native Americans*, and Gonzalez, "Prospero, Caliban, and Black Sambo."

66. According to Walter Meserve, the "vogue" reached its zenith in 1829 with Augustus Stone's melodrama, *Metamora; or the Last of the Wampanoags*, starring an enterprising young actor named Edwin Forrest; see *An Emerging Entertainment*, 294.

67. Grose, "Edwin Forrest," 191; Eugene Jones, *Native Americans as Shown on the Stage*, 2.

68. Deloria, *Playing Indian*, 37.

69. Consult Porter, *With an Air Debonair*, for production information; also, these repeat performances were especially rare in nineteenth-century U.S. theaters.

70. See Aldridge, *Memoir and Theatrical Career of Ira Aldridge*.

71. This dramatic figure is based on the Spanish priest who wrote *Devastation of the Indies* (1552), a treatise condemning the Spanish extermination of New World natives.

72. Aldridge, *Memoir and Theatrical Career of Ira Aldridge*, 10.

73. *National Advocate*, September 21, 1821, 2.

74. Aldridge, *Memoir and Theatrical Career of Ira Aldridge*, 10.

75. Brief production histories and commentary on *She Would Be a Soldier* can be found in Goldberg, *Major Noah*; Sarna, *Jacksonian Jew*; and Grimsted, *Melodrama Unveiled*.

76. Sarna, *Jacksonian Jew*, 48.

77. Noah, *She Would Be a Soldier*, 64–65.

78. Noah was a longtime member of Manhattan's Tammany Society, a fraternal order firmly rooted in Native American culture, and even rose to the rank of sachem, or leader, in this organization. He thus had a history of thoroughly fetishizing native culture and was committed to "interior" Indianness. The Jewish editor-playwright maintained this special affinity for Native Americans, or the "Lo" as he called them, because he believed they were actually "descendants of the lost tribes of Israel" taken captive by the king of Assyria and later dispersed to the New World. Historian Isaac Goldberg explains that Noah looked forward to and worked toward the day when the "Lo" and their Jewish brethren would be reunited; see *Major Noah*, 198.

79. *New York Evening Post*, November 30, 1821, 2.

80. Noah, *She Would Be a Soldier*, 6; *National Advocate*, December 15, 1821, 2.

81. Odell, *Annals of the New York Stage*, 3:35. Hewlett titled the piece a "pantomime," which David Mayer describes as a series of silent disconnected episodes that, like ballets, feature choreographed dramatic action set to orchestral accompaniment; see *Harlequin in His Element*, 19–20.

82. *New York American*, November 29, 1820, 3.

83. Gonzalez, "Prospero, Caliban, and Black Sambo," 26.

84. *National Advocate*, March 16, 1822, 2.

85. *New York Evening Post*, March 26, 1822, 2.

86. In *The Life of Olaudah Equiano*, the former slave Equiano remarked that this gender separation reminded him of most social dancing in West Africa.

87. *New York American*, June 16–17, 1823.

88. Odell, *Annals of the New York Stage*, 3:71.

89. See *Ready Reference: American Indians*, 3:762–63.

90. *Spectator*, January 16, 1822, 2.

91. Odell, *Annals of the New York Stage*, 3:70–71. Also see Hay, *African-American Theatre*, and "Into the Spotlight."

92. Hay, *African-American Theatre*, 11; *New York Evening Post*, January 10, 1822, 2; Carlyle Brown, *The African Company*, 53.

93. Odell, *Annals of the New York Stage*, 2:555.

94. The "official histories" I am drawing on are William Young, *An Account of the Black Charaibs in the Island of St. Vincent's* and *A Tour through Several Islands of Barbadoes, St. Vincent, Antigua, Tobago, and Grenada*; Shepard, *An Historical Account of the Island of St. Vincent*; and Bayley, *Four Years' Residence in the West Indies*. The modern scholarship, which includes Garifuna folklore, consists of Gonzalez, "Prospero, Caliban, and Black Sambo" and *Sojourners of the Caribbean*; Gullick, *Myths of a Minority*; Jinkins and Bobrow, *St. Vincent and the Grenadines*; Kirby and Martin, *The Rise and Fall of the Black Caribs*; Hadel, "Carib Folk Songs and Carib Culture"; Virginia Young, *Becoming West Indian*; Hulme and Whitehead, *Wild Majesty*; Craton, *Testing the Chains*; and Forbes, *Africans and Native Americans*.

95. Hill, "The Revolutionary Tradition in Black Drama," 409.

96. See William Young, *An Account of the Black Charaibs in the Island of St. Vincent's*, 106–7.

97. This folklore is recounted in Hadel, "Carib Folk Songs and Carib Culture," 7, and Kirby and Martin, *The Rise and Fall of the Black Caribs*, 64.

98. William Young, *An Account of the Black Charaibs in the Island of St. Vincent's*, 117–18.

99. Gonzalez, *Sojourners of the Caribbean*, 31.

100. Hay, *African-American Theatre*, 192.

101. Gullick, *Myths of a Minority*, 84.

102. John Collins, "American Drama in Anti-Slavery Agitation," 100. By the time Brown revived *Shotaway* in June 1823, two other American dramatists, Noah and J. H. Payne, had penned dramatic accounts of the Greek independence struggle against the Turks. M. M. Noah wrote *The Grecian Captive; or the Fall of Athens* (1822), and a year later, J. H. Payne penned *Ali Pacha; or The Signet Ring* (1823).

103. See Bolster, "To Feel like a Man," and Julius Scott, "Common Wind."

CHAPTER FOUR

1. Gottschild, *Digging the Africanist Presence*, 13.

2. *National Advocate*, August 9, 1822, 3.

3. The only details of these two productions come from Mr. Twaites's letter of August 13, 1822, published in the *Spectator*.

4. Interestingly, Thompson's document collection includes an 1823 Eighth Ward tax assessment record that officially listed Brown's Village theater on Mercer Street as the "African Theatre." Yet, publicly, Brown continued to advertise as the American Theatre.

5. *New York Evening Post*, March 3, 1823, 2.

6. *National Advocate*, June 21, 1823, 2.

7. For the increasingly difficult dynamics posed by free blacks, see Litwack, *North of Slavery*; Nash, *Forging Freedom*; and White, *Somewhat More Independent*.

8. This much abridged history of Old Word extratheatrical and theatrical encounters with racial others and the two varieties of stage Africans relies on Oldfield, "The 'Ties of Soft Humanity'"; Barthelemy, *Black Face, Maligned Race*; Ernest Baker, *The Novels of Mrs. Aphra Behn*; Jordan and Love, *The Works of Thomas Southerne*; Nicoll, *The World of Harlequin*; Inigo Jones, *The Theatre of the Stuart Court*; Eldred Jones, *Othello's Countrymen*; Quinn, *A History of the American Drama*; Belcher, "The Place of the Negro in the Evolution of the American Theatre"; Petit, "The Important American Dramatic Types to 1900"; Damon, "The Negro in Early American Songsters"; Dennison, *Scandalize My Name*; Boskin, *Sambo*; Meserve, *An Emerging Entertainment*; Toll, *Blacking Up*; and Cockrell, *Demons of Disorder*.

9. Barthelemy, *Black Face, Maligned Race*, 200–201.

10. Oldfield, "The 'Ties of Soft Humanity,'" 2.

11. Ibid., 9–11.

12. Murdock, *Triumph of Love*, 69.

13. *New York Evening Post*, March 29, 1822, 2.

14. The mark of a successful nineteenth-century play was the number of revivals during a season. Throughout the 1810s, half the plays produced were never seen again, but by the 1820s the best-attended plays reappeared with some frequency. See Burge, *Lines of Business*.

15. *New York American*, December 23–30, 1822.

16. Cockrell, *Demons of Disorder*, 19.

17. In his *Retrospectives on America, 1797–1811*, English comedian John Bernard claimed that both African and Irish Americans shared a lack of intelligence and an incomplete grasp of standard English. In terms of physical representations, an illustration accompanying the nineteenth-century Irish song "Corporal Casey"—occasionally performed by James Hewlett—depicts an Irish soldier with wild hair and exaggerated, apelike facial features similar to those later used to caricature African Americans during blackface minstrelsy. The song and illustration were published as part of R. W. Hume's London broadside series *The Lyre* during the early 1800s. The broadside can be viewed at the Performing Arts Division of the Library of Congress. For more accessible examples of nineteenth-century Irish imagery, see Curtis, *Apes and Angels*.

18. *National Advocate*, January 1, 1823, 2.

19. Perhaps as a warning to potential audience members, Park Theatre playbills emphasized that this piece was the *Serious Pantomime of Obi, or Three Fingered Jack*. See Park advertisements in the *National Advocate*, December 24–29, 1822.

20. *New York American*, January 13, 1823, 3.

21. Ibid., February 21–28, 1823.

22. Ibid., March 4, 1823, 3; Cockrell, *Demons of Disorder*, 16.

23. *National Advocate*, April 28, 1823, 2. The original French story was published in *New York Magazine*, February 1793, 114–19. In Colman's dramatic adaptation, Selico's "Foulah," or Fulani, village is overrun by Mandingo warriors, and Selico, along with his brothers, must devise a way to support his elderly mother. *The*

Africans is an extremely rare stage African drama because Colman sentimentally portrays a West African family and realistically depicts interethnic conflicts on the "dark continent."

24. For the critical reaction to *Africans*, see Odell, *Annals of the New York Stage*, 2:336, and *American Monthly Magazine*, June 1817, 139.

25. *New York Evening Post*, May 10, 1823, 2.

26. *American Monthly Magazine*, November 1817, 61.

27. Toll, *Blacking Up*, 272.

28. Huggins, *Harlem Renaissance*, 252–54.

29. For Pinkster background, see White, "Pinkster in Albany, 1803" and " 'It Was a Proud Day' "; Eights, "Pinkster Festivities in Albany"; Alice Earle, *Colonial Days in Old New York*; Cooper, *Satanstoe*; Williams-Myers, "Pinkster Carnival"; Stuckey, "The Skies of Consciousness"; and Lhamon, *Raising Cain*.

30. There is some disagreement on this issue. In his various articles on Pinkster, Shane White argues this New World festival was a complex syncretization of African and Dutch cultures. However, other scholars and eyewitnesses agree that Dutch colonists gradually lost interest in the festival and blacks began using Pinkster to exercise their surviving Old World African cultural practices. Sterling Stuckey and historian A. J. Williams-Myers have produced the most detailed investigations of African expressive culture at Pinkster rites.

31. Emery, *Black Dance*, 145. The Totau resembled the sensual dances practiced at New Orleans's Congo Square and throughout the Caribbean; also see Stearns and Stearns, *Jazz Dance*.

32. White, "Pinkster in Albany, 1803," 197, 199.

33. In *The Market Book*, 1:344–45, a butcher named Thomas DeVoe describes how slaves from Manhattan, Long Island, and New Jersey gathered at the slip for three days during Pinkster to sell roots, berries, herbs, fruits, and vegetables. After disposing of their produce, the slaves earned extra shillings by dancing for vendors interested in attracting customers to their booths. The dancers soon realized they could showcase their talents independently of vendors and raise a substantial collection for themselves through competitions that expanded well beyond Pinkster rites to regular market days. DeVoe noticed that crews of black dancers began overtaking the slip, with one dancer designated to perform various breakdowns on a shingle five or six feet wide, while another crew member kept time, and two others held the shingle in place. DeVoe recalls how the dancers mainly performed solo street dances like the jig and the breakdown. This Catherine Market breakdown was most likely a combination of various shuffles, double shuffles, and heel toes. As for the jig, historian Dena Epstein claims this primarily lower-body dance did not originate among "American Negroes" but was a popular dance dating back to sixteenth-century Ireland; see *Sinful Tunes and Spirituals*, 121–22. Black market dancers may have been adept at this Irish dance, but it is possible DeVoe never witnessed a jig. Dance historians Marshall and Jean Stearns indicate that, before minstrelsy, most African American dances were incorrectly labeled as "jigs"; see *Jazz Dance*, 49–50.

34. Lhamon, *Raising Cain*, 3–8.

35. White, "'It Was a Proud Day,'" 47.

36. This Old World inversion ritual originated somewhere between ancient Greece and eighteenth-century England. For the multiple origins of Callithumpian Bands, see Gilje, *The Road to Mobocracy*; Susan Davis, *Parades and Power*; and Cockrell, *Demons of Disorder*.

37. Cockrell, *Demons of Disorder*, 52–56.

38. Thanksgiving Day sermons can be found in Aptheker, *Documentary History of the Negro People*, vol. 1, and Dorothy Porter, *Early Negro Writing*.

39. See Sweet, "The Fourth of July and Black Americans in the Nineteenth Century," and Fabre, "African-American Commemorative Celebrations."

40. This box office report is taken from *Rambler's Magazine and New York Theatrical Register*, January 1810, 21.

41. Szwed, "Race and the Embodiment of Culture," 30.

42. Roediger, *Wages of Whiteness*, 97–104, 116.

43. After white rioters nearly dismantled Brown's theater, Noah reported that Brown retreated to Albany: "The African Company have closed their Theatre, in Mercer-street, in consequence of the epidemic, and have gone to Albany to perform a few nights"; *National Advocate*, October 12, 1822, 2. Brown's troupe performed Sheridan's *Pizarro* in a temporary Albany theater in order to earn enough funds to repair the damage to his American Theatre; see Phelps, *Players of a Century*, 56.

44. This playbill is included in Hutton, *Curiosities of the American Stage*, and Thompson, *A Documentary History*. Perhaps to capitalize on the singularity of his company, Brown charged his highest admission prices ever for the June 7 double bill of *Tom and Jerry* and *Obi; or Three-Finger'd Jack*. He increased box and pit tickets to seventy-five cents and fifty cents respectively, now identical to Park Theatre prices, and for the gallery, he set an admission price of thirty-seven and one-half cents, surpassing the Park's gallery price of twenty-five cents.

45. The March 1823 Hewlett playbill is reprinted in Thompson, *A Documentary History*.

46. Smith's race was first speculated on in Over, "New York's African Theatre," 9. Also see Odell, *Annals of the New York Stage*, 1:262.

47. Moncrieff, *Tom and Jerry*, iii.

48. Egan, *Life in London*, 321.

49. *Albion*, March 8, 1823, 303.

50. Moncrieff, *Tom and Jerry*, 84–85.

51. *New York Mirror*, October 11, 1823, 86.

52. Marian Winter, "Juba and American Minstrelsy," 30.

53. By the early 1840s female impersonators would become a major and well-received component of minstrel shows performed before predominantly male audiences; see Bean, "Transgressing the Gender Divide." Also, in *Love and Theft*, Eric Lott pursues the homoerotic possibilities of the minstrel body in the same-sex minstrel show context.

54. Odell, *Annals of the New York Stage*, 3:70.

55. For more on the Royal African Company, consult Davies, *The Royal African Company*, and Patterson, *Slavery and Social Death*.

56. Lorenzo Turner's article, "Anti-Slavery Sentiment in American Literature," examines these issues. And for plays depicting white slavery, see Susanna Rowson's *Slaves in Algiers; or A Struggle for Freedom* (1794); J. H. Payne's *The Fall of Algiers* (1825); and James Ellison's *The American Captive; or Siege of Tripoli* (1812).

57. Bates, *Harlequin Mungo*, 8.

58. Colman, *The Africans*, 42–45. Various slavery historians have covered African involvement in the slave trade, including Eric Williams, Philip D. Curtin, Basil Davidson, Orlando Patterson, and James Rawley.

59. See Fraser, *Charleston! Charleston!*, and Hagy, *This Happy Land*.

60. Rawley, *The Transatlantic Slave Trade*, 395–96.

61. In 1800 Fawcett published the two-act seriopantomime and an additional song collection titled *Songs, Duets, and Choruses in the Pantomimical Drama of Obi; or Three-Finger'd Jack*. The following discussion of Fawcett's pantomime relies on the published pantomime and an 1800 edition of the song collection.

62. This profile of Jack Mansong is based on Campbell, *The Maroons of Jamaica*; Reidel, "The Maroon Culture of Endurance"; Eyre, "Jack Mansong"; Burdett, *Life and Exploits of Mansong*; and Hill, *The Jamaican Stage*. Alan L. Eyre has uncovered roughly twenty biographies—two of them best-sellers—that immortalized the revolutionary turned hijacker. These biographies, many published anonymously, portrayed Jack Mansong as a Robin Hood–like hero who defended the poor and dispossessed the wealthy, a characterization that Eyre finds laughable; see Eyre, "Jack Mansong," 7, 14.

63. Fawcett, *Obi*, 16.

64. Ibid., 5.

65. Patterson, *Sociology of Slavery*, 188–90.

66. Fawcett, *Obi*, 9–10.

67. Ibid., 9.

68. Dallas, *The History of the Maroons*, 1:92–93.

69. Differing from Dallas and Fawcett, Caribbean scholar Edward Brathwaite contends that Afro-Jamaicans believed Obeah and Christianity—or "white obi"— were not mutually exclusive and could peacefully coexist; see "The African Presence in Caribbean Literature," 41.

70. Fawcett, *Obi*, 13.

71. Ibid., 19.

72. In the 1809 collection of pantomime songs, John Fawcett reveals Three-Fingered Jack had earlier prophesied "white obi" would ultimately defeat him; see *Songs, Duets, and Choruses*, 3–4.

73. In Jamaica, Jonkonnu developed from transplanted Gold Coast African cultures and was celebrated from roughly December 26 through January 1. Very similar to New York's Pinkster, Jonkonnu was an interracial, African-controlled, and white-financed celebration open to all Jamaicans. There were isolated instances of Afro-Jamaican entrepreneurs pooling resources to sponsor a Jonkonnu king, but

the king's tribute money was largely supplied by the white planter class. On rare occasions, a Euro-Jamaican merchant would sponsor a white Jonkonnu king. Following behind Jonkonnu, there were additional performers like the Set Girls, a group of synchronized, identically dressed females who promenaded singing Scottish and English songs, and the Actor Boys, a cadre of young men who performed scenes from Shakespeare and other dramatists. A highly commercialized and modernized version of the Jonkonnu is still performed in the Bahamas, primarily around the Christmas–New Year's season. For more on Jonkonnu, as practiced in Jamaica, see Bayley, *Four Years' Residence in the West Indies*; Barclay, *A Practical View of the Present State of Slavery in the West Indies*; Matthew Lewis, *Journal of a West India Proprietor*; Michael Scott, *Tom Cringle's Log*; Reid, "The John Canoe Festival"; Wright, *Revels in Jamaica*; Bettelheim, "Jonkonnu and Other Christmas Masquerades"; Hill, *The Jamaican Stage*; Cassidy, "Hipsaw and John Canoe"; and Richards, "Horned Ancestral Masks."

74. Fawcett, *Obi*, 13–14.

75. Ibid., 12.

76. Snipe, *Sports of New York* (1824), 10–11.

77. John Collins, "American Drama in Anti-Slavery Agitation," 100. "St. Domingo" refers to the Haitian Revolution, and the Prosser insurrection references an aborted uprising in August 1800 in Richmond, Virginia, allegedly involving more than one thousand slaves.

78. As a slave, Vesey served as a ship's steward and visited islands like Santo Domingo where he encountered revolutionary ideas that he would later incorporate into his insurrectionary agenda. After winning fifteen hundred dollars in a local lottery, he purchased his freedom and established a successful carpentry business in Charleston. He also began ministering as a lay preacher in the local African Methodist Episcopal Church, and from the pulpit, he blended the Declaration of Independence, French Revolution rhetoric, the Haitian Revolution, and the Bible to convince slaves in and around Charleston to take up arms. On the Vesey conspiracy and trial, see "Denmark Vesey," *Atlantic Monthly*, June 1861; Lofton, "Denmark Vesey's Call to Arms"; Killens, *The Trial Record of Denmark Vesey*; and Robertson, *Denmark Vesey*. For Manhattan's coverage, read the *National Advocate*, *New York Evening Post*, *New York American*, and *Spectator* from July 1 to September 3, 1822.

79. Obtaining accurate information was difficult because Charleston authorities were reticent on the alleged conspiracy; see "Denmark Vesey," *Atlantic Monthly*, June 1861, 742. One interesting piece of fiction circulating throughout the states was the rumor that the Vesey conspirators intended to murder all the white males so they could marry the white females.

80. Accompanying the "official" record, the *Spectator* published short biographies of the conspirators, including Vesey, Peter Poyas, Rolla, Monday Gell, and Gullah Jack, who became the leading men of the *Spectator*'s courtroom drama.

81. *National Advocate*, August 28, 1822, 2.

82. Mintz and Price, *The Birth of African-American Culture*, 51.

CHAPTER FIVE

1. See Ottley and Weatherby, *Negro in New York*; Langston Hughes, "The Negro and American Entertainment"; and Mitchell, *Black Drama*.

2. Fanon, *Black Skin, White Masks*, 64.

3. Hay, *African-American Theatre*, 6–9.

4. This brief overview of early New York politics, political parties, and suffrage rights relies on Fox, *The Decline of Aristocracy in the Politics of New York* and "The Negro Vote in Old New York."

5. *New York Evening Post*, August 28, 1821, 2.

6. *National Advocate*, April 12–28, 1820. Most Manhattan newspapers were funded and controlled by a political party, and, not surprisingly, Noah's *National Advocate* was Republican property. See O.P.Q.'s *Sketches of the New York Press*.

7. *National Advocate*, September 24, 1821, 2.

8. The Federalist and other speeches are included in *Reports of the Proceedings*.

9. *National Advocate*, September 25, 1821, 2.

10. The new constitution was printed in *Reports of the Proceedings*, 661.

11. Leslie Harris, "Creating the African-American Working Class," 49–50.

12. See Roediger, *Wages of Whiteness*, and for a detailed discussion of the Irish immigrant journey from despised outsider to somewhat assimilated insider, see Ignatiev, *How the Irish Became White*. Also, historian Ron Takaki discovered that, before the 1820s, federal legislation favored Irish immigrants over immigrants of color. The 1790 Naturalization Law specifically stipulated citizenship for "whites" only. See Takaki, *A Different Mirror*, 9.

13. Hirsch, "New York and the Negro," 417–18.

14. White and White, *Stylin'*, 92.

15. *New York Evening Post*, August 24, 1820, 2.

16. Two particular *Advocate* articles, from issues June 22, 1822, and July 9, 1822, are especially interesting.

17. White and White, *Stylin'*, 88–92.

18. *Freedom's Journal*, June 29, 1827.

19. The *Journal*'s concerns are part of a long-standing debate over how nineteenth-century African Americans should best engage in public celebration. John Zuille's *Historical Sketch of the New York African Society for Mutual Relief* recounts how this organization handled this issue for its various commemorations. Nash's *Forging Freedom* examines similar debates in Philadelphia, and White's *Somewhat More Independent* expounds on this intraracial issue in New York.

20. *Freedom's Journal*, August 24, 1827.

21. *National Advocate*, January 9, 1822, 2.

22. MacDonald, "Acting Black," 236.

23. *New York Evening Post*, January 10, 1822, 2.

24. Price unleashed municipal authorities on other theaters besides Brown's. He employed a similar strategy to undermine another rival institution, Hippolyte Barrère's canvas Pavilion Theatre. Price convinced New York's Common Council to

pass a law declaring canvas structures a fire hazard, and after the council passed his legislation, he promptly sent the fire warden to close the Pavilion Theatre. See Cowell, *Thirty Years Passed among the Players*; Glenn Hughes, *A History of the American Theatre*; and *Minutes of the Common Council*, 13:169.

25. Moody, "'Fine Word, Legitimate!,'" 238.

26. See Snipe, *Sports of New York* (1823), and Nielsen, *Recollections of a Six-Years' Residence in the United States of America*. Eighteenth-century critics declared *Douglas* the "Scottish declaration of literary independence" from England; see Tobin, *Plays by Scots*.

27. Levine, *High Brow, Low Brow*, 31.

28. Taylor, *Reinventing Shakespeare*, 6, 82–83.

29. *New York Evening Post*, February 5, 1822, 2.

30. Hay, *African-American Theatre*, 10, 238 n19.

31. MacDonald, "Acting Black," 236–37.

32. Ibid., 237.

33. Gilje, *The Road to Mobocracy*, 153–55.

34. *Spectator*, August 20, 1822, 2.

35. Thompson has included these articles from the *National Advocate*, November 19, 1821, 2, and *New York American*, November 21, 1821, 2, in his document collection.

36. *Spectator*, January 16, 1822, 2.

37. Snipe, *Sports of New York* (1823), 5.

38. Gilje, *The Road to Mobocracy*, 157.

39. Roediger, *Wages of Whiteness*, 56.

40. Ibid., 103, 154.

41. Samuel Hay claims that the integration dilemma began when Brown extended and Noah accepted his invitation to the "African Grove" opening; see *African-American Theatre*, 6–7.

42. A map in Thompson, *A Documentary History*, places the circus south of Canal Street on White Street, but that was an older circus building. In the 1820s, the new Broadway Circus was north of Canal between Grand and Howard/Hester Streets. All the other New York City sources place the new circus building further up the island. The large wood structure originally housed nomadic theater troupes, traveling circuses, and even a temporarily homeless African Methodist Episcopal Zion congregation. See Odell, *Annals of the New York Stage*, vol. 2; Ireland, *Records of the New York Stage*, vol. 1; and Rush, *A Short Account of the Rise and Progress of the African Methodist Episcopal Church in America*.

43. *Spectator*, August 20, 1822, 2.

44. The August 11, 1822, *Allen Royce et al. v. Robert Mitchell et al.* case is available at the New York City Municipal Archives. On the actual court document, there is a line through August West's name. Thompson has transcribed the case for *A Documentary History*.

45. Gilje, *The Road to Mobocracy*, 157.

46. In the early nineteenth century, before the advent of blackface minstrelsy, Irish

and English circus dancers created a lucrative niche by applying lamp black or burnt cork and executing Irish jigs, English clogs, European hornpipes, and break-downs as comical "Negro Boys." See Marian Winter, "Juba and American Minstrelsy."

47. See Thompson, *A Documentary History*, for transcriptions of these court documents.

48. Gilje, *The Road to Mobocracy*, 157.

49. *National Advocate*, August 9, 1822, 3.

50. See Thompson, *A Documentary History*.

51. Sanjek, *American Popular Music and Its Business*, 166–70.

52. Cowell, *Thirty Years Passed among the Players*, 64.

53. *National Advocate*, June 13, 1822, 3, and June 17, 1822, 3.

54. *New York Evening Post*, February 5, 1822, 2; *National Advocate*, July 15, 1822, 3.

55. Various articles from *Spectator*, July 26 to August 5, 1822.

56. *National Advocate*, August 26, 1822, 2.

57. Ibid., September 3, 1822, 2.

58. Gilje, *The Road to Mobocracy*, 159.

59. Thompson, *A Documentary History*, 104–5, 111–12.

60. Aldridge, *Memoir and Theatrical Career of Ira Aldridge*, 11.

61. Marshall and Stock, *Ira Aldridge*, 39.

62. Roediger, *Wages of Whiteness*, 104; Lott, *Love and Theft*, 39, 44–46.

63. James W. Johnson, *Black Manhattan*, 78–80.

64. This satiric humor at the expense of African Americans was not limited to the white press. Although committed to racial uplift, in various issues, Russwurm and Cornish's black-owned *Freedom's Journal* published jokes and humorous anec-dotes often composed in the most exaggerated black dialect. For a solid example, see *Freedom's Journal*, February 14, 1829.

65. The American Antiquarian Society's graphics collection houses several "Bobalition" broadsides, many of them published and perhaps authored by O. Shoe-maker. Shane White and Graham White have reprinted facsimiles of some broad-sides in *Stylin'*.

66. Hay, *African-American Theatre*, 17.

67. See *St. Tammany's Magazine*, December 4, 1821, 52. Professor Michael Warner of Rutgers University introduced me to this item, and Thompson includes the so-liloquy in his document collection. Warner, with several other authors, recently published an article, "A Soliloquy 'Lately Spoken at the African Theatre,'" which explores two potential authors for the speech. The two strongest candidates are James Hewlett, Brown's "chief" performer, and Robert C. Sands, a rising young au-thor who may have "ventriloquized" a black actor for the magazine.

68. *National Advocate*, July 1, 1823, 2.

69. Ibid., August 27, 1823, 2.

70. "Bob-link" is a reference to the Bobolink, a field bird whose underparts change from brown to black during the spring mating season; see Lhamon, *Raising Cain*, 4.

71. Malapropism, using the wrong word or a close approximation at the right comic moment, was first popularized on the American stage by rustic Yankee char-

acters and social-climbing white women, such as Richard Sheridan's Mrs. Malaprop. Apparently, a proper command of English was beyond the reach of not just African Americans but other early national Euro-Americans as well. See Lott, *Love and Theft*, 122, and Cockrell, *Demons of Disorder*, 20.

72. Curry, *The Free Black in Urban America*, 119.

73. See Snipe, *Sports of New York* (1824), 10–11.

74. Lott makes this point in *Love and Theft*. He also argues that performed minstrelsy often passes for the singular form of blackface because published caricatures were not sufficient for racial burlesque; they lacked the "crucial presence of the body"; see *Love and Theft*, 41. Lhamon agrees that printed minstrelsy merely circulated rigid images, which could hardly rival the improvisational skill of three-dimensional minstrel performers; see *Raising Cain*, 163–64.

75. This letter and others detailing Mathews's excursion to the New World can be accessed in the multivolume *Memoirs of Charles Mathews* (1839), edited by his wife Anne Jackson Mathews.

76. Mathews, *Mr. Mathews's Trip to America*, 11–12, 27.

77. Music historian Charles Hamm found that "Opossum" was published in London in 1824 as a "South Carolina Negro Air" and "an original Negro melody," but he contends the tune has a Scotch-Irish melodic structure and resembles an Irish folk melody called "The Lasses of Dublin." Furthermore, theater historian Hans Nathan discovered that in the early 1800s, "Opossum" was very popular among southern frontiersmen of Scottish-Irish extraction. Nathan claims white farmers shared this tune with plantation blacks in the South. So, "Opossum" was never a uniquely "Negro" air, and Mathews may have been more familiar with this song than Brown's urban black patrons. See Hamm, *Yesterdays*, and Nathan, "Charles Mathews, Comedian, and the American Negro."

78. Dennison, *Scandalize My Name*, 511–12.

79. *National Advocate*, September 21, 1821, 2. Samuel Hay accuses Mathews of plagiarizing the final *Richard III* section of "Black Tragedian" from Noah's brazenly satirical reviews; see *African-American Theatre*, 13, 254 n6.

80. *National Advocate*, May 8, 1824, 2.

81. *Memoirs of Charles Mathews*, 3:391.

82. See Dunlap, *A Trip to Niagara*, and Haywood, "Negro Minstrelsy and Shakespearean Burlesque," for more on the "Darkey Tragedian."

83. Marshall and Stock, *Ira Aldridge*, 44.

84. I found this information on the aforementioned 1840 playbill for the Aldridge performance at Caledonian Hall in Dingwall, Scotland, which is available at the Folger Shakespeare Library.

85. Aldridge, *Memoir and Theatrical Career of Ira Aldridge*, 11.

86. Susan Davis, *Parades and Power*, 161.

87. Gilje, *The Road to Mobocracy*, 157.

88. Specifically, I am building this discussion of class subversion and masking on Cockrell, *Demons of Disorder*; Lott, *Love and Theft*; and Lhamon, *Raising Cain*.

89. Lott, *Love and Theft*, 81.

90. Krasner, *Resistance, Parody, and Double Consciousness in African American Theatre*, 136.

91. Long after Brown's career ended, the New York press continued to associate "African Theatre" and disorder. Thompson's *A Documentary Collection* contains several articles or blurbs about allegedly riotous activity occurring at James Hewlett productions. Some of the incidents actually transpired; others sprung from the fertile imaginations of editors like M. M. Noah.

92. Gottschild, *Digging the Africanist Presence*, 94.

CONCLUSION

1. From May to July 1823, the *National Advocate* ran bankruptcy notices for a William Brown, which declared the gentleman "an insolvent debtor"; these documents are included in Thompson's collection. Although there were many William Browns in Manhattan, I suspect the theater manager was in financial trouble because of the June benefit performances that he held for himself.

2. Odell, *Annals of the New York Stage*, 3:70–71.

3. Ibid.

4. Hay, *African-American Theatre*, 182.

5. Lott, *Love and Theft*, 102.

6. *Spectator*, January 16, 1822, 2.

7. Aldridge, *Memoir and Theatrical Career of Ira Aldridge*, 11.

8. *National Advocate*, September 29, 1821, 2.

9. Ibid., August 28, 1823, 2.

10. Sarna, *Jacksonian Jew*, 11.

11. *Freedom's Journal*, March 16, 1827.

12. Ibid., August 24, 1827.

13. *National Advocate*, May 8, 1824, 2.

14. Thompson has collected several post-Brown articles in which a humor-starved Noah turned to Hewlett for satiric material. Noah printed stories on Hewlett performances, some accurate and some fictitious, in which mutinous crowds caused "rows" and even collapsed a floorboard. See *A Documentary History*.

15. *National Advocate*, May 8, 1824, 2.

16. Thompson has collected playbills from when Hewlett briefly assumed managerial control.

17. Thompson, *A Documentary History*, 167–71.

18. Roediger, *Wages of Whiteness*, 117–18.

19. The letter is included in *Memoirs of Charles Mathews*, vol. 3, and Thompson includes this reference to Hewlett in *A Documentary History*, 153.

20. Odell, *Annals of the New York Stage*, 3:536.

21. Barbara Lewis, "Dandy Blue," 262.

22. Thompson includes playbills and newspaper clippings, uncovered by Bernth Lindfors, which document Hewlett's performances in Trinidad; see *A Documentary History*, 222–24.

23. Ibid., 224.

24. Laurence Hutton includes the June 1823 playbill, which mentions Brown's plan to stage this Manhattan-centered version of *Tom and Jerry* in the upcoming weeks; see *Curiosities of the American Stage*, 97.

25. Marshall and Stock, *Ira Aldridge*, 236.

26. Lindfors, "The Signifying Flunkey," 7.

27. Ellison, "Change the Joke," 107.

28. Bethel, *The Roots of African-American Identity*, 26.

29. Lewis, "Dandy Blue," 260.

30. *New York Evening Post*, December 30 and 31, 1823, 2.

31. Thompson, *A Documentary History*, 144.

32. This quotation comes from the "Jitney" *Playbill*, October 31, 2000, 19:1. Wilson first called for the creation of this kind of arts organization in his famous 1996 speech, "The Ground upon Which I Stand," published in *American Theatre* (September 1996). Cook and Walker answered Wilson's call and convened a summit of black theater artists in March 1998, out of which AGIA emerged. In partnership with Dartmouth's Amos Tuck School of Business, AGIA also launched the Business/Performing Arts Partnership Initiative (BPAPI), designed to equip managers of African American and other minority theaters with the business expertise necessary to keep their theaters solvent. See the Amos Tuck School of Business press release, "Leading Business School Forms Unique Partnership with Minority Performing Artists."

33. When African American artists were allowed on the minstrel stage, innovative and dominant craftsmen like Billy Kersands, Bert Williams, George Walker, and Bob Cole faced an uphill battle as they worked to counter the disturbing racial assumptions embedded in this Euro-constructed performance tradition. But to some extent black vaudeville and musical performers, such as George Walker, who eventually performed free of blackface, and Bob Cole, who occasionally performed in whiteface, were successful in counteracting the presumptions of white superiority and black inferiority.

34. Quoted in Gottschild, *Digging the Africanist Presence*, 143.

35. Ibid., 78.

BIBLIOGRAPHY

MANUSCRIPT COLLECTIONS

Evanston, Illinois
  Northwestern University, Special Collections
    Ira Aldridge Manuscript Collection
New York, New York
  New York City Municipal Archives
    Allen Royce et al. v. Robert Mitchell et al., August 11, 1822, box 7437 (1822–23)
    Minutes of the Court of General Sessions (1821–23)
    Tax Assessment Records, 5th and 8th Wards (1820–24)
    Watch Returns, 5th and 8th Wards (June 1818–September 1822)
  New-York Historical Society
    C. Hunt, "A Crier Extraordinary," "Life in Philadelphia," Lithograph Series,
      London (1828)
    Anthony Imbert, "Life in New York," Lithograph Series, New York (1829–35)
Washington, D.C.
  Folger Shakespeare Library
    Ira Aldridge Scrapbook and Manuscript File
    William Shakespeare, *Richard III* Promptbooks (1830, 1860)
  Library of Congress, Performing Arts Division, Rare Books and
    Manuscripts
Worcester, Massachusetts
  American Antiquarian Society
    O. Shoemaker, "Bobalition," Broadside Series, Boston (1821–23)

NEWSPAPERS AND MAGAZINES

African Repository and Colonial Journal (Washington, D.C.), 1825
Albany Argus, 1823
Albion (New York), 1823
American Drama (New York), 1832
American Monthly Magazine and Critical Review (New York), 1817
American Quarterly Review (New York), 1827–32

Anglo-African Magazine (New York), 1859–60
Crisis Magazine (New York), 1926
Freedom's Journal (New York), 1827–28
National Advocate (New York), 1816–29
New York Advertiser, 1821–23
New York American, 1816–29
New York Evening Post, 1816–29
New York Gazette, 1820
New York Magazine, 1792–96
New York Mirror, 1823–29
New York Star, 1821–25
Playbill (New York), 2000
Rambler's Magazine and New York Theatrical Register, 1809–10
Spectator (New York), 1816–29
St. Tammany's Magazine (New York), 1821

BOOKS, PLAYS, PAMPHLETS, TRACTS,
ARTICLES, DISSERTATIONS

An Address, by Several Ministers, in New York, to Their Christian Fellow-Citizens, Dissuading Them from Attending Theatrical Representations. New York: New York Religious Tract Society, 1812.

Aldridge, Ira. *Memoir and Theatrical Career of Ira Aldridge, the African Roscius.* London: J. Onuhyn, 1849.

Allen, James. *The Negro in New York.* New York: Exposition Press, 1964.

Allen, Oliver E. *The Tiger: The Rise and Fall of Tammany Hall.* Reading, Mass.: Addison-Wesley, 1993.

Allen, Theodore. *The Invention of the White Race.* London: Verso, 1994.

Amos Tuck School of Business. "Leading Business School Forms Unique Partnership with Minority Performing Artists." ⟨http://www.dartmouth.edu/tuck/news/media/pr980521_bpapi.html⟩. September 15, 1998.

Anbinder, Tyler. *Five Points: The 19th-Century New York City Neighborhood That Invented Tap Dance, Stole Elections, and Became the World's Most Notorious Slum.* New York: Free Press, 2001.

Anderson, Benedict. *Imagined Communities: Reflections on the Origins and Spread of Nationalism.* New York: Verso Press, 1991.

Andrews, Charles C. *History of the New York African Free Schools.* 1830. New York: Negro Universities Press, 1969.

Aptheker, Herbert. *Documentary History of the Negro People.* Vol. 1. New York: Carol Publishing Group, 1951.

Arnold, Samuel J. *The Devil's Bridge; an Opera in Three Acts.* New York: Longworth, 1817.

Awkward, Michael. *Negotiating Difference: Race, Gender, and the Politics of Positionality.* Chicago: University of Chicago Press, 1995.

Axtell, James. "Colonial America without the Indians: A Counter-factual Scenario." In *Indians in American History: An Introduction*, edited by Frederick E. Hoxie, 47–65. Arlington Heights, Ill.: Newberry Library, 1988.

Baker, Ernest. *The Novels of Mrs. Aphra Behn*. Westport, Conn.: Greenwood Press, 1969.

Baker, Houston A., Jr. *Modernism and the Harlem Renaissance*. Chicago: University of Chicago Press, 1987.

Bakhtin, Mikhail. *Rabelais and His World*. Translated by Helene Iswolsky. Cambridge, Mass.: MIT Press, 1968.

Bank, Rosemarie K. *Theatre Culture in America, 1825–1860*. New York: Cambridge University Press, 1997.

Barclay, Alexander. *A Practical View of the Present State of Slavery in the West Indies*. London: Smith, Elder & Company, 1828.

Barker, J. N. *The Indian Princess; or La Belle Sauvage*. 1808. In *Representative Plays by American Dramatists, 1765–1819*. Vol. 1. New York: E. P. Dutton, 1918.

Barthelemy, Anthony G. *Black Face, Maligned Race*. Baton Rouge: Louisiana State University Press, 1987.

Barton, Andrew. *The Disappointment; or the Force of Credulity*. 1767. Gainesville: University of Florida Press, 1976.

Bates, William. *Harlequin Mungo; or A Peep into the Tower*. London: J. Skirven, 1788.

Bayley, F. W. *Four Years' Residence in the West Indies*. London: W. Kidd, 1830.

Bean, Annemarie. "Transgressing the Gender Divide: The Female Impersonator in Nineteenth-Century Blackface Minstrelsy." In *Inside the Minstrel Mask: Readings in Nineteenth-Century Blackface Minstrelsy*, edited by Annemarie Bean, James V. Hatch, and Brooks McNamara, 245–56. Hanover, N.H.: Wesleyan University Press, 1996.

Behn, Aphra. *History of the Royal Slave*. 1688. In *The Novels of Mrs. Aphra Behn*, edited by Ernest Albert Baker, 1–81. Westport, Conn.: Greenwood Press, 1969.

Belcher, Fanin. "The Place of the Negro in the Evolution of the American Theatre, 1767–1940." Ph.D. dissertation, Yale University, 1945.

Berlin, Ira. "The Structure of the Free Negro Caste in the Antebellum United States." *Journal of Social History* 9 (Spring 1976): 297–318.

Bernard, John. *Retrospectives of America, 1797–1811*. New York: Harper & Brothers, 1887.

Bethel, Elizabeth Rauh. *The Roots of African-American Identity: Memory and History in Free Antebellum Communities*. New York: St. Martin's Press, 1997.

Bettelheim, Judith. "Jonkonnu and Other Christmas Masquerades." In *Caribbean Festival Arts: Each and Every Bit of Difference*, edited by John Nunley and Judith Bettelheim, 39–83. Seattle: University of Washington Press, 1988.

Bhabha, Homi. *The Location of Culture*. London: Routledge, 1994.

Bickerstaff, Isaac. *The Padlock: A Comic Opera*. 1768. In *The Plays of Isaac Bickerstaff*, edited by Peter A. Tasch, 1–31. New York: Garland, 1981.

Blake, William. *Don Juan; or The Libertine Destroy'd, a Tragic Pantomimical Entertainment, in Two Acts*. 1795. London: J. Roach, 1820.

Bold, Alan. *A Burns Companion*. New York: St. Martin's Press, 1991.

Bolster, W. Jeffrey. *Black Jacks: African-American Seamen in the Age of Sail*. Cambridge: Harvard University Press, 1997.

———. "'To Feel like a Man': Black Seamen in the Northern United States, 1800–1860." *Journal of American History* 76 (March 1990): 1173–99.

Booth, Mary. *History of the City of New York*. New York: W. R. C. Clark & Meeker, 1859.

Booth, Michael. *English Melodrama*. London: Herbert Jenkins, 1965.

———, ed. *Hiss the Villain: Six American and English Melodramas*. New York: Benjamin Blom, 1967.

Boskin, Joseph. *Sambo: The Rise and Demise of an American Jester*. New York: Oxford University Press, 1986.

Boyer, Paul. *Urban Masses and Moral Order in America, 1820–1920*. Cambridge: Harvard University Press, 1992.

Brathwaite, Edward. "The African Presence in Caribbean Literature." *Bim* 17 (June 1979): 33–34.

Brawley, Benjamin. *A Social History of the American Negro*. New York: Macmillan, 1921.

Brown, Carlyle. *The African Company Presents Richard the Third*. New York: Dramatists Play Service, 1994.

Brown, T. Allston. *A History of the New York Stage: From the First Performance in 1732 to 1901*. Vol. 1. New York: Benjamin Blom, 1963.

Browne, Jackson. *A Brief History of the AMEZ Church*. Chattanooga: n.p., 1962.

Buckley, Peter George. "To the Opera House: Culture and Society in New York City, 1820–1850." Ph.D. dissertation, State University of New York at Stony Brook, 1984.

Burdett, William. *Life and Exploits of Mansong, Commonly Called Three-Finger'd Jack, the Terror of Jamaica*. London: A. Neil, 1800.

Burge, James C. *Lines of Business: Casting Practice and Policy in the American Theatre, 1752–1899*. New York: Peter Lang, 1986.

Cambridge History of the American Theatre. Vol. 1, *Beginnings to 1870*. Edited by Don B. Wilmeth and Christopher Bigsby. New York: Cambridge University Press, 1998.

Campbell, Mavis. *The Maroons of Jamaica, 1655–1796: A History of Resistance, Collaboration, and Portrayal*. Granby, Mass.: Bergin & Garvey, 1988.

Carmichael, Mrs. *Domestic Manners and Social Conditions of the White, Coloured, and Negro Population of the West Indies*. Vol. 2. London: Whittaker, Treacher, and Company, 1833.

Cassidy, Frederick G. "Hipsaw and John Canoe." *American Speech* 41 (February 1996): 45–51.

Children Now Foundation. "A Different World: Children's Perceptions of Race and Class in Media." ‹http://www.childrennow.org/media/mc98/DiffWorld.html›. May 1998.

Chong, Ping. "Notes for Mumblings and Digressions: Some Thoughts on Being an Artist, Being American, Being a Witness . . ." *Melus* 16:3 (Fall 1989–90): 62–67.

Cibber, Colley, ed. *The Tragical History of King Richard III.* In *Five Restoration Adaptations of Shakespeare*, edited by Christopher Spencer, 275–349. Urbana: University of Illinois Press, 1965.

Cobb, James. *Paul and Virginia, a Musical Entertainment in Two Acts.* In *The London Stage*, 4:10–16. London: Sherwood, Jones and Company, 1824–27.

Cockrell, Dale. *Demons of Disorder: Early Blackface Minstrels and Their World.* New York: Cambridge University Press, 1997.

Cohn, Michael, and Michael Platzer. *Black Men of the Sea.* New York: Dodd, Mead, 1978.

Cole, John. *The Minstrel: A Collection of Celebrated Songs.* Baltimore: F. Lucas, 1812.

Collins, John. "American Drama in Anti-Slavery Agitation, 1792–1861." Ph.D. dissertation, University of Iowa, 1963.

Collins, William. *The Works of William Collins.* Edited by Richard Wendorf and Charles Ryskamp. Oxford: Clarendon Press, 1979.

Colman, George, Jr. *The Africans; or War, Love, and Duty, a Play in Three Acts.* 180?. In *Cumberland's British Theatre*, vol. 43, edited by George Daniel, 1–62. London: Cumberland, 1826–61.

———. *Inkle and Yarico: An Opera in Three Acts.* 1787. In *The British Theatre*, edited by Mrs. Inchbald, 20:1–69. London: Hurst, Rees, and Orme, Paternoster Row, 1808.

The Complete Jefferson, Containing His Major Writings, Published and Unpublished, except His Letters. Edited by Saul K. Padover. New York: Tudor Publishing Company, 1943.

Connolly, L. W. *The Censorship of English Drama, 1737–1824.* San Marino, Calif.: Huntington Library, 1974.

Cooper, James Fenimore. *The Last of the Mohicans.* 1826. New York: Oxford University Press, 1998.

———. *The Pioneers.* 1823. New York: Oxford University Press, 1991.

———. *Satanstoe.* 1845. Albany: State University of New York Press, 1990.

Cowell, Joseph. *Thirty Years Passed among the Players.* 1828. Hamden, Conn.: Archon Books, 1979.

Craton, Michael. *Testing the Chains: Resistance to Slavery in the British West Indies.* Ithaca: Cornell University Press, 1982.

Curry, Leonard P. *The Free Black in Urban America, 1800–1850: The Shadow of the Dream.* Chicago: University of Chicago Press, 1983.

Curtis, L. Perry. *Apes and Angels: The Irishman in Victorian Caricature.* Washington, D.C.: Smithsonian Institution Press, 1971.

Dallas, R. C. *The History of the Maroons.* Vol. 1. London: T. N. Longman and O. Rees, 1803.

Damon, S. Foster. "The Negro in Early American Songsters." *Papers of the Bibliographical Society of America* 28 (1934): 132–63.

Davies, Kenneth Gordon. *The Royal African Company*. London: Longmans, 1957.

Davis, Natalie Zemon. *Society and Culture in Early Modern France*. Stanford: Stanford University Press, 1975.

Davis, Susan G. *Parades and Power: Street Theatre in Nineteenth-Century Philadelphia*. Philadelphia: Temple University Press, 1986.

Davison, Nancy Reynolds. "E. W. Clay: American Political Caricaturist of the Jacksonian Era." Ph.D. dissertation, University of Michigan, 1980.

Delany, Martin. *The Condition, Elevation, Emigration, and Destiny of the Colored People of the United States*. 1852. New York: Arno Press, 1968.

Deloria, Philip J. *Playing Indian*. New Haven: Yale University Press, 1998.

"Denmark Vesey." *Atlantic Monthly* 7 (June 1861): 728–44.

Dennison, Sam. *Scandalize My Name: Black Images in America Popular Music*. New York: Oxford University Press, 1982.

DeVoe, Thomas. *The Market Book: A History of the Public Markets of the City of New York*. 2 vols. New York: Thomas DeVoe, 1862.

Dewberry, Jonathan. "The African Grove Theatre and Company." *Black American Literature Forum* 16 (Winter 1982): 128–31.

Douglass, Frederick. *Narrative of the Life of Frederick Douglass*. In *The Classic Slave Narratives*, edited by Henry Louis Gates Jr., 243–331. New York: Mentor Books, 1987.

Du Bois, W. E. B. *The Souls of Black Folk*. 1903. New York: Penguin Books, 1989.

Dunlap, William. *History of the American Theatre*. 2 vols. New York: J. & J. Harper, 1832.

———. *A Trip to Niagara; or Travellers in America: A Farce, in Three Acts*. New York: E. B. Clayton, 1830.

Dwight, Timothy. *Travels in New England and New York*. Vol. 3. 1822. Cambridge: Harvard University Press, 1969.

Dyer, Richard. *White*. London: Routledge, 1997.

Earle, Alice M. *Colonial Days in Old New York*. 1896. New York: Ira J. Friedman, 1962.

Earle, William. *Obi; or The History of Threefingered Jack, in a Series of Letters from a Resident in Jamaica to His Friend in England*. London: Woodfall, 1804.

Egan, Pierce. *Life in London; or The Day and Night Scenes of Jerry Hawthorn, Esq. and His Elegant Friend Corinthian Tom in Their Rambles and Sprees through the Metropolis*. 1821. London: John Camden Hotten, 1869.

Eights, James. "Pinkster Festivities in Albany." In *Readings in Black American Music*, edited by Eileen Southern, 41–47. New York: W. W. Norton, 1983.

Ellis, David Maldwyn. *New York, State and City*. Ithaca: Cornell University Press, 1979.

Ellison, Ralph. "Change the Joke and Slip the Yoke." 1958. In *Collected Essays of Ralph Ellison*, edited by John F. Callahan, 100–112. New York: Modern Library, 1995.

Emery, Lynne F. *Black Dance: From 1619 to Today*. Princeton: Princeton Book Company, 1988.

Epstein, Dena J. *Sinful Tunes and Spirituals*. Urbana: University of Illinois Press, 1977.

Equiano, Olaudah. *The Life of Olaudah Equiano, or Gustavas Vassa, the African*. In *The Classic Slave Narratives*, edited by Henry Louis Gates Jr., 1–182. New York: Mentor Books, 1987.

Ernst, Robert. "Negro Concepts of Americanism." *Journal of Negro History* 39 (July 1954): 206–23.

Eyre, Alan L. "Jack Mansong: Bloodshed or Brotherhood." *Jamaican Journal* 7 (December 1973): 9–14.

Fabre, Geneviève. "African-American Commemorative Celebrations in the 19th Century." In *History and Memory in African-American Culture*, edited by Geneviève Fabre and Robert O'Meally, 72–91. New York: Oxford University Press, 1994.

Fairchild, Henry Pratt. *The Melting-Pot Mistake*. Boston: Little, Brown, 1926.

Fanon, Frantz. *Black Skin, White Masks*. 1952. Translated by Charles Lam Markmann. New York: Grove Press, 1967.

Fawcett, John. *Obi; or Three-Finger'd Jack, a Serio-Pantomime in Two Acts*. London: Duncombe & Moon, 1800.

———. *Songs, Duets, and Choruses in the Pantomimical Drama of Obi; or Three-Finger'd Jack*. 1800. In *Three Centuries of Drama: English (1751–1800)*, edited by Henry Willis Wells, 1–22. New York: Readex Microprint, 1966.

Foote, Thelma Wills. "Crossroad or Settlement? The Black Freedmen's Community in Historic Greenwich Village, 1644–1855." In *Greenwich Village: Culture and Counterculture*, edited by Rick Beard and Leslie Cohen Berlowitz, 125–33. New Brunswick, N.J.: Rutgers University Press, 1993.

Forbes, Jack. *Africans and Native Americans: The Language of Race and the Evolution of Red-Black Peoples*. Urbana: University of Illinois Press, 1979.

Fordham, Signithia, and John Ogbu. "Black Students' School Success: Coping with the 'Burden of Acting White.'" *Urban Review* 18:3 (1986): 176–206.

Fox, Dixon Ryan. *The Decline of Aristocracy in the Politics of New York*. New York: Harper & Row, 1965.

———. "The Negro Vote in Old New York." *Political Science Quarterly* 32 (February 1917): 252–75.

Francis, John. *Old New York: Reminiscences of the Past Sixty Years*. New York: C. Roe, 1858.

Fraser, Walter J. *Charleston! Charleston!* Columbia: University of South Carolina Press, 1989.

Freeman, Rhoda Golden. *The Free Negro in New York City in the Era before the Civil War*. New York: Garland, 1994.

Furer, Howard B. *New York: A Chronological Document, 1524–1970*. Dobbs Ferry, N.Y.: Oceana Publications, 1974.

Furman, Gabriel. *Antiquities of Long Island*. New York: J. W. Bouton, 1875.

Fusco, Coco. "The Other History of Intercultural Performance." *Drama Review* 38 (Spring 1994): 143–67.

Gale, Richard. "Archibald MacLaren's *The Negro Slaves* and the Scottish Response to British Colonialism." *Theatre Survey* 35 (November 1994): 77–93.

Garret, Thomas. "History of Pleasure Gardens in New York City, 1700–1865." Ph.D. dissertation, New York University, 1978.

Gates, Henry Louis, Jr. *The Signifying Monkey: A Theory of African-American Literary Criticism*. New York: Oxford University Press, 1988.

Genovese, Eugene. *Roll, Jordan, Roll: The World the Slaves Made*. New York: Vintage, 1976.

George-Graves, Nadine. *The Royalty of Negro Vaudeville: The Whitman Sisters and the Negotiation of Race, Gender, and Class in African American Theater, 1900–1940*. New York: St. Martin's Press, 2000.

Gilfoyle, Timothy J. *City of Eros: New York City, Prostitution, and the Commercialization of Sex, 1790–1920*. New York: W. W. Norton, 1992.

Gilje, Paul. *The Road to Mobocracy: Popular Disorder in New York City, 1765–1854*. Chapel Hill: University of North Carolina Press, 1987.

Gilroy, Paul. *The Black Atlantic: Modernity and Double Consciousness*. Cambridge: Harvard University Press, 1993.

———. "'. . . To Be Real': The Dissident Forms of Black Expressive Culture." In *Let's Get It On: Politics of Black Performance*, edited by Catherine Ugwu, 12–33. Seattle: Bay Press, 1995.

Ginsberg, Elaine K., ed. *Passing and the Fictions of Identity*. Durham, N.C.: Duke University Press, 1996.

Glazer, Nathan, and Daniel P. Moynihan. *Beyond the Melting Pot*. Cambridge: MIT Press, 1963.

Gluckman, Max. *Rituals of Rebellion in South-East Africa*. Manchester: Manchester University Press, 1954.

Goffman, Erving. *The Presentation of Self in Everyday Life*. New York: Anchor Books, 1959.

Goldberg, Isaac. *Major Noah: American-Jewish Pioneer*. Philadelphia: Jewish Publication Society of America, 1936.

Gonzalez, Nancie L. "Prospero, Caliban, and Black Sambo: Colonial Views of the Other in the Caribbean." *1992 Lecture Series, Working Paper No. 11*. College Park: Department of Spanish and Portuguese, University of Maryland, 1992.

———. *Sojourners of the Caribbean*. Urbana: University of Illinois Press, 1988.

Goodfriend, Joyce D. *Before the Melting Pot: Society and Culture in Colonial NYC, 1664–1730*. Princeton: Princeton University Press, 1992.

Gottschild, Brenda Dixon. *Digging the Africanist Presence in American Performance: Dance and Other Contexts*. Westport, Conn.: Greenwood Press, 1996.

Gramsci, Antonio. *Selections from the Prison Notebooks*. Edited and translated by Quinten Hoare and Geoffrey Nowell Smith. London: Lawrence and Wishard, 1971.

Grimsted, David. *Melodrama Unveiled: American Theater and Culture, 1800–1850*. Berkeley: University of California Press, 1987.

Grose, B. Donald. "Edwin Forrest, *Metamora*, and the Indian Removal Act of 1830." *Theatre Journal* 37 (May 1985): 181–91.

Gullick, C. J. M. R. *Myths of a Minority: The Changing Traditions of the Vincentian Caribs*. Assen, Netherlands: Van Gorcum, 1985.

Hadel, Richard E. "Carib Folk Songs and Carib Culture." Ph.D. dissertation, University of Texas at Austin, 1972.

Hagy, James William. *This Happy Land: The Jews of Colonial and Antebellum Charleston*. Tuscaloosa: University of Alabama Press, 1993.

Hall, Stuart. "Cultural Identity and Diaspora." In *Colonial Discourse and Post-Colonial Theory: A Reader*, edited by Patrick Williams and Laura Chrisman, 392–403. New York: Columbia University Press, 1994.

———. "Culture, Community, Nation." *Cultural Studies* 7:3 (October 1993): 349–63.

Hamm, Charles. *Yesterdays: Popular Song in America*. New York: W. W. Norton, 1979.

Hardie, James. *An Account of the Yellow Fever, Which Occurred in the Year 1822*. New York: Samuel Marks, 1822.

Harper, Philip Brian. "Passing for What? Racial Masquerade and the Demands of Upward Mobility." *Callaloo* 21:2 (Spring 1998): 381–97.

Harris, Leslie. "Creating the African-American Working Class: Black and White Workers, Abolitionists, Reformers in New York City, 1785–1863." Ph.D. dissertation, Stanford University, 1994.

Harris, M. A. *A Negro History Tour of Manhattan*. New York: Greenwood Publishing, 1968.

Hay, Samuel. *African-American Theatre: An Historical and Critical Analysis*. New York: Cambridge University Press, 1994.

Haywood, Charles. "Negro Minstrelsy and Shakespearean Burlesque." In *Folklore Society: Essays in Honor of Benj. A. Botkin*, edited by Bruce Jackson, 77–92. Hatboro: Folklore Associates, 1966.

Herskovits, Melville J. *The Myth of the Negro Past*. 1941. Boston: Beacon Press, 1990.

Hewitt, Barnard. "King Stephen of the Park and Drury Lane." In *The Theatrical Manager in England and America*, edited by Joseph W. Donohue Jr., 87–141. Princeton: Princeton University Press, 1971.

———. *Theatre U.S.A., 1665 to 1957*. New York: McGraw Hill Books, 1959.

Higginbotham, Leon A. *In the Matter of Color: Race and the American Legal Process*. New York: Oxford University Press, 1978.

Hill, Errol. *The Jamaican Stage, 1655–1900: Profile of a Colonial Theatre*. Amherst: University of Massachusetts Press, 1992.

———. "The Revolutionary Tradition in Black Drama." *Theatre Journal* 38 (December 1986): 408–26.

———. *Shakespeare in Sable*. Amherst: University of Massachusetts Press, 1984.

Hirsch, Leo H. "New York and the Negro." *Journal of Negro History* 16 (October 1931): 382–454.

Hitchcock, H. Wiley. *Music in the United States: A Historical Introduction*. Engle-wood Cliffs, N.J.: Prentice-Hall, 1974.

Hodge, Francis. "Charles Mathews Reports on America." *Quarterly Journal of Speech* 36 (December 1950): 492–99.

Holloway, Joseph E., ed. *Africanisms in American Culture*. Bloomington: Indiana University Press, 1990.

Homberger, Eric. *The Historical Atlas of New York City*. New York: Holland, 1994.

Home, John. *Douglas: A Tragedy*. 1771. Edited by Gerald D. Parker. Edinburgh: Oliver and Boyd, 1972.

hooks, bell. *Ain't I a Woman: Black Women and Feminism*. Boston: South End Press, 1981.

Huggins, Nathan. *Harlem Renaissance*. New York: Oxford University Press, 1971.

Hughes, Glenn. *A History of the American Theatre*. New York: Samuel French, 1951.

Hughes, Langston. "The Negro and American Entertainment." In *American Negro Reference Book*, edited by John Davis, 826–49. Englewood Cliffs, N.J.: Prentice-Hall, 1966.

Hulme, Peter, and Neil L. Whitehead, eds. *Wild Majesty: Encounters with Caribs from Columbus to the Present Day, an Anthology*. Oxford: Clarendon Press, 1992.

Hutton, Laurence. *Curiosities of the American Stage*. New York: Harpers and Brothers, 1891.

Ignatiev, Noel. *How the Irish Became White*. New York: Routledge, 1995.

"Into the Spotlight: A History of African-American Theatre." Transcript. February 14, 1993. Arena Stage's NEH Symposium Series. Washington, D.C.: Arena Stage, 1993.

Ireland, Joseph Norton. *Records of the New York Stage, from 1750 to 1860*. Vol. 1. New York: T. H. Morrell, 1866–67.

Jinkins, Dana, and Jill Bobrow. *St. Vincent and the Grenadines: A Plural Country*. London: Concepts Publishing, 1985.

Johnson, Claudia. *American Actress: Perspective on the 19th Century*. Chicago: Nelson Hall, 1984.

Johnson, James Weldon. *Black Manhattan*. New York: A. A. Knopf, 1930.

Jones, Eldred. *Othello's Countrymen*. London: Oxford University Press, 1965.

Jones, Eugene. *Native Americans as Shown on the Stage, 1753–1916*. London: Scarecrow Press, 1988.

Jones, Inigo. *The Theatre of the Stuart Court; Including the Complete Designs for Productions at Court*. Edited by Stephen Orgel and Roy Strong. Berkeley: University of California Press, 1973.

Jones, Sally L. "The First but Not the Last of the 'Vanishing Indian': Edwin Forrest and Mythic Recreations of the Native Population." In *Dressing in Feathers: The Constitution of the Indian in American Popular Culture*, edited by S. Elizabeth Bird, 13–28. Boulder, Colo.: Westview Press, 1996.

Jordan, Robert, and Harold Love, eds. *The Works of Thomas Southerne*. Oxford: Oxford University Press, 1988.

Jordan, Winthrop. *White over Black: American Attitudes toward the Negro, 1550–1812*. Chapel Hill: University of North Carolina Press, 1968.

Killens, John O., ed. *The Trial Record of Denmark Vesey*. 1822. Boston: Beacon Press, 1970.

Kilroe, Edwin. *St. Tammany and the Origin of the Society of Tammany or the Columbia Order in the City of New York*. New York: Edwin P. Kilroe, 1913.

King, C. Richard. *Colonial Discourses, Collective Memories, and the Exhibition of Native American Culture and Histories in the Contemporary United States*. New York: Garland, 1998.

Kirby, I. E., and C. L. Martin. *The Rise and Fall of the Black Caribs*. St. Vincent: n.p., 1972.

Krasner, David. *Resistance, Parody, and Double Consciousness in African American Theatre, 1895–1910*. New York: St. Martin's Press, 1997.

Lanier, Henry Wysham. *Greenwich Village*. New York: Harper & Brothers, 1949.

Lapsansky, Emma Jones. "Since They Got Those Separate Churches: Afro-Americans and Racism in Jacksonian Philadelphia." *American Quarterly* 32 (Spring 1980): 54–78.

Levine, Lawrence. *Black Culture and Black Consciousness: Afro-American Folk Thought from Slavery to Freedom*. New York: Oxford University Press, 1977.

———. *High Brow, Low Brow: The Emergence of Cultural Hierarchy in America*. Cambridge: Harvard University Press, 1988.

Lewis, Barbara. "Dandy Blue: The Evolution of the Dark Dandy." In *Inside the Minstrel Mask: Readings in Nineteenth-Century Blackface Minstrelsy*, edited by Annemarie Bean, James V. Hatch, and Brooks McNamara, 257–72. Hanover, N.H.: Wesleyan University Press, 1996.

Lewis, Earl. "To Turn on a Pivot: Writing African Americans into a History of Overlapping Diasporas." *American Historical Review* 100 (June 1995): 765–87.

Lewis, Matthew Gregory. *Journal of a West India Proprietor*. 1834. New York: Houghton Mifflin, 1929.

Lhamon, W. T., Jr. *Raising Cain: Blackface Performance from Jim Crow to Hip Hop*. Cambridge: Harvard University Press, 1998.

Lindfors, Bernth. "The Signifying Flunkey: Ira Aldridge as Mungo." *Literary Griot* 5 (Fall 1993): 1–11.

Linebaugh, Peter. "All the Atlantic Mountains Shook." *Labour* 10 (Autumn 1982): 87–121.

Lippman, Monroe. "Stephen Price: The American Theatre's First Commercial Manager." *Southern Speech Journal* 15 (March 1940): 13–17.

Lipsitz, George. *Time Passages: Collective Memory and American Popular Culture*. Minneapolis: University of Minnesota Press, 1990.

Litwack, Leon. *North of Slavery: The Negro in the Free States, 1790–1860*. Chicago: University of Chicago Press, 1961.

Lofton, John M. "Denmark Vesey's Call to Arms." *Journal of Negro History* 33 (October 1948): 395–413.

Longworth's American Almanac; a New York City Directory. New York: Thomas Longworth, 1821–26.

Lott, Eric. *Love and Theft: Blackface Minstrelsy and the American Working Class*. New York: Oxford University Press, 1993.

MacDonald, Joyce Green. "Acting Black: Othello, Othello Burlesques, and the Performance of Blackness." *Theatre Journal* 46 (May 1994): 231–50.

MacLean, Fitzroy. *Highlanders: A History of the Scottish Clans*. New York: Viking Studio Books, 1995.

———. *Scotland: A Concise History*. London: Thames & Hudson, 1993.

Mahar, William J. *Behind the Burnt Cork Mask: Early Blackface Minstrelsy and Antebellum American Popular Culture*. Urbana: University of Illinois, 1998.

———. "Black English in Early Blackface Minstrelsy: A New Interpretation of the Sources of Minstrel Show Dialect." *American Quarterly* 37 (Summer 1985): 260–85.

Manual of the Corporation of the City of New York. Edited by D. T. Valentine. New York: Edmond Jones & Company, 1864.

Marshall, Herbert, and Mildred Stock. *Ira Aldridge, the Negro Tragedian*. Carbondale: Southern Illinois University Press, 1958.

Masters, Roger D., and Christopher Kelly. *The Collected Writings of Rousseau*. 6 vols. Hanover, N.H.: University Press of New England, 1990.

Mathews, Charles. *Mr. Mathews's Trip to America*. Philadelphia: Simon Probasco, 1824.

Mayer, David. *Harlequin in His Element*. Cambridge: Harvard University Press, 1969.

McConachie, Bruce A. *Melodramatic Formations: American Theatre and Society, 1820–1870*. Iowa City: University of Iowa Press, 1992.

———. "Towards a Postpositivist Theatre History." *Theatre Journal* 37 (December 1985): 465–86.

McCready, William. *The Irishman in London; or the Happy African, a Farce in Two Acts*. New York: De Witt Publishing House, 1850.

McDermott, Douglass. "The Theatre and Its Audience: Changing Modes of Social Organization in the American Theatre." In *The American Stage: Social and Economic Issues from the Colonial Period to the Present*, edited by Tice Miller and Ron Engle, 6–17. Cambridge: Cambridge University Press, 1993.

McLaren, Peter. *Revolutionary Multiculturalism: Pedagogies of Dissent for the New Millennium*. Boulder, Colo.: Westview Press, 1997.

McManus, Edgar. *A History of Negro Slavery in New York*. Syracuse, N.Y.: Syracuse University Press, 1960.

McWhorter, John H. *Losing the Race: Self-Sabotage in Black America*. New York: Free Press, 2000.

Memoirs of Charles Mathews, Comedian. Vol. 3. Edited by Anne Jackson Mathews. London: R. Bentley, 1839.

Meserve, Walter J. *An Emerging Entertainment: The Drama of the American People to 1828*. Bloomington: Indiana University Press, 1977.

Miller, John J. *The Unmaking of Americans: How Multiculturalism Undermined the Assimilation Ethic*. New York: Free Press, 1998.

Mintz, Sidney W., and Richard Price. *The Birth of African-American Culture: An Anthropological Perspective*. 1976. Boston: Beacon Press, 1992.

Minutes of the Common Council of the City of New York. 1794–1831. 21 vols. Edited by Arthur E. Paterson. New York: New-York Historical Society, 1917.

Mitchell, Loften. *Black Drama: The Story of the American Negro in the Theatre*. New York: Hawthorn Books, 1967.

Mitchison, Rosalind. *A History of Scotland*. 2nd ed. London: Routledge, 1990.

Mohl, Raymond. *Poverty in New York, 1783–1825*. New York: Oxford University Press, 1971.

Molette, Carlton W., and Barbara J. Molette. *Black Theatre: Premise and Presentation*. Bristol, Ind.: Wyndham Hall Press, 1986.

Moncrieff, William Thomas. *Tom and Jerry; or Life in London: A Musical Extravaganza*. Edinburgh: James L. Huie, 1826.

Moody, Jane. "'Fine Word, Legitimate!': Toward a Theatrical History of Romanticism." *Texas Studies in Literature and Language* 38 (Fall–Winter 1996): 223–44.

Moore's Irish Melodies. Dublin: M. H. Gill & Son, 1888.

Morrison, Toni. *Playing in the Dark: Whiteness and the Literary Imagination*. New York: Vintage Books, 1992.

Morton, Thomas. *The Slave; or The Triumph of Generosity, a Musical Drama*. New York: D. Longworth, 1817.

Moya, Paula, and Michael R. Hames-Garcia, eds. *Reclaiming Identity: Realist Theory and the Predicament of Postmodernism*. Berkeley: University of California Press, 2000.

Muñoz, José Esteban. *Disidentifications: Queers of Color and the Performance of Politics*. Minneapolis: University of Minnesota Press, 1999.

Murdock, John. *Triumph of Love; or Happy Reconciliation*. 1795. In *Three Centuries of Drama: American (1714–1830)*, edited by Henry Willis Wells, 12–84. New York: Readex Microprint, 1967.

Mushkat, Jerome. *Tammany: The Evolution of a Political Machine, 1789–1865*. Syracuse, N.Y.: Syracuse University Press, 1971.

Nash, Gary. *Forging Freedom: The Formation of Philadelphia's Black Community, 1720–1840*. Cambridge: Harvard University Press, 1988.

Nathan, Hans. "Charles Mathews, Comedian, and the American Negro." *Southern Folklore Quarterly* 10 (September 1946): 191–97.

Nicoll, Allardyce. *The World of Harlequin: A Critical Study of the Commedia dell'Arte*. London: Cambridge University Press, 1963.

Nielsen, Peter. *Recollections of a Six-Years' Residence in the United States of America, Interspersed with Original Anecdotes*. Glasgow: D. Robertson, 1830.

Noah, M. M. *The Grecian Captive; or the Fall of Athens*. New York: E. E. Murden, 1822.

——. *She Would Be a Soldier; or the Plains of Chippewa*. New York: D. Long-worth, 1819.

Odell, George C. D. *Annals of the New York Stage*. Vols. 1–3. New York: Columbia University Press, 1927–49.

——. *Shakespeare from Betterton to Irving*. Vol. 2. New York: Dover Publications, 1966.

O'Keefe, John. *The Poor Soldier*. 1782. In *The Plays of John O'Keefe*, edited by Frederick M. Link, 2:265–311. New York: Garland, 1981.

Oldfield, J. R. "The 'Ties of Soft Humanity': Slavery and Race in British Drama, 1760–1800." *Huntington Library Quarterly* 46 (1993): 1–13.

Olson, Edwin. "Negro Slavery in New York, 1626–1827." Ph.D. dissertation, New York University, 1938.

——. "Social Aspects of Slave Life in New York." *Journal of Negro History* 26 (January 1941): 66–77.

O.P.Q. *Sketches of the New York Press*. New York: n.p., 1844.

Ottley, Roi, and William J. Weatherby, eds. *Negro in New York: An Informal Social History*. New York: Oceana Publications, 1967.

Over, William. "New York's African Theatre: The Vicissitudes of the Black Actor." *Afro-Americans in New York Life and History* 3 (July 1979): 7–13.

Panton, Kenneth J., and Keith A. Cowland. *Historical Dictionary of the United Kingdom*. Vol. 2. London: Scarecrow Press, 1998.

Patterson, Orlando. *Slavery and Social Death: A Comparative Study*. Cambridge: Harvard University Press, 1982.

——. *Sociology of Slavery: An Analysis of the Origins, Development, and Structure of Negro Slave Society in Jamaica*. Rutherford, N.J.: Fairleigh Dickinson University Press, 1967.

Payne, Aaron. "The Negro in New York prior to 1860." *Howard Review* 1 (June 1923): 1–64.

Payne, Daniel A. *History of the African Methodist Episcopal Church*. 1891. New York: Johnson Reprint Corporation, 1968.

Payne, J. H. *Ali Pacha; or The Signet Ring*. New York: Murden, 1823.

Perlman, Daniel. "Organizations of the Free Negro in New York City, 1800–1860." *Journal of Negro History* 56 (July 1971): 181–97.

Petit, Paul B. "The Important American Dramatic Types to 1900: A Study of the Yankee, Negro, Indian, and Frontiersman." Ph.D. dissertation, Cornell University, 1943.

Phelps, H. P. *Players of a Century: Records of the Albany Stage*. Albany: Joseph McDonough, 1880.

Porter, Dorothy. *Early Negro Writing, 1760–1837*. Boston: Beacon Press, 1971.

Porter, Susan L. *With an Air Debonair: Musical Theatre in America, 1785–1815*. Washington, D.C.: Smithsonian Institution Press, 1991.

Powers, Bernard E., Jr. *Black Charlestonians: A Social History, 1832–1885*. Fayetteville: University of Arkansas Press, 1994.

Poyer, John. *The History of Barbados from the First Discovery of the Island in the Year 1605 til the Accession of Lord Seaforth.* London: Frank Cass, 1971.

Putney, Martha S. "Black Merchant Seaman of Newport, 1803–1865: A Case Study in Foreign Commerce." *Journal of Negro History* 57 (April 1972): 156–68.

Quinn, Arthur Hobson. *A History of the American Drama, from the Beginning to the Civil War.* New York: F. S. Crofts, 1943.

Rawley, James. *The Transatlantic Slave Trade.* New York: W. W. Norton, 1981.

Ready Reference: American Indians. Vol. 3. Edited by Harvey Harkowitz. Pasadena: Salem Press, 1995.

Reed, Ishmael, ed. *Multi-America: Essays on Cultural War and Cultural Peace.* New York: Penguin Books, 1998.

Reid, Ira De A. "The John Canoe Festival." *Phylon* 3 (1942): 349–70.

Reidel, Heidi. "The Maroon Culture of Endurance." *Americas* 42 (1990): 46–49.

Reports of the Proceedings and Debates of the New York Constitutional Convention. 1822. New York: Da Capo Press, 1970.

Richards, Sandra. "Horned Ancestral Masks, Shakespearean Actor Boys, and Scotch-Inspired Set Girls: Social Relations in Nineteenth-Century Jamaican Jonkonnu." In *The African Diaspora: African Origins and New World Identities,* edited by Isidore Okpewho, Carole Boyce Davies, and Ali A. Mazrui, 254–74. Bloomington: Indiana University Press, 1999.

Roach, Joseph. *Cities of the Dead: Circum-Atlantic Performance.* New York: Columbia University Press, 1996.

———. "The Emergence of the American Actor." In *The Cambridge History of American Theatre,* vol. 1, edited by Don B. Wilmeth and Christopher Bigsby, 338–72. New York: Cambridge University Press, 1998.

Robertson, David. *Denmark Vesey: The Buried Story of America's Largest Slave Rebellion and the Man Who Led It.* New York: Knopf, 1999.

Robinson, Amy. "Forms of Appearance of Value: Homer Plessy and the Politics of Privacy." In *Performance and Cultural Politics,* edited by Elin Diamond, 237–61. London: Routledge, 1996.

Roediger, David R. *The Wages of Whiteness.* New York: Verso Press, 1991.

Rogers, Robert. *Ponteach; or the Savage of America.* 1766. In *Representative Plays by American Dramatists, 1765–1819,* vol. 1, edited by Montrose Jonas Moses, 115–208. New York: B. Blom, 1964.

Rosenwaike, Ira. *Population History of New York City.* Syracuse, N.Y.: Syracuse University Press, 1972.

Rush, Christopher. *A Short Account of the Rise and Progress of the African Methodist Episcopal Church in America.* New York: n.p., 1843.

Sanjek, Russell. *American Popular Music and Its Business: The First Four Hundred Years.* Vol. 2. New York: Oxford University Press, 1988.

Sarna, Jonathan D. *Jacksonian Jew: The Two Worlds of Mordecai Noah.* New York: Holmes & Meir Publishers, 1981.

Saxton, Alexander. *The Rise and Fall of the White Republic: Class Politics and Mass Culture in Nineteenth-Century America.* London: Verso, 1990.

Schechner, Richard. *Between Theater and Anthropology.* Philadelphia: University of Pennsylvania Press, 1985.

Scott, James. *Domination and the Arts of Resistance.* New Haven: Yale University Press, 1990.

―――. *Weapons of the Weak: Everyday Forms of Peasant Resistance.* New Haven: Yale University Press, 1985.

Scott, Julius. "Common Wind: Currents of Afro-American Communication in the Era of the Haitian Revolution." Ph.D. dissertation, Duke University, 1986.

Scott, Kenneth. "The Slave Insurrection in New York in 1712." *New York Historical Society Quarterly* 45 (January 1961): 43–74.

Scott, Michael. *Tom Cringle's Log.* London: William Blackwood and Sons, 1899.

Shakespeare, William. *Richard III.* In *The British Theatre*, vol. 1, edited by Mrs. Inchbald. London: Longman, Hurst, Rees, and Orme, Paternoster Row, 1808.

Shattuck, Charles H. *Shakespeare on the American Stage: From the Hallams to Edwin Booth.* Washington, D.C.: Folger Shakespeare Library, 1976.

Shepard, Charles. *An Historical Account of the Island of St. Vincent.* 1831. London: Frank Cass, 1971.

Sheridan, Richard. *Pizarro: A Tragedy in Five Acts.* 1799. In *The London Stage*, 1:1–16. London: Sherwood & Company, 1827.

Smith, James McCune. "Ira Aldridge." *Anglo-African Magazine* 2 (January 1860): 27–32.

Snipe, Simon. *Sports of New York: Containing an Evening at the African Theatre.* New York: Simon Snipe, 1823.

―――. *Sports of New York: Containing a Peep at the Grand Military Ball, Hewlett at Home, Simon in Regimentals, etc.* New York: Simon Snipe, 1824.

Sollors, Werner. "National Identity and Ethnic Diversity: Of Plymouth Rock and Jamestown and Ellis Island; or Ethnic Literature and Some Redefinitions of America." In *History and Memory in African-American Culture*, edited by Geneviève Fabre and Robert O'Meally, 92–121. New York: Oxford University Press, 1994.

Southern, Eileen. *The Music of Black Americans: A History.* 2nd ed. New York: W. W. Norton, 1983.

Southerne, Thomas. *Oroonoko.* Lincoln: University of Nebraska Press, 1976.

Sprague, Arthur Colby. *Shakespeare and the Actors: The Stage Business in His Plays (1660–1905).* Cambridge: Harvard University Press, 1948.

Stansell, Christine. *City of Women: Sex and Class in New York, 1789–1860.* Urbana: University of Illinois Press, 1987.

Stearns, Marshall, and Jean Stearns. *Jazz Dance: The Story of American Vernacular Dance.* New York: Da Capo Press, 1994.

Stewart, J. *A View of the Past and Present State of the Island of Jamaica.* 1823. New York: Negro Universities Press, 1969.

Stott, Richard B. *Workers in the Metropolis: Class, Ethnicity, and Youth in Antebellum New York City.* Ithaca: Cornell University Press, 1990.

Stuckey, Sterling. "The Skies of Consciousness, African Dance at Pinkster in New York, 1750–1840." In *Going through the Storm: The Influence of African American Art in History,* edited by Sterling Stuckey, 53–80. New York: Oxford University Press, 1994.

———. *Slave Culture: Nationalist Theory and the Foundations of Black America.* New York: Oxford University Press, 1987.

Swan, Robert J. "John Teasman: African-American Educator and the Emergence of Community in Early Black New York City, 1787–1815." *Journal of the Early Republic* 12 (Fall 1992): 331–56.

Sweet, Leonard. "The Fourth of July and Black Americans in the Nineteenth Century: Northern Leadership Opinion within the Context of the Black Experience." *Journal of Negro History* 61 (July 1976): 256–75.

Swift, David E. *Black Prophets of Justice: Activist Clergy before the Civil War.* Baton Rouge: Louisiana State University Press, 1989.

Szwed, John F. "Race and the Embodiment of Culture." *Ethnicity* 2 (June 1975): 19–33.

Takaki, Ron. *A Different Mirror: A History of Multicultural America.* New York: Little, Brown, 1993.

Taylor, Gary. *Reinventing Shakespeare: A Cultural History, from the Restoration to the Present.* New York: Oxford University Press, 1989.

Thomas, Lamont D. *Rise to Be a People: A Biography of Paul Cuffee.* Urbana: University of Illinois Press, 1986.

Thompson, George A., Jr. *A Documentary History of the African Theatre.* Evanston, Ill.: Northwestern University Press, 1998.

Tobin, Terrence. *Plays by Scots.* Iowa City: University of Iowa Press, 1974.

Toll, Robert. *Blacking Up: The Minstrel Show in Nineteenth Century America.* New York: Oxford University Press, 1974.

Tompkins, Jane. *Sensational Designs: The Cultural Work of American Fiction, 1790–1860.* New York: Oxford University Press, 1985.

Trollope, Frances. *Domestic Manners of the Americans.* 1832. New York: Oxford University Press, 1984.

Turner, Lorenzo D. "Anti-Slavery Sentiment in American Literature." *Journal of Negro History* 14 (October 1929): 373–416.

Turner, Patricia. *I Heard It through the Grapevine: Rumor in African-American Culture.* Berkeley: University of California Press, 1993.

Turner, Victor. *Drama, Fields, and Metaphors.* Ithaca: Cornell University Press, 1974.

———. *From Ritual to Theatre: The Human Seriousness of Play.* New York: PAJ Publications, 1982.

———. *Schism and Continuity in an African Society.* Manchester: Manchester University Press, 1957.

Twiss, Horace. *The Carib Chief: A Tragedy in Five Acts*. London: Longman, Hurst, Rees, Orme, and Brown, Paternoster Row, 1819.

Vernon, Greensville. *Yankee Doodle-Doo: A Collection of Songs of the Early American Stage*. New York: Benjamin Blom, 1972.

Walker, Alice. *In Search of Our Mothers' Gardens: Womanist Prose by Alice Walker*. New York: Harcourt Brace Jovanovich, 1983.

Warner, Michael, with Natasha Hurley, Luis Iglesias, Sonia Di Loreto, Jeffrey Scraba, and Sandra Young. "A Soliloquy 'Lately Spoken at the African Theatre': Race and the Public Sphere in New York City, 1821." *American Literature* 73:1 (March 2001): 1–46.

Wemyss, Francis Courtney. *Twenty-Six Years of the Life of an Actor and Manager*. New York: Burgess, Stringer, and Company, 1847.

———. *Wemyss' Chronology of the American Stage, from 1752 to 1852*. 1852. New York: Benjamin Blom, 1968.

Wesley, Charles H. "The Negroes of New York in the Emancipation Movement." *Journal of Negro History* 24 (January 1939): 65–72.

West, Cornel. *Race Matters*. Boston: Beacon Press, 1993.

White, Shane. "'It Was a Proud Day': African Americans, Festivals, and Parades in the North, 1741–1834." *Journal of American History* 81 (June 1994): 13–50.

———. "Pinkster in Albany, 1803: A Contemporary Description." *New York History* 70 (April 1989): 191–99.

———. "A Question of Style: Blacks in and around New York City in the Late 18th Century." *Journal of American Folklore* 102 (January–March 1989): 23–44.

———. *Somewhat More Independent*. Athens: University of Georgia Press, 1991.

White, Shane, and Graham J. White. *Stylin': African-American Expressive Culture from Its Beginnings to the Zoot Suit*. Ithaca: Cornell University Press, 1998.

Widdicombe, Toby, ed. "New York Theatre in the 1830s: An Eyewitness Account." *19th Century Theatre* 19 (Summer 1991): 45–50.

Wilentz, Sean. *Chants Democratic: New York City and the Rise of the American Working Class, 1788–1850*. Oxford: Oxford University Press, 1984.

Williams, Patricia J. *The Alchemy of Race and Rights: Diary of a Law Professor*. Cambridge: Harvard University Press, 1991.

Williams-Myers, A. J. "Pinkster Carnival." *Afro-Americans in New York Life and History* 9 (January 1985): 7–18.

Wilson, August. "The Ground upon Which I Stand." *American Theatre* (September 1996): 14–16, 71–74.

Winter, Marian H. "Juba and American Minstrelsy." *Dance Index* 6 (February 1947): 28–48.

Winter, William. *Shakespeare on the Stage*. New York: Moffat, Yard, 1911.

Wright, Richardson. *Revels in Jamaica, 1682–1838*. New York: Dodd, Mead, 1937.

Young, Virginia Heyer. *Becoming West Indian: Culture, Self, and Nation in St. Vincent*. Washington, D.C.: Smithsonian Institution Press, 1993.

Young, William. *An Account of the Black Charaibs in the Island of St. Vincent's.*
1795. London: Frank Cass, 1971.
———. *A Tour through Several Islands of Barbadoes, St. Vincent, Antigua, Tobago,
and Grenada, in the Years 1791 and 1792.* London: J. Stockdale, 1801.
Zuille, John. *Historical Sketch of the New York African Society for Mutual Relief.*
New York: n.p., 189?.

INDEX

Bates, Mr., 94, 116, 126, 128, 168
Bates, William, 109, 120–21
Beers, Charles. *See* Taft, Charles
Behn, Aphra, 106, 109
Belle sauvage, 87, 88, 90, 92–94, 100
Bellmont, George, 147, 149
Bellmont, James, 146, 147, 148, 149
Bethel, Elizabeth Rauh, 14, 70, 71, 179
Bhabha, Homi, 5, 6, 13, 103
Bickerstaff, Isaac, 106–7, 109, 111, 178
Black Caribs. *See* Afro-Indian Caribs
Blackface minstrelsy, 105, 130, 133, 175;
  and early national masking, 4–6;
  impact on African American imaging, 7, 151, 166, 169, 175, 186 (n. 15),
  202 (n. 17); revisionist scholarship
  on, 15, 56, 111, 162, 186 (n. 15); as distinct from whiteface minstrelsy, 15–
  16; early pioneers of, 18–19, 147,
  148, 150, 157, 160, 182–83, 208–9
  (n. 46), 212 (n. 33); and white working class, 56, 113, 162–64, 165, 181;
  connections to stage Africans, 110–
  11, 115, 157; and written minstrelsy,
  151–57, 158, 160, 175, 183, 210 (n. 74)
Bowery Theatre, 162–63
Broadway Circus, 146–49, 166, 208
  (n. 41)
Brothels, 27, 28, 134
Brown, William: background of, 1, 3,
  27, 29, 43, 95, 119, 126, 190 (n. 43);
  and legendary sign, 2, 9, 131–33, 185
  (n. 5); key managerial decisions of,
  4, 7, 8–9, 27–28, 35–36, 41–42, 44,
  46–48, 66, 69, 71–72, 75–76, 77,
  104, 116, 117, 128–29, 142–43, 145–
  46, 163–64, 169, 204 (n. 44), 208
  (n. 41); managerial demise of, 5, 9,
  94, 129, 150, 153, 165–66, 167–68,
  181, 211 (n. 1); as playwright, 8, 50,
  70, 87, 89, 95–100, 101, 116, 120–21,
  123, 168, 201 (n. 102), 212 (n. 24);
  legacy of, 9, 65, 165, 167, 169, 173,
  175–83; influence of maritime cul-

ture on, 29, 35, 95, 100, 122; and August 1822 riot, 79, 115, 146–47, 149–
  50, 204 (n. 43). *See also* African Company; African Grove; American
  Theatre; *Drama of King Shotaway*;
  Minor Theatre

Callithumpian Bands, 4, 111, 113, 114,
  115, 186 (n. 9), 204 (n. 36)
Catherine Market, 112–13, 203 (n. 33)
Charleston, S.C., 20, 25, 40, 119, 121,
  122, 127–28, 206 (nn. 78, 79)
Chatham Gardens. *See* Barrère,
  Hippolyte
City Hall Park, 27, 40, 44, 48, 190
  (n. 44)
City Hotel, 42, 192 (n. 10)
City Theatre. *See* Baldwin, Mrs.
Cockrell, Dale, 15, 16, 56, 108, 111, 113,
  186 (n. 9), 210 (n. 88). *See also* White-
  face minstrelsy
Coleman, William, 72, 93, 104, 139
Collins, John, 99, 127
Colman, George, Jr., 87, 88, 90, 92–93,
  109, 110, 114, 120–21, 178, 202–3
  (n. 23)
Commedia dell'Arte, 106
Common Council (New York), 22, 44,
  112, 135, 190–91 (n. 51), 198 (n. 48),
  207–8 (n. 24)
Constitutional Convention (1821), 134–
  36, 145
Cooke, George Frederick, 40, 54, 59,
  194 (n. 48)
Cooper, James Fenimore, 85, 199
  (n. 60)
Cornish, Samuel. See *Freedom's
  Journal*
Cowell, Joseph, 148, 192 (n. 8)
Cuffee, Paul, 70–71, 190 (n. 49)

Dancing cellars, 28, 30, 36, 137
Dandyism, 22–23, 34, 188 (n. 30);
  white dandies, 22–23, 24, 33, 34,

36; "black dandys and dandizettes,"
22–26, 28, 30, 32, 33, 34, 35, 37, 132,
137, 138, 145, 151, 164, 176, 189 (n. 37)
Davis, Natalie Zemon, 20, 189 (n. 37)
Davis, Susan G., 162
Davis, Vaginal, 52–53
Delany, Martin, 43, 81
Deloria, Philip, 82–83, 85–86, 87, 88,
91, 186 (n. 12)
Dennison, Sam, 159–60
Disidentification, 51–53, 55, 58, 60,
64–65, 66, 80. *See also* Muñoz,
José; Welsh, S.
Don Juan (William Blake), 104, 147
Douglas (John Home), 140, 208 (n. 26)
Douglass, Frederick, 20, 21
Drama of King Shotaway (William
Brown), 8, 87, 89, 95–100, 168
Du Bois, W. E. B., 6, 13, 71, 103, 196
(n. 19)
Dunlap, William, 83, 160
DuValle, 97
Dwight, Timothy, 68–69, 101, 182, 185
(n. 4), 196 (n. 8)

Ellison, Ralph, 4, 35, 186 (n. 15)
Equiano, Olaudah, 94, 200 (n. 86)
"Eveleen's Bower," 61–63, 64, 164

Fanon, Frantz, 131
Fawcett, John, 108–9, 114, 116, 122–26,
127, 128, 129, 205 (n. 72). See also
Obi; or Three-Finger'd Jack
Federalist Party, 31–33, 36, 133–35, 151
Five Points, 27–30, 32, 36, 138, 145,
153, 155, 163, 190 (n. 44)
Fortress of Sorrento (M. M. Noah), 73
Free blacks: social status of, 6, 29, 30,
33, 36; institutions of, 14, 28, 33, 143,
145, 151, 153, 157, 179; and philanthropy, 14, 111, 180–81, 193 (n. 19);
occupations of, 23, 29, 190 (n. 49),
193 (n. 26); residential patterns of,
27, 44, 45; voting rights and political

affiliations of, 30, 31, 34, 71, 132, 134–
37, 145; and African colonization,
70–71; and U.S. citizenship, 71; as
depicted onstage, 106, 107, 110; public celebrations of, 113–14, 138, 207
(n. 19)
Freedom's Journal, 28, 70, 138, 161,
170–71, 209 (n. 64)
Fusco, Coco, 82, 85, 198 (n. 55)

Garifuna. *See* Afro-Indian Caribs
Gates, Henry Louis, 19–20, 24, 52
Gilje, Paul, 143, 147, 162
Gilroy, Paul, 6, 15, 29
Gottschild, Brenda Dixon, 3, 6, 13, 166,
182
Gramsci, Antonio, 17, 188 (n. 17)
Greek independence struggle, 180–81,
201 (n. 102)
Greenwich Village, 2, 22, 44–46, 73–
74, 84, 103, 145, 163, 169, 179, 180,
185 (n. 2)

Haiti. *See* Santo Domingo
Hall, Stuart, 3, 13–14, 103, 185 (n. 7)
Hamlet, 62, 158–60, 161, 173
Hampton's Hotel, 48–50, 73, 116, 142
Hay, Samuel, 95–96, 99, 133, 141, 151,
169, 185 (nn. 3, 6), 189 (n. 41), 208
(n. 41), 210 (n. 79)
Herskovits, Melville, 12, 13, 18
Hewlett, James: as actor/performer, 7,
9, 43, 47, 51, 56, 57, 58, 79–82, 89–
90, 92, 98, 99, 104, 116, 142, 143, 157,
173; various occupations of, 30, 43,
144, 192 (n. 17); background of, 43,
66; as choreographer, 70, 89, 90,
92–95, 100, 119, 168, 200 (n. 81);
confronts Charles Mathews, 160,
171–76; as theatrical manager, 172,
181, 211 (n. 91); understanding of
blackface representations, 175; as
playwright, 177; Trinidadian tour of,
177

Hill, Errol, 97, 185 (nn. 3, 6)
Hooks, bell, 58, 60–61, 63, 195 (n. 69)
Hornpipe, 80, 118, 119, 154, 168, 169,
    197 (n. 43), 209 (n. 46)
Huggins, Nathan, 110–11, 114, 115
Hughes, Langston, 131, 185 (n. 5)

Indian Removal Act of 1830, 88
Integration: as Brown's primary
    agenda, 2, 4, 7, 9, 28–29, 66, 129,
    145, 146, 150, 153, 169, 173, 179, 182;
    at African Grove, 27, 28, 35–36, 208
    (n. 41); in Manhattan neighbor-
    hoods, 27, 101, 145; in maritime cul-
    ture, 29; at Minor Theatre, 41, 42,
    46–47, 48, 50; at American Theatre,
    69, 76–77, 78, 82, 93, 101, 161, 164,
    167, 180
Irish Americans, 67, 68, 185 (n. 4),
    196 (n. 5), 207 (n. 12); social and res-
    idential relations with Afro–New
    Yorkers, 27–28, 29, 32, 142, 145,
    157; and Republican Party, 32, 34,
    36, 133, 134, 136; artistic compar-
    isons with African Americans, 108,
    202 (n. 17)
"Is There a Heart That Ever Lov'd,"
    81, 197–98 (n. 45)

Jackson, Andrew, 23, 33
Jackson, Mr., 116, 119
Johnson, James Weldon, 150, 167
John Street Playhouse, 83–84
Jonkonnu, 124, 125–27, 205–6 (n. 73).
    See also Whiteface minstrelsy

Kean, Edmund, 40, 43, 54, 55, 58,
    59–60, 65, 194 (n. 48)
Kotzebue, August von. See Pizarro
Krasner, David, 51, 168, 194 (n. 39)

Levine, Lawrence, 58, 140, 191 (n. 56)
Lewis, Barbara, 176, 179
Lewis, Earl, 12–13

Licensing Act (1737), 39–40
Lindfors, Bernth, 178
Lipsitz, George, 35
Lott, Eric, 56, 111, 169, 186 (n. 15), 204
    (n. 53), 210 (n. 74)

Macbeth, 48, 65, 177
Mahar, William J., 6
Mansong, Jack, 109, 116, 122, 126, 205
    (n. 62). See also Obi; or Three-
    Finger'd Jack
Mathews, Charles, 18, 40, 43, 47, 58,
    109, 132, 150, 158–61, 166, 171–76,
    178, 188 (n. 20), 210 (nn. 77, 79)
Minor Theatre, 2, 4, 103, 167, 182;
    repertoire of, 8, 41, 44, 48, 50–51,
    54, 62, 66, 72, 81, 95; debut of, 39,
    49, 192 (n. 8); relation to Price and
    Park Theatre, 39, 50–51, 66, 149,
    170; and audience integration and
    dynamics, 41, 44–48, 49, 50, 62, 66,
    81, 141–42; and "upstairs theater,"
    41–42, 44, 74, 143, 151; acting com-
    pany of, 42–44, 46, 47–48, 49, 50,
    62, 66; and 1822 Shakespeare ar-
    rests, 49, 73, 96, 138–42, 167, 170;
    as counterpublic sphere, 51–53, 66,
    81, 132, 151, 163–64; as political tar-
    get, 132, 135, 136. See also Stage
    Europeans
Mintz, Sidney, 13, 129
Missouri Compromise, 34, 154
Molette, Barbara and Carlton, 12
Moody, Jane, 39–40, 44, 52, 140, 141
Morrison, Toni, 72
Morton, Thomas, 109–10
Mr. Mathews's Trip to America
    (Charles Mathews), 158, 159, 161.
    See also Mathews, Charles
Muñoz, José, 52–53. See also
    Disidentification
Murdock, John, 107, 111
Murphy, Eddie, 11, 17

Royal African Company, 120

Russwurm, John. See *Freedom's Journal*

Saint Vincent (West Indies), 3, 8, 95, 96–97, 99, 100, 101, 199 (n. 65)

Santo Domingo (Haiti), 50, 95, 96, 100, 127, 206 (nn. 77, 78)

"Scots, wha hae wi' Wallace bled" (Robert Burns), 56–57, 98. *See also* Wallace, William

Scott, James, 21, 25–26, 52, 188 (n. 17)

Shakespeare, William: black appropriations of, 8, 41, 42, 43, 48, 49, 50–51, 53–55, 57, 58–60, 62, 64–65, 80, 82, 132, 133, 135, 140, 142–43, 156, 159, 165–66, 170, 173–75, 177, 206 (n. 73); significance in America, 40, 49, 53–54, 58, 73, 83, 140–43. *See also individual plays*

Sheridan, Richard. See *Pizarro*

She Would Be a Soldier (M. M. Noah), 72–73, 83, 87, 89, 90–91, 99, 100

Shotaway (Joseph Chatoyer), 50, 97–99, 101

Shotaway; or the Insurrection of the Caribs of St. Domingo, 50

Simpson, Edmund, 40, 108, 109, 114, 170

Slavery: New World slave culture, 6–7, 8, 12–13, 15, 17–18, 20–21, 28, 63–64, 100, 111–12, 124–25, 203 (n. 13); stage representations of, 9, 87, 106–7, 109, 110, 116, 120–21, 126, 194 (n. 55), 205 (n. 56); slave presence at African Grove, 12, 30, 33, 35–36, 45, 121, 164; conditions and laws, 20, 24, 31–32, 34–35, 56–57, 60–61, 96, 97, 189 (n. 37), 190–91 (n. 51); abolition legislation and emancipation, 32, 34–35, 57, 70, 99, 105, 133–34, 138, 151, 154, 155, 196 (n. 10); slave trade, 113–14, 119–20, 122, 181, 191 (n. 60), 205 (n. 58)

Smith, James McCune, 29–30, 190 (n. 49)

Smith, Mr., 116–17, 121

Snipe, Simon, 75, 77, 78, 79–80, 81–82, 116–17, 126, 140, 144, 153, 157

Southerne, Thomas, 106–7, 109

Stage Africans, 7, 12, 51, 115, 116, 118, 119, 143, 159, 160, 175, 177, 203–4 (n. 23); and Brown's balancing act, 8, 104–5, 115, 121–27, 128, 167, 177; and Manhattan vogue, 8, 108–11, 113, 114, 115, 117, 120, 129, 168; relation to blackface minstrelsy, 105, 110–11, 115, 150, 157; two varieties of, 106–8, 123, 129, 142, 150, 174, 178; and black actors, 116, 119, 121, 126, 127, 128–29, 130, 148, 175

Stage Europeans, 7, 16, 51, 101, 168, 175; defined, 7, 8, 41, 51, 52–53, 55; on Brown's stage, 8, 41, 48, 54–66, 80, 103, 104, 121; as social transgression and training, 9, 20, 51–52, 56–57, 64–65, 136–37, 151, 178–79; in various theaters, 65, 173, 177, 193–94 (n. 38). *See also* Whiteface minstrelsy

Stage Indians, 7, 12, 51, 82, 92, 152, 169, 175; Afro-constructed versions of, 8, 89, 92–101, 119, 132, 167, 168; Euro-constructed versions of, 69, 70, 72–73, 82, 85–89, 90–91, 92, 95, 100, 101, 103, 106, 110, 115, 121, 177, 182, 199 (n. 63); Indio-constructed versions of, 69, 70, 82–85, 89, 94, 100, 101, 103, 121

Stansell, Christine, 23, 61

Stuckey, Sterling, 12–13, 14, 112, 203 (n. 30)

Susquehannock Nation, 95

Szwed, John, 16

Taft, Charles: stars in *Richard III*, 42, 55, 59, 60, 143, 151, 160; criminal activity of, 42, 144, 156; background of, 42–43, 54, 65, 179, 192 (nn. 10–11)

Teasman, John, 14

Thanksgiving Day, 111, 113–14, 181, 191 (n. 60)

Thompson, George A., Jr., 147, 185 (n. 3), 192 (nn. 10–11, 17), 193 (n. 33)

Tom and Jerry; or Life in London (William Moncrieff), 116, 117–19, 121–22, 128

Transcripts, public and private, 21–22, 24–26, 31, 35, 36, 52, 123, 162–63, 189 (n. 34), 191 (n. 60). *See also* Scott, James

Trinidad (West Indies), 173, 177

Trollope, Francis, 18, 47, 132, 188 (n. 20)

Turner, Victor, 20, 186 (nn. 9, 12), 189 (n. 34)

Twaites, Mr., 75, 76–77, 80–81

Twiss, Horace, 96

Vauxhall Gardens, 31, 44, 84, 94, 185 (n. 2)

Vendue Range (Charleston, S.C.), 122

Vesey, Denmark, 127–28, 206 (nn. 78–80)

Walker, David, 71, 72

Wallace, William, 56, 164

Welsh, S., 7, 41, 51, 65, 80, 116, 143, 161, 182, 183; feminist potential of, 41, 58, 60, 61, 63–64, 65, 142; background of, 42, 43, 90, 100, 179; acting style

and textual revisions of, 42, 58–60, 61–65, 80, 140, 159; as dancer, 92–93. *See also* Stage Europeans

West, Mr. *See* Broadway Circus

West Side (Manhattan), 1, 2, 3, 4, 14, 27–29, 30, 44, 169, 190 (nn. 43–44)

White, Shane, 113, 137, 189 (n. 37), 190 (n. 46), 191 (n. 63), 203 (n. 30)

Whiteface minstrelsy, 6, 13, 14, 51, 65, 115, 194 (n. 39); defined, 7, 8, 12, 15; in African Grove, 7, 26, 30–36, 42, 90, 93, 132, 133, 151, 164; transgressive and training potential of, 9, 11, 19–21, 22, 33, 35–36, 51, 53, 136–38, 142, 164, 168, 178–79, 212 (n. 33); and Eddie Murphy, 11, 17; and Jonkonnu, 15; as theorized by Dale Cockrell, 15, 16; as defined by Joseph Roach, 16, 31; and Homer Plessy, 16–18; relation to passing, 16–18; and Broadway promenaders, 20, 22, 24–25, 28, 30, 105, 111, 132, 137, 145, 189 (n. 37); in Charleston, S.C., 20, 25

White Like Me, 11, 17

Williams, Miss, 80–81, 118, 119, 154

Williams, Peter, Jr., 14, 70, 113

Wilson, August, 181, 212 (n. 32)

Wolfe, George, 182

Womanism, 41, 60, 64, 65, 142, 159, 195 (n. 69)

Yellow fever, 105, 149

Young, Sir William, 97–98

Contents

Note: Sculpture appears at the end of Volume II

List of Advertisers

Apollo Magazine - UK — Vol 1 rear end papers

Art Newspaper - UK — page 28 & 29

Braswell Galleries - USA — adjacent to DREWES, Werner

Christie's - UK — Vol I front cover

Dobiaschofsky Auktionen - Switzerland — Vol 1 front end papers

Eberhart Auktionen - Switzerland — Vol I spine

Edmund Peel - Spain — Vol I page 22 & Vol II front end papers

Hanzel Galleries - USA — adjacent to NICHOLS, Dale

Hindman - USA — Vol II rear cover

International Directory of Art - Germany — Vol II rear end papers

Irish Arts Review - Ireland — page 6

Leonard Joel - Australia — Vol I rear cover

G A Key - UK — adjacent to BEAVIS, Richard

Kunstpreis Jahrbuch - Germany — page 16

Lawrence - UK — Vol 1 front end papers

Mystic Fine Arts - USA — adjacent to BUTTERSWORTH, James E

Phillips, Leeds - UK — adjacent to KRAMER, Jacob

Skinner, Inc - USA — adjacent to HARTMANN, Ludwig

C G Sloan & Company - USA — adjacent to SOROLLA Y BASTIDA, Joaquin

Tennants Auctioneers - UK — adjacent to GODWARD, John William

Trace Publications Ltd — page 21

Watercolours, Drawings & Prints Magazine - UK — Vol II rear end papers

Weltkunst - Germany — Vol 1 rear end papers

William Doyle Galleries - USA — adjacent to CAMPIGLI, Massimo

Wolf's Auctioneers - USA — Vol II spine & Vol II front end papers

Woolley & Wallis - UK — adjacent to O'CONOR, Roderick

Young Fine Arts Gallery Inc - USA — Vol II Contents page

IRISH
ARTS REVIEW
YEARBOOK 1991-1992

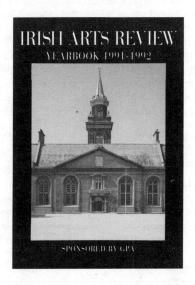

This superb publication can be ordered from the editorial office
of Irish Arts Review, 22 Crofton Road, Dun Laoghaire, Co Dublin. Ireland
Telephone +353-1-2808415. Fax +353-1-2808309
Hardback: Stg£29.00 to Ireland and England, Stg£31.00 to the rest of
Europe, US$53.00 to North America and other continents.
Paperback: Stg£19.00 to Ireland and England, Stg£21.00 to the rest of
Europe, US$37.00 to North America and other continents.